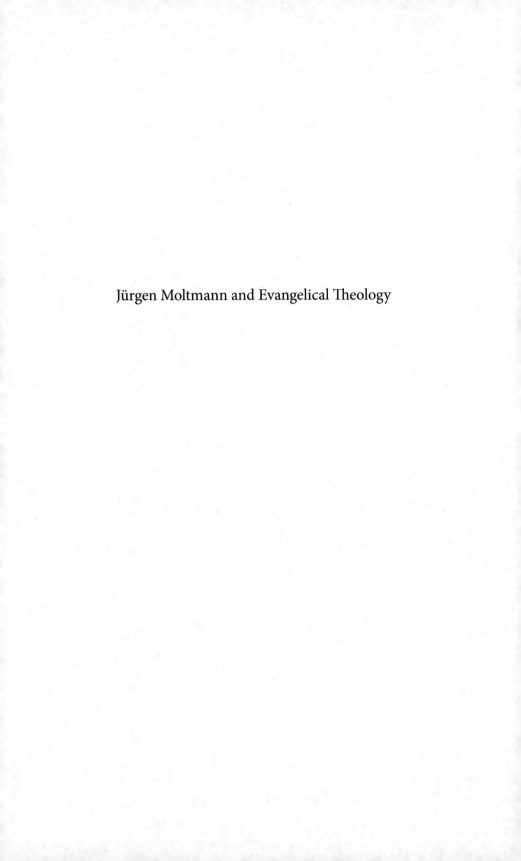

Jürgen Moltmann and Evangelical Theology

Jürgen Moltmann and Evangelical Theology

A Critical Engagement

Edited by
Sung Wook Chung

PICKWICK *Publications* · Eugene, Oregon

JÜRGEN MOLTMANN AND EVANGELICAL THEOLOGY
A Critical Engagement

Pickwick Publications
An Imprint of Wipf and Stock Publishers
199 W. 8th Ave., Suite 3
Eugene, OR 97401

www.wipfandstock.com

ISBN 13: 978-1-61097-890-3

Cataloging-in-Publication data:

Jürgen Moltmann and evangelical theology : a critical engagement / edited by Sung Wook Chung.

XVI + 250 p. ; 23 cm. Includes bibliographical references and index.

ISBN 13: 978-1-61097-890-3

1. Moltmann, Jürgen. 2. Evangelicalism. I. Chung, Sung Wook, 1966–. I. Title.

BX4827.M6 C48 2012

Manufactured in the U.S.A.

Contents

Contributors

Timothy Bradshaw is Senior Tutor and Tutor in Christian Doctrine at Regents Park College, Oxford, and University Research Lecturer. He is a member of the Anglican Orthodox International Theological Commission. His most recent publications are *Pannenberg: A Guide for the Perplexed* (2009) and *Chaos or Control? Authority in Crisis in Church and State* (2010). He has also written on the contemporary debate about sexual ethics, on ecclesiology, and on Karl Barth.

Lanier Burns is Research Professor of Theology and Senior Professor of Systematic Theology at Dallas Theological Seminary, Dallas, Texas. He is the author of numerous books and articles on trinitarianism, anthropology, hamartiology, angelology, eschatology, theology and society, and theology and science.

Graham Buxton is Head of Postgraduate Studies in the School of Ministry, Theology, & Culture at Tabor Adelaide in Australia, where he is also Director of the Graeme Clark Research Institute. He is the author of *Dancing in the Dark: The Privilege of Participating in the Ministry of Christ* (2001), *The Trinity, Creation, and Pastoral Ministry: Imaging the Perichoretic God* (2005) and *Celebrating Life: Beyond the Sacred-Secular Divide* (2007).

Daniel Castelo is Associate Professor of Theology at Seattle Pacific University, Seattle, Washington. He is the author of *The Apathetic God* (2009) and the forthcoming work titled *Theological Theodicy*.

Sung Wook Chung is Associate Professor of Theology at Denver Seminary, Littleton, Colorado. He is the author of *Admiration and Challenge: Karl Barth's Theological Relationship with John Calvin* (2002) and editor of *Karl Barth and Evangelical Theology: Convergences and Divergences* (2008) and *John Calvin and Evangelical Theology: Legacy and Prospect* (2009).

David Höhne is a Senior Lecturer in Theology and Philosophy at Moore Theological College in Sydney, Australia. He is the author of *Spirit and Sonship* (2010), *The Last Things* (forthcoming) and has contributed chapters to a number of volumes including *Engaging with Calvin* (2009).

Veli-Matti Kärkkäinen is Professor of Systematic Theology at Fuller Theological Seminary in Pasadena, California, and Docent of Ecumenics at the University of Helsinki. He is the author of about 200 articles and more than ten books, including *The Trinity: Global Perspectives* (2007). He is also the co-editor of *The Global Dictionary of Theology* (2008).

Paul Parker is the Baltzer Distinguished Professor of Religious Studies and Chair of the Department at Elmhurst College in Illinois. He teaches courses in Christian ethics and has written about prayer, suffering, God, and religious dimensions of the conflict between Israel and Palestine.

Kurt Anders Richardson (DTh, Basel) is Professor in the Faculty of Theology, Department of Philosophy, McMaster University and an adjunct with University of Toronto and Toronto School of Theology. He works in the fields of systematic theology and comparative theology (Abrahamic traditions). Some of his publications are: *The New American Commentary: James* (1997), *Reading Karl Barth: New Directions for North American Theology* (2004).

M. Daniel Carroll Rodas is Distinguished Professor of Old Testament at Denver Seminary, Colorado. Prior to his appointment to Denver Seminary, he was Professor of Old Testament and Ethics at El Seminario Teológico Centroamericano in Guatemala City, Guatemala. He remains an adjunct professor there. Dr. Carroll recently was named to the board of the National Hispanic Christian Leadership Conference, which is the Hispanic arm of the National Association of Evangelicals. He has authored and edited numerous books both in English and Spanish. Presently he is working on a major commentary on Amos for the *New International Commentary on the Old Testament*. His latest book is *Christians at the Border: Immigration, the Church and the Bible*.

Stephen N. Williams is Professor of Systematic Theology at Union Theological College, Belfast. He has published in the fields of biblical studies, theology, and intellectual history. His most recent publications are *The Shadow of the Antichrist: Nietzsche's Critique of Christianity* (2006) and a commentary on *Joshua* in the Two Hoirzons series, co-authored with J. Gordon McConville (2010).

Foreword

WRITING A FOREWORD, WHILE a privilege, can be a peculiar exercise. One is invited to add a comment as an outsider to a collection of essays with its own purpose and feel. In other words, one is a guest. The goal is to enhance the conversation respectfully and engagingly. This is quite the challenge, especially when the object for discussion is the thought of someone of singular status.

Jürgen Moltmann has been one of the giants in theology over the last fifty years, not only in his native Germany, of course, but also around the world. He has been the subject of innumerable articles and many full-length book studies and doctoral theses. The breadth of topics to which Moltmann has given attention is impressive, as the range of essays by the theologians in this volume attests. How is it that I, an Old Testament scholar, come to participate?[1] It is interesting that one of the most prominent interpreters of Moltmann's work in the English language is another biblical studies person, the British New Testament scholar, Richard Bauckham.[2] So, I am in good company!

I encountered Moltmann in an indirect way many years ago. I am half-Guatemalan and was on my way to teach at a seminary there, so I began to read Latin American Liberation Theology. Armed conflict was racking the countries of Central and South America, and this new formulation was trying to wrestle with the meaning of Christian faith and practice in that context. It quickly became apparent that Moltmann

1. An Old Testament scholar who repeatedly references Moltmann is Walter Brueggemann. See, e.g., Bruegemann, *Theology of the Old Testament: Testimony, Dispute, Advocacy, passim.*

2. Bauckham, *Moltmann: Messianic Theology in the Making*; Bauckham, *The Theology of Jürgen Moltmann*, and Bauckham, *God Will Be All in All: The Eschatology of Jürgen Moltmann.*

was a formative influence on the thinking of these theologians. So, I purchased and read *Theology of Hope*.[3] That was my introduction to his provocative thought. As I reflect on my ongoing interest in Moltmann, I appreciate that it has been stimulated in large measure by my experience in Latin America.

Liberation Theology's engagement with Moltmann began in uncomfortable fashion. Rubén Alvez, José Míguez Bonino, and Gustavo Gutiérrez, among others, appreciated much of what he had to say about the need to reorient theology toward the future and ground it in the kingdom of God.[4] At the same time, however, these Latin Americans launched a fundamental criticism of Moltmann's thought. They argued that his understanding of the future and the divine promise was too transcendent. It was, they said, not some vague hope of a different future that could pull humanity forward; rather, it was the injustices of the present that demanded change and would drive the option to work for transformation on the way to realizing that future. The exchange between Moltmann and these liberation theologians was not only formal, in print. It was also personal, since this disapproval had been voiced publicly in his presence. He published a response, which circulated widely in several languages.[5]

Over time, though, the mutual appreciation between Moltmann and Liberation Theology grew.[6] A significant contribution to this change was his book, *The Crucified God*.[7] Latin American theologians, in particular Jon Sobrino, stimulated Moltmann's focus on the centrality of praxis for Christian reflection and the identification of God in Christ with human suffering, even as his reflections deepened theirs.[8]

---

3. Moltmann, *Theology of Hope: On the Ground and Implications of a Christian Eschatology.*

4. Alvez, *A Theology of Human Hope*, 55–68; Míguez Bonino, *Doing Theology in a Revolutionary Situation*, 132–53; Gutiérrez, *A Theology of Liberation*, 13–15, 160–68, 215–25. Also note Assmann, *Theology for a Nomad Church*, 94–96.

5. Moltmann, "An Open Letter to José Míguez Bonino: On Latin American Liberation Theology," 57–63. See his reflections on the personal dimension in Moltmann, *Experiences in Theology: Ways and Forms of Christian Theology*, 217–220, and in *A Broad Place: An Autobiography*, 222–32.

6. See Moltmann, *Experiences in Theology*, 220–48; Míguez Bonino, "Reading Jürgen Moltmann from Latin America," 105–14.

7. Moltmann, *The Crucified God*. Moltmann's thinking on ecclesiology and ecology also has made an impact on Latin American theologians.

8. Sobrino, *Christology at the Crossroads*, 28–33, 228–29, 251–53, *passim*; and

These discussions sparked a reassessment in the 1980s and 1990s of my own thinking in relationship to two primary areas. A third has come to the fore more recently. The first element of my theological framework that found a voice in Moltmann's work was his stress on the relevance of eschatology for present socio-political realities and ideological commitments.

I came to faith in an evangelical tradition that put a lot of emphasis on the future, and at a popular level in local churches this interest could take on quite a sensationalistic tone. Debates centered on determining the timing of the Rapture of the church and of Christ's return. Battle lines were drawn over charts and differences in the interpretation of biblical passages offered by premillennialism (especially of the dispensationalist variety) and amillennialism. Questions began to form in my mind. What was the point of all of this? Did not the hope of the cessation of war, of just governance under Messiah, and of a time of abundance have something to say to Latin America, which was burdened by violence, oppressive systems, poverty, hunger, and disease? What was the purpose of those prophetic announcements to ancient Israel? Through Moltmann, I found an articulation of my conviction that eschatology—in particular premillennial eschatology—matters and has socio-ethical relevance for contemporary life.[9] The importance of the resolution of injustice within *our* history and in *this* world leads him to argue for the necessity and relevance of a millennial reign of Christ. Evangelical scholars have critically evaluated details of his thinking on the topic; some disagree with his premillennialism.[10] Fair enough. For me, however, Moltmann's work proved to be a stimulus to reread the prophets in order to comprehend their description of the Messiah and his reign and its significance, the power of that hope to sustain and encourage the faithful in difficult circumstances, and the possible options for world transformation that such a word generates.

The second, and related topic, that Moltmann's work prompted me to contemplate, was the importance of the horizons of history. During

Sobrino, *Jesus the Liberator,* 117–20, 240–45, *passim.*

9. In addition to *Theology of Hope,* see esp. Moltmann, *The Coming of God: Christian Eschatology.* Two related topics deserve mention. Moltmann's eschatology connects strongly with the resurrection of Jesus, a central tenet of evangelical faith, and argues for a place for Israel, a basic element of the premillennialism I espouse.

10. See the publications by Bauckham cited in fn. 2 above. Recent critiques include Chester, *Mission and the Coming of God,* and Neal, *Theology as Hope.*

the decades of revolutionary conflict in Latin America there was a wide-spread sense that its history was fated to a repetitive cycle of inescapable violence without viable alternatives to the status quo of injustice. This frustration, even despair, was reflected in the dictator novel, a genre found throughout the continent.[11] One of Latin America's most decorated authors, Nobel laureate Gabriel García Márquez, communicated this conviction in a powerful way in *One Hundred Years of Solitude*, in which natural disasters, murderous events, and damaging character types recur in self-destructive fashion in the land of Macondo, a symbolic reflection of his native Columbia and of all Latin America.[12] Early on, Moltmann and liberation theologians (for whom history's realities and direction were also crucial) appeared to take dissimilar stances on whether the future beckoned the present or whether from today's crises arose efforts to create a different future. Either way, history was an arena of the work of God. The evangelicalism of which I was a part either eschewed such thinking or restricted the purposes of God and his church to the salvation and nurture of souls; if history were a consideration, it was usually in connection with the end times. Yet, prophetic texts announce that judgment and disaster are not the final word of God. Beyond lies a renewed world under Messiah (e.g., Isa 65:17–25; Amos 9:11–15). In other words, there is a vibrant hope for a very different concrete existence, the reversal of the present.[13]

The third area in which Moltmann has impacted my theology concerns the relationship of God to evil and the suffering of the innocent. The question of theodicy is a human one that occupies every culture and all religions. It has, of course, always been a topic for Christian reflection, but in the last few years these concerns have taken on new importance in theological circles and in the public square. Lay people, biblical scholars, and theologians, and the voices of the "new atheism" wonder if the God of Scripture truly is good and if the Bible itself is not inherently a violent text whose deity is no longer acceptable. Moltmann's discussion of the solidarity of God with humanity in its pain, evident at the Exodus and culminating in the cross of Jesus, reoriented my thinking in profound

11. Carroll R., "The Prophetic Text and the Literature of Dissent in Latin America," 76–100.

12. García Márquez, *One Hundred Years of Solitude*.

13. Carroll R., "God and His People in the Nations' History," 39–70; Carroll R."Living Between the Lines," 50–64.

ways. He points out that the suffering of God on the cross says something about the trinitarian God himself; it is a window into God's nature
and not only the substance of atonement. The cross assumes a central
role in Christian identity and life and in the understanding of God. I am
aware that Moltmann's reflections have some problematic edges, but the
essence of his thought here is crucial to guide sufferers to Golgotha and
to the God who loves them and stands with them in unimaginable ways.

I have traced in brief fashion my own interaction with Moltmann.
Each person will have come to his thought in a different way. My approach has not been one that seeks to assess the particulars of his corpus
or their internal coherence; I am not a professional theologian. Rather,
in Moltmann I have found a voice that has pushed me to think for the
first time about fundamental issues of human existence in relationship
to Christian faith and to look at traditional concepts in fresh ways. My
reading of his work, therefore, has been a bit selective. I do appreciate
that he has dealt with the spectrum of Christian doctrines, always in
open-minded dialogue with the realities of the entire globe and with
a wide spectrum of perspectives both within and outside Christian
circles.[14] This incessant probing, characterized by a gracious ecumen-
ist spirit, is a gift to the church worldwide. In sum, for me Moltmann
has been, as it were, a theological stimulator, even though his method is
quite dissimilar from my own (due in part, I am sure, to his European
training and context, and his life experiences).

In contrast to this limited, more generalized personal appreciation,
you the reader have before you a series of essays that present careful
examination of Moltmann's publications. These theologians come from
diverse traditions and represent several theological institutions, thus
underlining the extent of Moltmann's influence. To analyze a theologian's thinking, especially one whose work is so wide-ranging and influential, is part and parcel of the theological enterprise. The authors
review and evaluate Moltmann's thinking on key systematic theological
categories from the confessional stance of evangelicalism. Not surprisingly, in a volume of this sort the degree of acceptance of his positions
varies. Some champion Moltmann's work, at least in part, while others

---

14. His memoir, *A Broad Place*, and *Experiences in Theology* are a demonstration of
this fact. An overview and assessment of Moltmann's interaction with minority voices,
other religions, and specific ethical issues would require another volume.

demand greater clarity in his formulations or profoundly disagree. This is a stimulating read.

I would hazard a guess that our German theologian would be pleased that he impacts thinking arising in the crucible of life and in educators' offices, classrooms, and conferences. Christian faith always needs reformulation in new contexts, even as it must respond to and connect itself with historic roots. It should inspire and challenge the church for mission in the world, even as it must be articulated clearly and constructively. Jürgen Moltmann's work has provided the material to do all of this, and we are all the richer for it.

M. Daniel Carroll R.

Preface

IN SPITE OF CONTROVERSIES around him, Jürgen Moltmann (1926–)
should be regarded as one of the most influential Christian theologians since Karl Barth (1886–1968). Ever since the publication of his
major theological work, *The Theology of Hope*, in the middle of 1960s,
Moltmann's creative and innovative theology has been making a considerable impact upon not only Euro-American but also majority world
theologians. For example, it is evident that Latin American liberation
theologians were heavily indebted to his theology for its foundation as
well as consolidation. Furthermore, Korean *Minjung* Theology, given
birth to in the context of the Korean democratization movement in the
1970s, was considerably influenced by Moltmann's theological insights
and inspirations. In addition, his theology has made an impact upon
global Pentecostalism, feminist liberation theology, and environmental
theology. More than anything else, his trinitarian theological reflection
has made a great impact upon the renaissance of trinitarian theology in
the global theological context in the last thirty years.

However, because of his revisionist positions on several areas
of Christian doctrines, evangelical theologians have engaged with
Moltmann's theology insufficiently and hesitatingly. For example,
Moltmann's universalistic tendencies have caused evangelical theologians to accuse him of championing an extreme or heterodox view of
soteriology. Evangelical theologians and Christians have shown a tendency to sweepingly criticize Moltmann without a serious and responsible engagement with his theological arguments. This book aims to fill
the gap, envisioning a critical engagement with major loci of Moltmann's
dogmatic theology from a solidly evangelical perspective. I have invited
evangelical theologians of caliber with various backgrounds to analyze

and reflect upon major doctrinal positions of Moltmann. Among these doctrinal areas are Scripture, Christology, pneumatology, ecclesiology, and eschatology, to name a few. This critical engagement is geared to test Moltmann's theology, taking the good and leaving the bad aside. Unless evangelical theology wants to remain in a fundamentalist ghetto, it should learn how to engage responsibly with non-evangelical theologians and theological movements. Such an engagement, I hope, will demonstrate the intellectual maturity and dynamics of evangelical theology and its commitment to the Lord's command to "test the spirits to see whether they are from God."

Sung Wook Chung

1

Moltmann on Scripture and Revelation

Sung Wook Chung

INTRODUCTION

IN SPITE OF CONTROVERSIES around him, Jürgen Moltmann (1926–) should be regarded as one of the most influential Christian theologians within the camp of ecumenical theology since Karl Barth (1886–1968). However, because of his revisionist positions on many areas of Christian doctrines, evangelical theologians have engaged with Moltmann's theology insufficiently and hesitatingly. This chapter aims to fill the gap, envisioning a critical engagement with a major locus of Moltmann's dogmatic theology, that is, his doctrine of revelation and Scripture, from a consensual evangelical perspective. This critical analysis, engagement, and reflection is geared to test Moltmann's theology, taking the good and leaving the bad aside.

EVANGELICAL CONSENSUS

Revelation

Evangelical theologians have defined revelation as the infinite God's self-manifestation and self-communication toward finite humans.[1] They have also divided revelation into two categories: *general* or

1. Erickson, *Christian Theology*, 178.

universal revelation and *special* or specific or particular revelation. General revelation refers to the sort of divine revelation which is available to all human beings, at all places, and at all times. A great example of general revelation is the natural order, which reveals "God's invisible qualities—his eternal power and divine nature since the creation of the world" (Rom 1:20). In addition, evangelical theologians have agreed that human history and human constitution and conscience are also channels of general revelation through which some genuine, albeit confused and distorted, knowledge about God's existence and attributes is offered to all people all over the world. However, because of human sin, human beings cannot enter into a salvific and personal relationship with God through general revelation. This makes another revelation, namely, special revelation necessary.

Special revelation refers to divine self-communication that is available to specific people, at specific places, and at specific times. The purpose of special revelation is to give sinners authentic knowledge of God that leads them to redemptive and personal relationship with God. Evangelical theologians have consented that the triune God revealed himself through a variety of channels including prophetic oracles, visions, dreams, miracles, mighty acts, and appearances. The climax of divine special revelation came with the incarnation, life, death, and resurrection of Jesus Christ, the Son of God (Heb 1:1–2). Christ's apostles were appointed to be receivers and deliverers of special revelation.[2]

Scripture

According to the evangelical tradition, divine special revelation was inscripturated into sixty-six canonical books through divine inspiration. These inspired books of the Bible are considered to be authoritative for faith and practice of all Christians. As a natural corollary of divine inspiration of the Bible, most evangelical theologians have acknowledged that the Scripture is inerrant or infallible in what it affirms, whether it is related to history, archeology, geography, and science as well as to matters of faith and salvation.[3]

2. For a powerful discussion of the idea of revelation from an evangelical perspective, see Lewis and Demarest, *Integrative Theology*, 59–128.

3. Undoubtedly, some progressive evangelical theologians may argue that the Bible is infallible only in relation to the matters of faith and salvation. Still, these progressive evangelicals are a minority group within the global evangelical movement.

Evangelical theologians have also agreed that theology as a scientific discipline should be understood to be the study and discourse about God on the basis of biblical revelation. So theology should pursue the knowledge of God that is available primarily in and through the Bible. In that sense, Scripture is the only norming norm of theological discourse, which is differentiated from norms such as tradition, reason, and experience.[4] This means there is a close and inseparable connection between theology and the Scripture. The Bible defines the boundary of theology and theology is bound by biblical presuppositions and conceptions. Thus, for evangelicals, genuine theology must be revealed theology, that is, theology grounded upon biblical revelation. Although most evangelicals acknowledge that natural knowledge of God, albeit confused, is available through general revelation, natural theology as a theological discipline independent of revealed theology is anathema.

MOLTMANN ON REVELATION

Then, what about Moltmann's idea of revelation? Does he endorse evangelical ideas of revelation? Does he consent to evangelical categories such as general revelation and special revelation? In short, what on earth is revelation for Moltmann?

It is clear that Moltmann does not endorse evangelical ideas of revelation. For him, when traditional theology—including its evangelical version—discusses revelation, it reduces everything to the problem of the knowledge of God and as a result it "brings about the much lamented formalism of revelation theology."[5] In contrast to the traditional evangelical notion of revelation, which is identified with divine self-disclosure and self-manifestation, Moltmann highlights the biblical notion of the promise of God in terms of God's revealing action. In so doing, he makes the notion of revelation clothed with radically eschatological character and reduces everything to the problem of "hope" in God, not to the problem of the "knowledge" of God. This means that for Moltmann the idea of knowledge of God is not a framework regulating and governing the idea of revelation any longer. Rather, the ideas of promise and hope

---

4. For an excellent discussion of issues related to norms of theology by a postconservative evangelical theologian, see Franke, *The Character of Theology*, 130–63.

5. Moltmann, *The Theology of Hope*, 42.

dominate his discussion of revelation. Moltmann states, "But now the more recent theology of the Old Testament has indeed shown that the words and statements about the 'revealing of God' in the Old Testament are combined throughout with statements about the 'promise of God.' God reveals himself in the form of promise and in the history that is marked by promise."[6]

Moltmann continues to argue that Israelite faith was radically distinguished from the faith of the world around Israel in that the former was religion centered on the God of promise while the latter was focused on the gods of epiphanies. The essential difference between them did not lie in the fact that Israelite faith was a religion of revelation while Babylonian faith was not. Rather, the difference did lie in "the different ways of conceiving and speaking of the revelation and self-manifestation of the deity."[7]

Therefore, while traditional theology, including its evangelical version, has acknowledged that God reveals what he is like, what he does, and what he requires of humans through his self-manifestation and self-communication, Moltmann's new theology recognizes that God reveals primarily his "faithfulness, and in it himself and his presence,"[8] by making and fulfilling promises. And God's action of making and fulfilling promises transforms his revelation into something radically eschatological. Moltmann contends, "But if promise is determinative of what is said of the revealing of God, then every theological view of biblical revelation contains implicitly a governing view of eschatology . . . The Christian doctrine of the revelation of God must be eschatologically understood, namely, in the field of the promise and expectation of the future of the church."[9]

Another rationale behind his radical reinterpretation of the biblical idea of revelation lies in his acceptance of the Reformation theology of promise and rejection of the post-Reformation theology of revelation. Moltmann argues that "the correlate of faith is for the Reformers not an idea of revelation, but is expressly described by them as the *promissio dei: fides et promissio sunt correlativa*. Faith is called to life by promise and is therefore essentially hope, confidence, trust in the God who will

6. Ibid.
7. Ibid., 43.
8. Ibid.
9. Ibid.

not lie but will remain faithful to his promise."[10] This means that for the Reformers, Christians are called to trust God's faithfulness and to hope that God's promise will be fulfilled on account of his faithfulness, not to have faith in the generic and abstract idea of divine revelation.

It is important to appreciate that in this context Moltmann contrasts the Reformers' theology of promise with Protestant orthodoxy's theology of reason and revelation. He continues to argue, "it was only in Protestant orthodoxy that under the constraint of the question of reason and revelation, nature and grace, the problem of revelation became the central theme of dogmatic prolegomena. It was only when theology began to employ a concept of reason and a concept of nature which were not derived from a view of promise but were now taken over from Aristotle, that the problem of revelation appeared in its familiar form."[11] This means that for Moltmann ever since the ascendancy of Protestant orthodoxy, the biblical idea of revelation based on God's promise has been suppressed and suffocated and the theme of divine revelation based on God's self-communication has taken the place of the theme of divine promise and divine faithfulness to that promise. For this reason, Moltmann attempts to retrieve the "eschatological outlook"[12] in which revelation is interpreted to be God's promise and human hope in its fulfillment.

On the basis of the above discussion, we can conclude that Moltmann's ideas of revelation are radically different from the evangelical consensus on the notion of revelation. In addition, the typical evangelical division of revelation into the two categories of general and special revelation has no significance for Moltmann's eschatologically redefined idea of revelation. Another essential difference between evangelical notion of special revelation and Moltmann's idea of revelation lies in the fact that the motif of redemption, reconciliation, and salvation is systematically dismissed in Moltmann's discussion of revelation. For evangelical theology, special revelation is necessary for reconciliation between the righteous God and sinful humans.

Although Moltmann argues that promise as the mode of divine revelation is the promise of liberation and redemption, his motif of liberation is reinterpreted to be primarily horizontal liberation from the

10. Ibid., 44.
11. Ibid.
12. Ibid.

power of an unjust government or economic system, not vertical liberation from rebellion against God and the spiritual power of the kingdom
of darkness. It seems undeniable that the evangelical ideas of forgiveness
of sins and justification of sinners are suppressed in Moltmann's discussion of revelation.

In spite of these demerits of Moltmann's theology of revelation,
evangelical theology can be appreciative of Moltmann's reconstruction
of the idea of revelation from the perspective of God's promise and
fulfillment. In particular, by emphasizing God's promise as the mode
of divine revelation, Moltmann presented a timely antidote and viable
alternative to the Barthian and Brunnerian reinterpretation of revelation as essentially personal and existential, which dismisses outright
the propositional dimension of divine revelation. For both Barth and
Brunner, revelation is understood to be essentially a personal encounter
between God and humans with no necessity of propositional communication. However, Moltmann struck a keen balance between propositional and personal dimensions of divine revelation by reinterpreting
it from the perspective of making and fulfilling promises. It is because
an action of making promises is both personal and propositional in its
essential character. A promise should be made personally and narrated
with cognitive content[13] if it intends to stand. Without delivering some
information about the future, a promise cannot be made genuinely.

Another positive point that evangelicals can reappropriate from
Moltmann's theology of revelation is his emphasis upon the intercon-
nection between divine revelation and God's faithfulness. Evangelicals
have traditionally argued that through the action of self-communication God reveals his manifold attributes including divine faithfulness.
However, by connecting revelation with the framework of the history of
promise and fulfillment, Moltmann stresses correctly God's faithfulness
on which the entire Bible unashamedly focuses. Evangelicals may agree
with Moltmann that divine faithfulness is one of the most significant
attributes of God on which the entire history of redemption hinges.

13. Cf. Thiemann, *Revelation and Theology*, 112–77.

MOLTMANN ON SCRIPTURE

Then, what about Moltmann's view of Scripture? Does Moltmann agree with evangelical ideas of the Bible such as inspiration, inerrancy, infallibility, and authority? Does he regard the Bible as supernaturally inscripturated and preserved revelation and the Word of God?

First of all, as a Christian theologian, Moltmann seems to think of the Scripture as somewhat authoritative for theological reflection and discussion. However, he does not endorse the traditional evangelical idea of the divine authority of Scripture. He states,

> But in my dealings with what the biblical writings say I have also noticed how critical and free I have become towards them. Of course I want to know what they intend to say, but I do not feel bound to take only what they say, and repeat it, and interpret it. I can quite well conceive that it is possible to say what they say in a different way. In other words, I take Scripture as a stimulus to my own theological thinking, not as an authoritative blueprint and confining boundary.[14]

It is crystal clear from the above statement that Moltmann's view of the Bible is considerably different from an evangelical consensus. For most evangelicals, Scripture remains divinely authoritative and absolutely binding in what it speaks about, whereas Moltmann wants to enjoy relative freedom to take Scripture as one of many stimulating resources for theological endeavors.

In addition, Moltmann seems to regard the traditional evangelical view of Scripture as a "fundamentalist" option and so he rejects it outright. In particular, he does not champion the idea of the verbal inspiration of Scripture. He contends, "We find independent status being given to Scripture in the various doctrines about the *verbal inspiration* of Scripture. These writings are then holy in the literal sense, because the holy Spirit itself guided the pens of the writers . . . To see the Spirit at work only in the verbal inspiration of Scripture is a reduction of the mighty efficacy of God the Spirit which does not accord with 'the matter of scripture.' 'The matter of scripter' does not receive its due through fundamentalism."[15]

---

14. Moltmann, *Experiences in Theology*, xxii.
15. Ibid., 136.

It is regrettable that Moltmann does not differentiate evangelical-ism from fundamentalism in the above statement.[16] In the context of North American evangelicalism, fundamentalism cannot be identified with evangelicalism in spite of their common heritage in relation to a high view of the Bible. For sure, evangelicals are willing to agree with fundamentalists in terms of the idea of verbal inspiration of Scripture and biblical inerrancy as its corollary. However, evangelical theology does reject the fundamentalist idea of "dictation," a more rigid and al-most *docetic* form of inspiration, and the fundamentalist practice of extremely literalistic hermeneutics without a proper concern for genre differences and diversity of historical background of the text.

Thus, evangelical theologians have advocated the idea of "organic" inspiration and the hermeneutical practice which respects the genre differences, historical backgrounds, and diverse contexts of biblical texts. However, Moltmann seems to ignore these seemingly minute but practically very significant differences between evangelicalism and fun-damentalism at least in the context of the North American evangelical movement and the church in the global South.[17]

The above statement gives us an impression that for Moltmann evangelicals (for him fundamentalists) see the Spirit at work only in the verbal inspiration of Scripture. This is a regrettable statement based on his prejudice and bias against evangelicalism (for him fundamentalism). Most evangelicals in North America, even fundamentalists, do see the Spirit at work in other areas beyond the verbal inspiration of Scripture. I will discuss it in more detail in later sections of this paper. However, it would be sufficient to note here that most evangelicals and even some fundamentalists believe that the Holy Spirit enables and empowers us to understand the true meaning of the Bible by illuminating us with his supernatural light.

In the process of his rejection of the evangelical notion of verbal inspiration, Moltmann introduces the idea of "the matter of Scripture" against which all scriptural texts and passages must be judged. Moltmann argues, "In comparing the different traditions, we have to examine the

16. We can find the same tendency in Karl Barth's *Church Dogmatics* as well. Barth identifies evangelicalism with fundamentalism without distinguishing them properly.

17. It is important to appreciate that most evangelical Christians in the global South concur with the North American evangelical view of Scripture presented here. Cf. Jenkins, *The New Faces of Christianity: Believing the Bible in the Global South*.

Scriptures with a view to seeing how they bring out 'the matter' they share. Objective hermeneutics presupposes the difference between 'the matter of Scripture' and the scriptural text, and the interior circle of the two; and it is open to objective criticism of what is written."[18] As a result, while some biblical texts and passages are more directly related to "the matter of Scripture" and so more authoritative and substantially contributive and stimulating for theological reflection, others are more indirectly related to it and so less authoritative.

Thus, he seems to advocate a new version of "the canon within the canon" approach. His approach seems to be squarely opposed to the Reformation approach which is characterized by the idea of *tota scriptura*, which means that the totality and entirety of Scripture must be taken to be authoritative, not some portion of it. It is undeniable that evangelical theologians have concurred with this Reformation idea, at least in theory, although one may argue that evangelicals have not practiced it consistently.

Then, what is "the matter of Scripture" for Moltmann? He contends,

> "The matter of Scripture" in the Tenach/Old Testament is God's covenant with Israel and the divine promises given in that covenant, promises which point beyond Israel to the salvation of all peoples and the peace of the whole creation . . . In the New Testament "the matter of Scripture" is the unconditional endorsement and universal enactment of God's promises through and in Christ, and the beginning of their fulfillment in the experiences of God's Spirit. The Christian Scriptures are "holy" inasmuch as they correspond to God's promise in Christ and in the Spirit; they are "hallowed" or sanctified by their function for the proclamation of the gospel to the nations, and for the new life in the Spirit. They are writings on which the church is founded, and life-renewing texts of the promise.[19]

Probably, many evangelical theologians would agree that the central gist or the red thread running through the entire Old Testament is "God's covenant with Israel and the divine promises given in that covenant, promises which point beyond Israel to the salvation of all peoples and the peace of the whole creation," as Moltmann understands. In this sense, evangelical theologians may conclude that Moltmann has read

18. Moltmann, *Experiences in Theology*, 135.
19. Ibid., 135–36.

the Old Testament attentively and correctly. It is important to note, however, that evangelicals would not endorse Moltmann's contention that "God's covenant with Israel and the divine promises given in that covenant, promises which point beyond Israel to the salvation of all peoples and the peace of the whole creation" is the "matter of Scripture" against which biblical texts and passages should be judged and as a result of this judgment some biblical texts and passages might be dismissed as non-canonical, less authoritative, or unsubstantially contributive.

In a similar vein, many evangelicals would find Moltmann's reading of the New Testament to be appropriate in that he emphasizes correctly the fulfillment dimension of God's promises of the new life in Christ and the Holy Spirit. Nevertheless, many evangelicals would not accept Moltmann's assertion that "the matter of Scripture" in the New Testament should play a role of "the canon within the canon" because it abrogates the Reformation affirmation of *sola et tota scriptura*. For most evangelicals, the entire Scripture including Old and New Testaments is the canon, the ruler or the standard, which has divine authority for their faith and practice. Unquestionably, it is absolutely appropriate for evangelicals to attempt to find the red thread or so-called central theme running through both the Testaments. However, it is inappropriate for evangelicals to identify a theme or a text as "the matter of Scripture" which regulates the canonicity of other biblical themes and texts. Furthermore, many evangelicals would criticize Moltmann's idea of "the matter of Scripture" and his definition of it, as they seem to make his theological judgment an arbitrary exercise, rather than a principled and balanced action in congruence with the evangelical presuppositions that they inherited from the Reformation.

In line with the above discussion, we may raise another serious question. Does Moltmann think that the canon of the Scripture is closed or open? The question whether the canon is closed or not has been perennially raised in evangelical circles and beyond. The evangelical consensus in relation to the question is that the canon is closed with the finishing of the Book of Revelation. Therefore, after the closing of the canon, no new revelation can be identified and added as "canonical" or "divinely authoritative." According to the authoritative confessions of the Reformation, adding any other book or text to the canon should be condemned and cursed.

It is important to appreciate, however, that Moltmann does not consent to the evangelical consensus on the closing of the canon. He argues,

> If we look only at the scriptural texts themselves, we have to con-
> sider the canon to be closed, or at most open for the addition
> of other writings. But if we look at the scriptural texts from the
> angle of "the matter of Scripture," then the canon remains open:
> we can, for objective reasons, judge the Epistle of James to be
> "an epistle of straw," as Luther did, and might prefer to exclude
> the book of Revelation; but we can also preach from non-biblical
> texts if they accord with "the matter of Scripture." A quotation
> from the Bible is not enough to guarantee the truth of what is
> said. And what would happen if someone found what proved to
> be a Third Epistle of Paul to the Corinthians?[20]

It is undeniable that Luther was suspicious about the canonic-ity of the Epistle of James and the Book of Revelation. It is important to remember, however, that later Lutheran and Reformed confessions agreed unanimously that the canon is closed and that only the sixty-six books of the Old and New Testaments are the divinely inspired Word of God. And evangelical tradition has unanimously endorsed this Reformation affirmation. Thus, it is regrettable that Moltmann argues that even non-biblical texts can be preached if they are consistent with "the matter of Scripture."

It is even more regrettable that Moltmann contends that "a quota-tion from the Bible is not enough to guarantee the truth of what is said." From an evangelical perspective, his contention seems to be contradic-tory to the Lord Jesus' own view and use of Scripture. For example, when the Lord Jesus was tempted by Satan, he rejected Satan's temptation by quoting the Old Testament passages and by using the same phrase, "it is written." For Jesus Christ, the phrase "it is written" had the same meaning as the phrase "God has spoken." This means Jesus Christ identified the Bible with the Word of God written, which cannot be broken, not merely a fallible human testimony of faith. Of course, evangelicals would agree with Moltmann that when a quotation from the Bible is made out of its context and without proper hermeneutical exercise, "it is not enough to guarantee the truth of what is said." However, it is important remember that for evangelicals a verse—quoted within its own context and with

20. Ibid., 138–39

the help of proper hermeneutical exercise—*is* "enough to guarantee the truth what it said."

In this context, we should raise another decisive question in relation to Moltmann's view of Scripture. Is the Bible the Word of God for Moltmann? If so, what does he mean by that? It is interesting to point out that for Moltmann the Bible can be identified with both the Word of God and a human testimony of faith. For Moltmann, as the Word of God the Christian Scripture requires "a hermeneutics from above" and as a human testimony of faith the Bible requires "a hermeneutics from below." According to Moltmann, "a hermeneutics from above" has been associated with "orthodox Protestantism, and in Protestantism the Reformed tradition particularly" and Karl Barth has also advocated this approach to the Bible.[21]

It is very important to appreciate, however, that both Moltmann and Barth understand the Bible to be a witness to divine address and divine history, not to be divinely inspired and inscripturated Word of God *per se*. The idea of divine inspiration is dismissed in this context as well. As a result, the Bible itself cannot be the inerrant Word of God for either Moltmann or Barth. Therefore, it is important to appreciate that even when Moltmann uses the phrase "the Word of God" in relation to the Bible, he does *not* mean the same thing that evangelicals ordinarily do.

On the other hand, Moltmann states, "A 'hermeneutics from below' develops[22] once the biblical writings are viewed as human testimony of faith, which have been historically, socially, and culturally conditioned. Then, their determining subject is not the sovereign self-revealing God; it is the historically existing and responding human being." "A hermeneutics from below," according to Moltmann, has been associated with liberal theology and its adoption of historical-critical methodology in relation to the Bible. A fundamental presupposition of this approach is that the Scripture has errors and fallacies in matters of history, geography, archeology, and science. While evangelical theologians have been consistently rejecting the viability of historical-critical methodology and some of them have advocated a responsible employment of it in the con-

21. Ibid., 139. It is questionable that Barth took the same approach to Scripture as orthodox Protestantism and the Reformed tradition. Barth never endorsed the idea of biblical inerrancy and supernatural inspiration although it is undeniable that he retained a higher view of the Bible than German liberal Protestantism.

22. Ibid., 141

text of the acknowledgement of the supernatural, Moltmann believes that the Bible should be investigated by the historical-critical method at least in the beginning stage of believers' engagement with the Bible. This is another example of significant differences between evangelicals and Moltmann in their views of the Bible.

Because of his energetic endorsement of the validity of historical-critical methodology, Moltmann does not accept the historicity of Genesis 1–3. The opening three chapters of the Book of Genesis are a record of myth, "which offers a mythological interpretation of the physical history of the world."[23] Moreover, for him, Adam was not a historical figure and the fall was not a historical event. It is evident that Moltmann's view of the beginning chapters of the Book of Genesis makes a seriously negative impact upon his doctrines of humanity, sin, and redemption. For example, Moltmann comments on the Pauline and Protestant doctrine of original and universal sin as follows: "Collective guilt of this kind makes people blind to specific, practical guilt. Indeed it can actually be used as an excuse for specific, practical guilt. The universality of sin leads to a universal night in which everything is equally black, and even to use weapons of mass extermination is no longer special."[24]

The final question that should be raised in relation to the doctrine of Scripture is who the real interpreter of the Bible is. Is it the Holy Spirit, the Bible, or the reader? The Reformers argued that Scripture itself is its true interpreter by saying "Scripture interprets itself (*Scriptura sacra sui ipsius interpres*)." Evangelicals have demonstrated a tendency to accept this hermeneutical axiom.

However, Moltmann is critical of it and presents an alternative to it from the perspective of the "matter of Scripture." He argues that although the Reformation principle of Scripture's self-interpretation made a great contribution to the renewal of the old church, it "also meant that the interpretative authority of enlightened or inspired reason was denied too—not only rationalist interpretation, but 'pneumatological exegesis' as well."[25] As a result, the post-Reformation Protestant orthodoxy made

23. Moltmann, *Spirit of Life*, 125–26.
24. Ibid., 126.
25. Ibid., 128.

Scripture "a kind of Protestant pocket-pope, infallible and inerrant"[26] and the Bible became "no less than Jesus Christ existing as Scripture."[27]

For Moltmann, since "the matter of Scripture" is God's promissory history, the Holy Spirit must be regarded as its real interpreter. He argues,

> What the Spirit of truth communicates is knowledge of Christ the Lord and of the God who has raised him. But the fact that the Spirit communicates this is something new and specific to the Spirit, over against what Christ and God the Father have done and do. Why   did Christ come, die, and rise again? The answer is: in order to send the Spirit who sanctifies life and opens up the future of the eternal kingdom . . . From time immemorial, the Holy Spirit has been understood as the eternal light which enlightens and illuminates. Because, as we are told, God is known only through God, it is in his light alone that we see light (Ps 36:9). It is not only the knowledge of God that proceeds from God; it is the knowing too. Just as no one knows the Father except the Son (Matt 11:27), so no one confesses Jesus as Lord except in the Holy Spirit (1 Cor 12:4). This is formulated as if it were a limiting condition, but what it means is the very reverse—a marvelous de-limitation of the trinitarian circle: the person who knows Christ and believes the God who   raised him from the dead is illuminated by God the Spirit, and enters into the eternal light.[28]

Moltmann continues to argue that, as the giver of life, the Holy Spirit interprets and communicates to us what furthers life in the biblical texts. The Holy Spirit also "subjects to criticism whatever is hostile to life."[29] For him, the Holy Spirit is not only the Spirit of the truth but also the Spirit of *life*. As the Spirit of life, for Moltmann, the Holy Spirit interprets the Scripture for the purpose of furthering life. In this context, Moltmann urges theologians to pay attention to "a new, extended version of the Calvinist doctrine about the inner testimony of the Holy Spirit (*testimonium Spirituus Sancti internum*)."[30] According to Calvin's

26. Ibid., 129.

27. Ibid., 139. It is undeniable that Moltmann's perception of the post-Reformation Protestant Orthodox theology is distorted and biased. Richard A. Muller has made a great contribution to revising such a negative view about Protestant Orthodoxy that heavily influenced Moltmann. See Muller, *Post-Reformation Reformed Dogmatics.*

28. Ibid., 145–46.

29. Ibid., 149.

30. Ibid., 143.

original idea of *testimonium Spirituus Sancti internum*, the Holy Spirit is the One who convinces us of the divine authority and truthfulness of the Scripture by giving us mysterious and internal testimonies about the Scripture, which he inspired to be written and inscripturated.

It is important, however, to appreciate here that although Calvin endorsed the idea of *testimonium Spirituus Sancti internum*, he never acknowledged that the idea of *testimonium Spirituus Sancti internum* can be contradictory to the idea of *tota et sola scriptura* because Calvin believed that the entire Bible is the product of the Holy Spirit's inspiration. This means that, for Calvin, the Holy Spirit respects the authority of the *entire* Scripture simply because he is the real Author of the Bible in its totality. In stark contrast, although Moltmann endorses Calvin's idea of *testimonium Spirituus Sancti internum*, he innovatively reinterprets it in a manner that the principle of *testimonium Spirituus Sancti internum* overrides the idea of *sola et tota scriptura*. As a consequence, for Moltmann, some portion of biblical testimony can be contradictory to the Holy Spirit's agenda of furthering life. This makes the adoption of the canon within the canon approach necessary and inevitable for him. However, Calvin never endorsed the idea of the canon within the canon.

Therefore, it seems evident from the above discussion that evangelicals cannot endorse many points of Moltmann's view of Scripture and his hermeneutics in spite of his many other insightful points that we can reappropriate in proper contexts.

CONCLUDING REMARKS

On the basis of the above discussion, we may conclude that Moltmann's ideas of revelation and Scripture have many divergences from those of evangelical tradition. Nevertheless, if we as evangelicals endeavor to learn from his insights and proposals, we may reappropriate creatively some of his insights in the context of evangelical theological discussions. It is important for us as evangelicals to engage with all new theological proposals and ideas from all perspectives. It is because of the fact that the Lord commands us to "test the spirits to see whether they are form God" (1 John 4:1) in order to take what is good and consistent with the Word of God and leave aside what is inconsistent with the Bible. This means that evangelicals cannot help maintaining an ambivalent attitude, both love and serious suspicion, toward Moltmann.

2

Moltmann's Communitarian Trinity

Kurt Anders Richardson

MOLTMANN'S THEOLOGICAL STARTING POINT

THE FIRST CRISIS OF modern theology (mid-fifteenth century to today) was two-fold: soteriological and trinitarian. The former was embodied in the polemic between the Papacy and the Reformers; the latter appeared in conflicts with anti-trinitarians (Socinians, etc). An extension of the second came with the advent of Deism in the Enlightenment theses of "natural religion"—from which "natural theology" has its origins and most "natural" affinity—which became an underlying agenda for many liberal and culturally Protestant theological agendas.[1] Schleiermacher is incorrectly credited with theologically de-centering the Trinity, but this he did not do, even though consigning trinitarian doctrine to the appendix of his *Glaubenslehre*.[2] The doctrine of the Trinity certainly ceased to be the foundational link to all other

1. Concerning, "Natural theology"/*natürliche Theologie*, an immense topic reflecting the encounter with "natural science"; cf., Alexander and Numbers, *Biology and Ideology from Descartes to Dawkins*; Crocker, *Religion, Reason, and Nature in Early Modern Europe*; Brunner, *Natur und gnade: zum gespräch mit Karl Barth*; Hart, *Karl Barth vs. Emil Brunner*. Moltmann's bigger issue is with monotheism and the history of theology's yielding to the idea at the expense of trinitarian reasoning.

2. *The Christian Faith*, 1831; did not deny the doctrine but demurred in providing a new formulation, this was a signal of its dislocation from essential theological exposition for over a century.

theological *topoi* as it had functioned in the traditions. On the traditionalist side, however, a surfeit of apologetics and dogma had virtually created the skepticism that would plague modern theological discourse. Ultimately, modernist liberal theology would lose its grip on soteriology as well in the social and cultural crises of the twentieth century.

Karl Barth is credited with having re-centered the doctrine of the Trinity within Christian theology. Jürgen Moltmann, publishing in time for Barth to read his first theology, had begun his theological studies at Göttingen under Otto Weber, one of Barth's eminent students. As with Barth, essential to understanding the rejection of natural theology is the identification of revelation in Christ with salvation and therefore the non-functionality of natural revelation as an agent of divine redemption. God is known only if God is known soteriologically in Christ and therefore as Trinity. This Trinity/soteriology linkage is also key to understanding Moltmann's contribution that will be discussed in this chapter, particularly as formulated in his books: *The Crucified God* (1974) and yet more fully in his, *Trinity and the Kingdom of God* (1980). Although the earlier work received some criticism for a binitarian tendency (the Western foregrounding of the Father/Son relation with the Holy Spirit as the eternal bond of their relation), the second book provided a kind of corrective based in the social analogy of the Trinity.[3] Liberal Christian theology has tended to reject the notion of God as triune and Jesus as Son of God incarnate. But where modern theologians embraced the liberal tradition in theology,[4] most notably that of Paul Tillich, Moltmann has been, from the beginning of his career, what for our purposes here is a "modern orthodox" theologian.[5]

---

3. Characteristic of the Cappadocian Fathers: Basil of Caesarea, Gregory of Nazianzen, and Gregory of Nyssa; most recently and Anglo-American theology: Richard Swinburne, Cornelius Plantinga, Jr., and William Lane Craig.

4. It must be remembered that "liberalism" in theology was originally connected with the notion of free will in salvation as over against predestination. One could embrace every aspect of traditional doctrine concerning God and Jesus Christ while asserting a "liberal" theology of the human will. The move to reduce Christian doctrine to only those features which supposedly comported with reason in "natural religion" was a separate and superseding development.

5. No one has much appreciated the moniker, "neo-orthodoxy" although it may perhaps be best applied to the likes of Emil Brunner, where some degree of reductionism of doctrinal understanding is in evidence. By contrast, "modern orthodoxy" (also in Judaism) seeks to avoid all reductionism of doctrine and to restate classic accounts of the epistemology of revelation. "Orthodox and modern" has received a helpful

Moltmann took his cues early from Barth and others of the so-called "theology of crisis" of the inter-war period of the Weimar Republic. In various senses these theologians took the revelation of God in Jesus Christ with utmost seriousness. Although Barth was committed to rational, critical analysis of Scripture he was simultaneously committed to "churchly" theology; i.e., that the church of Jesus Christ contributes to the actual knowledge of the world through its reception of revelation. This was Barth's theological realism, which is evident in Moltmann's own theological epistemology and is evident from the beginning of his many writings and teaching career within the theological faculty of the University of Tübingen.[6]

In his early lengthy assessment of the theology of crisis Moltmann would be sympathetic both to Bonhoeffer's concern about "revelational positivism" in Barth, as well as the radical rejection of the Reformed tradition of natural theology as expounded by Emil Brunner. Indeed, it can be said that part of the theological rationale for Moltmann's first and still most well known work, *The Theology of Hope*,[7] is in some ways an extension of the Brunnerian method. Before the emergence of the latest generation of Barthians, theologians who embraced the Reformed tradition, resisting the agendas of Tillich and Bultmann, largely embraced that of Brunner—as yet unwilling to buck the trends of many centuries where employing natural or "rational" arguments were allied to the classic appeal to the unique authority of revelation.

The theology of hope by Moltmann is certainly trinitarian and yet there is a massive "point of contact" (*Anknüpfungspunkt*) with general revelation in the principle of hope itself—particularly as articulated in the philosophy of Ernst Bloch (himself a kind of political theologian for Marxist/Jewish dialogue). In a sense, this was the book of and for the Marxist/Christian dialogue in Europe—what it was to become in Latin America would be quite different. It cannot be underestimated how terribly traditional theology had fared under the conditions of the time: not only under Nazism, but also under the many fascist and other types

definition in McCormack, *Orthodox and Modern*.

6. Cf. Moltmann, *A Broad Place*; Moltmann, *Sun of Righteousness, Arise!*.

7. Cf. Moltmann, *Theologie der Hoffnung*; Moltmann, *Theology of Hope*; also, Bauckham, ed. *God Will Be All in All*; Rossi-Keen, "Jürgen Moltmann's Doctrine of God," 447–63; Conyers, *God, Hope, and History*; Harvie, *Jürgen Moltmann's Ethics of Hope*.

of dictatorships in Europe in the first half of the twentieth century. Over and over again traditionalists had allied themselves to dictatorial regimes to their own massive discredit and consequently, to manipulation by many religious conservative adjuncts of these regimes. In Germany, "de-nazification" after WWII was a necessary process to which all of Moltmann's teachers would have had to submit or to recognize as unavoidable. The growing Soviet Block of nations had been "allies" during the war and this meant that communist philosophy became a fact of life among many within most institutions of higher learning. Intellectually, this fact of life meant that democratic and representative politics were in constant debate with varieties of Marxism. These were the bidders in the European "marketplace of ideas" and Moltmann, along with many other committed Christian theologians, were not about to surrender to the Marxists. *The Theology of Hope* was actually a non-Marxist, Christian answer to the Marxists.

As a typical approach of Christian apologists and theologians, Moltmann acquired a profound understanding of his dialogue partners' philosophy, seeking to introduce a theology with the social significance in post-War Europe. He drew out of the tradition of Christian soteriology and eschatology a christologically-centered political theology of hope that would supersede the Marxist model of the future communist state and community. The trinitarian God is already in evidence in the *Theology of Hope* (1964) but was not yet prominent and certainly not agenda-setting.

By the early 60s, Barth's trinitarian influence was still coming to fruition. Absent the full effects of this reorientation, the trinitarian dimension appears as an intentional notice of Moltmann's modern orthodoxy but without a full-orbed theology of God. From the perspective of his contemporaries, the Hegelian "left-wing" of Marxism was being confronted by Moltmann's "right-wing" Christian theology of hope. Bloch's philosophy had already been a Messianic Jewish interpretation of Marxist eschatology with Moltmann produced his christological messianism that was none the less liberationist in it political program. Although there is no radical dichotomizing of a Christology from below and one from above in Moltmann's theology, this eschatological orientation clearly dominates for the time being because of its close connection with the concreteness of God's action toward human beings and the actions he call them to in Jesus Christ. *Theology of Hope* demonstrated the strong praxis orientation of Moltmann's theology. In addition, his great burden was is to engage Marxism at the point of theodicy and the problem of evil and suffering as interpreted through the work of Christ.

The *Theology of Hope* is more of an exercise in apologetics than doctrine or dogmatics or, as Moltmann preferred to understand it, preparatory study (*prolegomena*) in theology. Moltmann regarded "theology of hope" as coming from the eschatological orientation of all Christian faith. It was therefore left undeveloped for the moment until he later integrated it into the full range of Christian doctrines and within the knowledge of God itself. This point was legitimate and important with respect to the work's inherent dialogical presupposition but also in terms of the influential critique of monotheism in political theory as highlighted in the work of Erik Petersen.[8] Indeed, at this point, any recovery or retention of the trinitarian tradition is very Augustinian and monarchical in spite of itself. Nevertheless, a theological triad (one of many in Moltmann's work) appears: promise, hope, mission. Beyond this, there are three themes that tie the book together: scriptural-narratival, soterio-centric, doxological-political orientation. Each one, the scriptural, the soteriological, and the missional are expressed in terms of both tradition and new construction for new contexts.

TRINITARIAN RELATIONS AND DIVINE SUFFERING IN MOLTMANN'S *THEOLOGIA CRUCIS*

In the book, *The Crucified God* (1974) Moltmann offers a powerful dialectic of cross and resurrection for theological understanding of the being of God revealed in Christ. This work highlights the theological triad: love, suffering, and solidarity. The mutual and eternal trinitarian relation of love between Father and Son engenders a reality of suffering in two modes: the Father's sacrificial giving up of the eternal Son to dereliction and death and the Son's personal experience of that death on the cross, both in solidarity with suffering, dying humanity for its redemption. The cross is the trinitarian event of divine self-giving and therefore of the trinitarian history of God in and with the world. Indeed, Moltmann's guiding principle: *crux probat omnia*: "the cross is the test of everything" is programmatic: no Christian theology appropriately asserts divine

---

8. Peterson, "Der Monotheismus als politisches Problem," 45–147.

impassibility in the face of the reality of the suffering of God in the cross of Christ.[9] It pointed out here that while Moltmann's formulations are trinitarian, the triadic relationality is not as fully developed as in later theology. Of course, every theology of the atonement foregrounds the relations between Father and Son. Also, Moltmann's trinitarianism will develop according to the social analogy of the Trinity and include a hefty critique of the psychological analogy in his later work as he thinks in a full-orbed way about creation/redemption/consummation in God's being and in relation to humanity.

Running through the *Crucified God* (CG) is Moltmann's critical stance toward anything in the tradition that has utilized analogies or metaphors that import notions of deity that are at variance with the biblical doctrines and narratives of God. Along with his critique of philosophical monotheism, Moltmann is also opposed to the strategies of describing Christ, the true Son of God incarnate, according to a schema of two natures. For him, any properly biblical Christology "must begin from the totality of the person of Christ" rather that an incipient dualism of two natures doctrine.[10] Moltmann wants to rid theological discourse of its entirely artificial strategy of having to make a distinction between divine and human experience of suffering in the life of Christ. "God's being is in suffering and . . . suffering is in God's being itself," as Moltmann insists based upon the high Christology if the fully divine, incarnate Son who is Jesus of Nazareth.[11] He goes on to point out that,

> Traditional Christology came very near to Docetism, according to which Jesus only appeared to suffer and only appeared to die abandoned by God: this did not happen in reality. The intellectual bar to this came from the philosophical concept of God, according to which God's being is incorruptible, unchangeable, indivisible, incapable-of-suffering, and immortal; human nature, on the other hand, is transitory, changeable, divisible, capable of suffering, and mortal. The doctrine of the two natures in Christ began from this fundamental distinction.[12]

---

9. Indeed, Moltmann acknowledges his theological indebtedness on the suffering of God in Christ in the likes of Studdart Kenedy, C.E. Rolt, Kazoh Kitamori, Miguel de Unamuno, Dietrich Bonhoeffer.

10. Moltmann, *Crucified God*, 206.

11. Ibid., 227.

12. Ibid., 227f.

Moltmann elided nature language from his theology on the basis of a biblical priority argument and proceeded to refer to the real, eternal, and mutual relations of Father, Son, and Spirit in the event and experience of the cross.

The being and life of God on God's own terms has been altered because of God's will to embrace humanity redemptively and victoriously in solidarity with its suffering and dying. In so doing, and in his own Reformed way of thinking according to divine election and action toward creation, Moltmann formulates an all-inclusive soteriology based upon the cross of Christ for the godforsaken: "Because God 'does not spare' his Son, all the godless are spared. Though they are godless, they are not godforsaken, precisely because God has abandoned his own Son and has delivered him up for them. Thus the delivering up of the son to god-forsakenness is the ground for justification of the godless."[13]

All humanity suffers under the collective condition of godlessness and god-forsakenness of sin and death. In solidarity with them, God's Son is offered upon effectively for them, enduring and conquering this condition for them so that they are no longer what he had become for them. In resurrection, they will in turn, share in the eternal blessedness of his glorified humanity. This, of course, would bring on the charge of universalism against Moltmann, one which he boldly faces referring over and over to the radical suffering and evil of human events and God's omnipotent determination to exhaust all of it with his grace.[14]

But Moltmann's primary focus is upon the inter-relationality in his eternal being with respect to suffering. Throughout the CG he is careful to distinguish fundamentally between the suffering of Father and Son, including the experience of death. He rejects theopaschite notions: God did not die, the Father "suffers the death of the son in the infinite grief of love." Indeed, in Christ's real experience of death, there is no cessation of existence or activity.[15] The theological formulation runs thusly: Death *in* God but not *of* God. In following the implications of the gospel story, Moltmann highlights the effect of the triune work upon triune relations:

13. Ibid., 242.

14. Cf., "There cannot be any other Christian answer to the question of this torment [tortuous death of an innocent young man in WWII], to speak here of a God who could not suffer would make God a demon. To speak here of an absolute God would make God an annihilating nothingness," ibid., 274.

15. Ibid., 243.

"The Son suffers dying, the Father suffers the death of the Son . . . The Fatherlessness of the Son is matched by the Sonlessness of the Father."[16] Since all that happens within the life of God is determined utterly by the freedom of the divine will, unconditionally willing the expressing of divine love in the way, there is actually no loss of divinity to God, only the gaining of lost humanity for its ultimate participation in divine glory. As such, the crucified God is a trinitarian narrative: "The doctrine of the Trinity is [not] . . . an exorbitant and impractical speculation . . . but is nothing other than a shorter version of the passion narrative of Christ."[17]

Toward the end of CG, Moltmann writes in a way that sums up the work trinitarianly as well as anticipating the work yet to be done in trinitarian theology: "If the cross of Christ is understood as a divine event, i.e., as an event between Jesus and his God and Father, it is necessary to speak in trinitarian terms of the Son and the Father and the Spirit . . . the form of the crucified Christ is the Trinity."[18] What is crucial always in CG is the soteriology of the trinitarian being in relation to humanity:

> God suffers, God allows himself to be crucified and is crucified, and in this consummates his unconditional love that is so full of hope. But that means that in the cross he becomes himself the condition of this love. The loving Father has a parallel in the loving Son and in the Spirit creates similar patterns of love in man in revolt. The fact of this love can be contradicted. It can be crucified, but in crucifixion it finds its fulfillment and becomes love of the enemy.[19]

At every point in reading CG, this sovereign relation of God to every aspect of the cruciform history of redemption is key: unconditional love and the conditionality of the cross, the latter particularly as this unique event for salvation.

The great critical issue in this book is the contention that God has united himself in Christ to the mutability and possibility of the creation. Of course, in classic Reformation evangelical terms, this should not be problematic—everything about creation, the incarnation, and resurrection is an expression of the absolutely sovereign God being whom he will be and doing what he will do in his own utterly unique freedom.

16. Ibid.
17. Ibid., 246.
18. Ibid.
19. Ibid., 248.

But for those that ground their theologies in the classic metaphysical tradition, this presents a massive problem. Although Moltmann's Christology would not violate the negations of Chalcedon, "*sine confusion*," the metaphysically committed take this as a warrant and guide for identifying when and where a "confusion of attributes" and therefore a denial of divine sovereignty or divinity itself may be evident or at least suspect. Unfortunately, this theological move has always straight jacketed revelation as it comes to us in the Gospels and the rest of the narratives of Scripture. Biblical narrative has to be downgraded in this tradition; anti-anthropomorphism is always lurking and rewriting the revelatory truth claims.[20] Most importantly, the line of argument that follows is not ultimately between metaphysical and anti-metaphysical but how theological exegesis in the twentieth century and beyond must now ground theology in a fundamental way. Trinitarian doctrine, like every other in Christianity, is grounded in the biblical narrative and nowhere else; many of the classic problems of theology have been caused and exacerbated by imposing, say, a Christianized, trinitarian version of the classic ontological categories of the supreme Being and evaluating all other claims, including exegetically based ones, in light of it.

When Moltmann writes of the economic Trinity in CG, his formulations reflect the Western tradition since Augustine: "the form of the Trinity which is revealed in the giving up of the Son (i.e., the cross) appears as follows: (1) the Father gives up his own Son to death in its most absolute sense, for us; (2) the Son gives himself up, for us; (3) the common sacrifice of the Father and the Son comes about through the Holy Spirit, who joins and unites the Son in his forsakenness with the Father."[21]

We have the distinction of Persons in the One God, who is not divided in an activity and yet are differentiated in their actions, most especially with respect to the word and works of Jesus Christ. It must be clear what orthodox trinitarian doctrine requires: the eternal relations of the one God in three persons. But how God is thus is never defined with utter precision. Unity can be numerical oneness but it is preferably the one God who is ever named according to three distinct yet inseparable persons. Their inseparability constitutes their oneness rather than numerical oneness, which threatens the actuality of their relations. In maintaining orthodoxy, it must be realized that ultimately

20. Cf., also, Rahner, *The Trinity*; Zizioulas, *Being as Communion*.
21. Moltmann, *Crucified God*, 241.

the matter is about maintaining boundaries within quintessential defini-
tions. Thus, while Nicea (381), Chalcedon (451) are the benchmarks of
orthodoxy but not the particular writings of the theologians themselves,
e.g., Athanasius, Basil, etc.

Thus, in the quote above, and in the entire work of Moltmann's
theology of the cross, accounting for the trinitarian gospel of Christ's
sacrifice as the trinitarian work, Moltmann is interested in explicating
the implication of the text in the truest way. Any other kind of thinking
posits a cleft between the truth of salvation history through Scripture
and the doctrine of the Trinity. Moltmann is convinced, as should all
Christian theologians be, that this cannot be allowed to become a dilemma. Happily, many of the Fathers understood this as well. Athanasius,
in the *Four Discourses against the Arians*, realizes that the best grounding for the doctrine of the Trinity is the high priestly prayer of Jesus in
John 17, and, consequently, it is far and away the most frequently cited
passage of the Bible. Indeed, the trinitarian language of Nicea is almost
entirely Johannine.

Of course, Moltmann states clearly that God's eternal nature is triune. He is ready to follow the text in its salvation historical priority and
therefore the reality of God's full participation in history and humanity's
participation in God, precisely on the trinitarian basis of perichoresis.
This will be discussed further below. The crucial factor for theology is
that it avoid a breach between scripturally grounded and exegetically
sound accounts of salvation history and essential doctrine. The creed
already does this, although negatively and also by almost completely
avoiding details from the words and works of Christ as found in the
Gospels. This has created a problem in the history of theology that
has only begun to get resolved, e.g., making the Jewishness of Jesus
something almost completely obscured up until recent decades. In the
final analysis, it must be reasserted that the Protestant principle of *sola
scriptura* is the basis of its views on doctrinal definition. Scripture is the
norma normans "norming norm" whereas even the most central creed is
always at most *norma normata* "normed norm," i.e., by Scripture itself.
The theological agenda that Moltmann set for himself—to work solely
based upon scriptural reasoning for his theology—was undertaken not
to find ways of eliminating doctrinal authority but because he had come
to recognize that all essential doctrines had been formulated in ways
that anticipated this move.

God embraces suffering and death out of his triune sovereignty over them; his self-constituting act as Creator and his self-determining act as Redeemer—therefore God's own rejection of impassibility. Thus: "the nucleus of everything that Christian theology says about 'God' is to be found in this Christ event."[22] In the cross of Christ, the triune God actually and truly has identified with humanity and drawn suffering and death into himself in order to triumph over them; otherwise they would defeat and destroy humanity. Moltmann's approach is driven by a desire to come to grips with the engagement of the deity with his creation that is so evident in the biblical narrative. He is not searching for a kind of apologetic that will be persuasive where others have not been. While many traditional apologists have tried to infer a necessary connection between divine impassibility and divine immutability, they forget, first of all, that the latter attribute is not founded on God's substance anyway but in God's sovereign will to be whom he will be and to be unwaveringly faithful to his promises. Thus, can God sovereignly enter into and engage creation by the incarnation and the mission of the Holy Spirit, suffering with it and yet with no loss of sovereignty whatsoever. Thus, when Moltmann says of the incarnation that God has subjected himself to helplessness and powerlessness, it is ultimately out of God's sovereign will that he identifies with human beings in their condition and for their redemption. This is the God who truly loves, who is more than merely benevolent, but who is like us in all things excepting sin: "for a man who is aware of the riches of his own nature in his love, his suffering, his protest and his freedom, such a God is not a necessary and supreme being, but a highly dispensable and superfluous being."[23]

It is really quite strange and unfortunate that the classical tradition essentially argued against the Gospel narratives on the nature of the loving God, but this is the case. Actually, this is the most insidious of all impositions from the classical Greek tradition: that God actually does not love because love entails desire and since desire necessarily only arises because of lack and God lacks nothing, therefore God does not love but merely wills in infallible benevolence. The gospel utterly dispenses with this tradition in that the living God, incarnate in Jesus Christ, reveals no necessary connection between desire and lack.

22. Ibid., 205.
23. Ibid., 223.

More importantly for Moltmann, God's freedom is constituted in love, which always suffers, since the creation includes the maladies of sin and death. Not that God is in any way subject to these realities but that his love leads him to subject himself to them so that even death will not be foreign to him. His love alone will prove stronger than death. Jesus' cry of dereliction (Matt 27:46; Mark 15:34; cf. Ps 22:1) is, of course, nothing other than the despair of the dying, faithful Son of God whose natures are both *sine confusione* and *sine divisione*. In the unity of the one and the same Jesus Christ, he endures death on the cross according to the will of the Father and achieves this faithful goal through the endurance supplied by the Holy Spirit.[24] In the triunity of God, the cross of Christ reveals that "God is not more glorious than he is in this self-surrender. God is not more powerful than he is in this helplessness. God is not more divine than he is in this humanity. The nucleus of everything that Christian theology says about 'God' is to be found in this Christ event."[25]

The event of Christ's death is a real experience for the Son of God, a mystery since death cannot hold him, and his immortality is not undone. Nevertheless, death is, along with the God-forsakenness of the Son, his actual condition in those moments where and when it was his destiny. In all this it is so very important to understand that while Moltmann in no way abandons the traditional objectivity of trinitarian reality as revealed through the incarnation, he is equally affirming the subjective aspect of Christ's exemplarity for its effect upon all who put their faith in him. The modern apologetic battle between subjectivity and objectivity is sublated by Moltmann's theological project.

In Moltmann's critique of Barth, he cites the latter's "use of the reflection structure to secure God's subjectivity, sovereignty, selfhood, and personality" that is (following a Fichtean model) "through self-distinction and self-recollection . . . God shows himself to be the absolute subject." This is because such "a reflection subjectivity . . . has not necessarily anything whatsoever to do with the biblical testimony to the history of God" because it "can be conceived even without any biblical reference at all." Moltmann see this as an original problem of the *Church Dogmatics* where the very model of revelation is based upon "that reflection logic," and is problematic thereafter and throughout as "problems of

24. Cf., ibid., 146–47.
25. Ibid., 205.

pneumatology." By this he means that Barth cannot refer to God "in his state-of-revelation, the Holy Spirit."[26]

He basically sees in Barth a continuation of a virtual binitarianism, God as "a duality," where the real relation is between Father and Son, only the mere unity of the two being the Spirit who "loses every centre of activity." This then was "a non-trinitarian concept of the unity of the one God . . . the concept of the identical subject," which is the problem of the exclusivist, Hellenistic monotheism Moltmann so ardently critiques elsewhere on political grounds in favor of a trinitarianism of the Judaic biblical conceptuality.[27] Unfortunately, Moltmann's analysis breaks off at the point of maintaining that only Barth's notion of covenant, with its model of mutual freedom in relation between God and man, saves Barth's theology from the power model of his own monotheist trinitarianism. Needless to say, it is this, and also Barth's development of election behind his model of covenant, that has to be taken as his own filling out of trinitarian doctrine, which could have balanced Moltmann's own view. And it is to that we turn now.

THE TRINITARIAN REDEEMER

As in all Reformed theology, so with Moltmann, the doctrine of salvation and creation are inseparable. Both are the *ad extra* works of God, the so-called "economic Trinity." In his book, *The Trinity and the Kingdom of God* (TK, 1980), Moltmann extends his contributions to theology beginning with exegetical-theological insights and extending them to the most fundamental analogies of person and community. In so doing Moltmann also extends not only his critique and constructive contribution to political theology but also to the analysis of the political theologies of ancient and modern Christianity. He considers dire the effects of the embrace of monotheism and earthly models of lordship.

Moltmann's critique of monotheism is simultaneously a political matter as much as a deeply theological matter and this takes him to reject what he regards as the addition of the "single substance" metaphysics of divine identity in unity to biblical revelation. Instead of a unity of relations in the one God, a prioritizing of single substance as

26. Ibid., 142.
27. Cf. Otto, "Moltmann and the Anti-Monotheism Movement," 293–308.

the monotheistic additive makes impossible the true subjectivity and therefore relationality of Father, Son, and Spirit. Modalism has been a temptation for trinitarianism since it's appearance in the third century and never lets go; only a re-prioritized biblical narrative can remedy this. Instead of single substance, it is the inseparable "at-oneness"[28] of the three that is their unity. From Moltmann's reading, the biblical notion of person is one in which personhood requires a unitary principle: there is no personhood without community and vice versa. His guiding principle is *perichoresis*, the model of relations that is mutual indwelling of persons constituting together a unity of being as over against the fundamentally incompatible "homogeneity" model of substantial oneness and therefore essential singularity of God.

The first order of business in TK is, in effect, to pick up where CG left off and to consider the immanent and economic Trinity according to the uncreated and created relations. The inseparable creation/redemption nexus within and without the divine being is elaborated according to the "room" God makes for space and time, not panentheistically or according to process models of God, but kenotically, by embracing a suffering that passionately wills the other so as to open up the perfection of the divine triune life to finite, deficient, perishable creation. "God does not suffer out of the deficiency of his being, like created being . . . But he suffers from the love which is the superabundance and overflowing of his being."[29] In this context, Moltmann highlights the work of "the Holy Spirit who 'opens' the Trinity to the world and at the same time unites the world to the Son and the Father."[30] The knowledge of the triune God must be recognized as the ground and grammar of all theology and as such, "God's revelation and communication is not passing on of "information" but it is a dialogic process with concrete effects on life like the sacraments and on the relation of men with the ultimate being."[31] As in the Reformed tradition, grace is the foundation of creation itself, ultimately becoming manifest in the redemptive work of Christ on the way to the drawing up of humanity and the cosmos into glorified relations with God—revelation itself is determined by and contained with this divine *oikonomia*. The revelation of the triune God is therefore wholly

28. Moltmann, *Trinity and the Kingdom of God*, 150.

29. Ibid., 23.

30. Ibid., 23.

31. Ibid., 24.

at odds with divine isolationism of philosophical monotheism, which Moltmann continues to reject throughout TK.

Moltmann believes that a scriptural guarding of his relational trinitarianism is maintained through a consistent salvation-historical and doxological logic. By holding strictly to this logic, monarchic and therefore monadic, homogeneic, single-substance (and therefore single-subjectivity) logic will not gain a foothold. Thus, *as God manifests himself in salvation history, so he in fact is in himself.* The Scripture therefore narrates what for Moltmann is the trinitarian history of God. Indeed, beginning with the creation text of the *imago Dei*, Moltmann points out that there is no personhood apart from other persons and that this is grounded upon the interpersonal personhood of the one God.[32] This is in contrast to the modern, individualistic concept of "person," which is ultimately based upon an image of God as sovereign Self, many-sided, but not interdependently relational; conditioned as is all love by mutuality. But in the praise that grounds Christian theology of the triune God, beginning with salvation in Christ, worship becomes elevated even further where God is loved for who God is as his own triune loving Being of three eternal persons-in-relation. This God "can never be reduced to a single identical subject (even if the subject is a threefold one) . . ."

It is impossible that there can be a reductionism such that "the three Persons to three modes of subsistence of the one God cannot illuminate salvation history in the fullness of God's open trinitarian relationships" of covenantal fellowship.[33] It is in God's eternal at-oneness of Father, Son, and Spirit—identical both immanently and economically, following Karl Rahner—that the biblical narrative can make sense in a way that is consistent with God's self-revelation.[34] Moltmann regards as insufficient Augustine's formula that externally God is undivided and internally divided.[35] The cross of Christ by God's own will has had an effect retroactively on God; which is far more than saying that the economic

---

32. Ibid., 155.

33. Ibid., 157.

34. There is immense controversy over Rahner's formula: "the economic Trinity is the immanent Trinity, and vice versa"; cf., Moltmann, *Trinity and the Kingdom of God*, 65; cf., vehemently attacked in singularly overwrought fashion in Molnar, *Divine Freedom and the Doctrine of the Immanent Trinity*; Cf., the fundamentally positive assessment of Rahner's formula, according to systematic and historical theology criteria in McGrath. *Christian Theology*, 309.

35. Moltmann, *Trinity and the Kingdom of God*, 160 (cf., 167).

Trinity reveals the immanent. This effect through the cross is for God, by God, a self-cause of "infinite pain."[36] Only in this way—Moltmann most emphatically contends—can God as love be understood.

The eschatological dimension is taken into the life of God from eternity to eternity. Moltmann properly identifies the Fatherhood of the Father in relation to the Son and not at all with the creation as Creator. It is an inner-trinitarian reality and thus precedes the creation eternally. The Father is the eternal "origin" (*arche*) of the Son. The Son is not *ex nihilo* created but has his eternal procession from the Father. "Consequently he is one in substance or essence with the Father and has everything in common with him, except his 'Personal' characteristics." While denying creatureliness to the Son, unfortunately—and this is due to too little exegetical and biblically comprehensive reference—Moltmann denies the imago Dei to the Son[37]—obviously ignoring the central text of Col 1:15. This does not mean the Moltmann is thinking extra-biblically. On the contrary, there is much that is more biblical than the classic trinitarianism of speculative theology. It must be realized that all of the non-personal metaphors for Trinity are extra-biblical. What counts are the relational metaphors and signs of eternal relationship. This relationship cannot be conceived tri-theistically, since the triune essence is one of another. "The generation and birth of the Son come from the Father's nature, not from his will. That is why we talk about the eternal generation and birth of the Son. The Father begets and bears the Son out of the necessity of his being. Consequently the Son, like the Father, belongs to the eternal constitution of the triune God. In Christian terms, no deity is conceivable without the eternal Father of the Son and without the eternal Son of the Father."[38]

Thus, the Father is the sole "origin" of the Son who receives eternally everything from the Father except this eternally generative role vis-à-vis the Son. In this sense, the Eastern tradition testifies to the correct understanding of two missions, two processions, where the Son is not generative *together with* the Father, but the *Father alone* is the eternal "origin" of Son and Spirit. In a way unique to the Son as eternally begotten of the Father: "Creation proceeds from the Father's love for the eternal Son. It is destined to join in the Son's obedience and in his responsive love to the

---

36. Ibid.

37. Ibid., 166: "Man is God's image, not his Son."

38. Ibid., 167.

Father, and so to give God delight and bliss." The redemptive destiny of creation from the particular action of the Son comes also into view here, where "the Son's sacrifice of boundless love on Golgotha is from eternity already included in the exchange of the essential, the consubstantial love which constitutes the divine life of the Trinity."[39]

But is the Spirit fully "person" together with the persons of Father and Son? This Moltmann answers entirely affirmatively; the Spirit is a *full divine subject.* The Spirit and the Son together are understood according also to the dual mission of Word and Spirit from the Father. Two logics are implied here for Moltmann: 1) Father and Son, and 2) Word and Spirit; the latter is based upon "the Father utters his eternal Word in the eternal breathing out of his Spirit."[40] Citing John 14:26 and 15:26, the Spirit emanates *from* the Father *through* the Son, although the Son "in time" sends the Spirit to believers "from" himself. Moltmann guards himself against the charge of tri-theism with an affirmation of Augustinian interpersonal logic: "the three divine Persons possess the same individual, indivisible, and one divine nature, but they possess it in varying ways. The Father possesses it of himself; the Son and the Spirit have it from the Father. There are three relations in the Trinity: fatherhood, sonship, the breathing of the Spirit (*paternitas, filatio, spiratio*). The inner being of the Persons is molded by these relationships in accordance with the relational difference."[41]

While affirming one divine essence and the inseparability of the eternal divine persons, their individuality and independence must also be affirmed in order that their person defining relations of eternal perichoresis can be seen as yet more greatly constituting their oneness. There must be no reduction of person to relation either.

Finally, precisely through the personal characteristics that distinguish them from one another, the Father, the Son, and the Spirit dwell *in* one another and communicate eternal life to one another. In their perichoresis and because of it, the trinitarian persons are not to be understood as three different individuals, who only subsequently enter into relationship with one another (which is the customary reproach, under the name of "tritheism"). But they are not, either, three modes of being or three repetitions of the one God, as the modalistic intepretation

39. Ibid., 168.
40. Ibid., 170.
41. Ibid., 172.

suggests. The doctrine of perichoresis [as in John of Damascus] links together in a brilliant way the threeness and the unity, without reducing the threeness to the unity, or dissolving the unity in the threeness.[42]

And, of course, subordinationism is ruled out. The Father is constitutionally the source of the triune Godhead from all eternity, but only constitutionally; in perichoresis there is circulation of the one divine life of the three. Their co-equality is their consummation. In a very beautiful and scripturally penetrating passage, Moltmann reflects on their coequal eternal glory:

> From all eternity the Father is "the Father of glory" (Eph 1:17), the eternal Word is "the reflection of glory" (Heb 1:3) and the Holy Spirit is "the Spirit of glory" (1 Pet 4:14). The Persons of the Trinity make one another shine through that glory, mutually and together. They glow into perfect form through one another and awake to perfected beauty in one another. In all eternity the Holy Spirit allows the Son to shine in the Father and transfigures the Father in the Son. He is the eternal light in which the Father knows the Son and the Son the Father. In the Holy Spirit the eternal divine life arrives at consciousness of itself, therein reflecting its perfect form. In the Holy Spirit the divine life becomes conscious of its eternal beauty. Through the Holy Spirit the eternal divine life becomes the sacred feast of the Trinity.[43]

Surely this statement is one of the most poignant and memorable in the Moltmann oeuvre. What is crucial here is that co-eternal oneness and three-ness are perfectly balanced according to Moltmann's biblical metaphysic of the divine life. Far from any tri-theist confusion, his dynamic conceptuality significantly aids trinitarian understanding.

Moltmann goes on to provide one of the great summative comments in the book:

> In the history and experience of salvation this illumination is perceived through the Spirit first of all. It is in the power of the Spirit that doxology begins. The perichoretic unity of the triune God is perceived in salvation history and reflected in salvation history. Lastly, the monarchy of the Father is perceived in the Trinity because everything in the history of salvation comes from him and strives toward him. To throw open the circulatory movement of the divine light and the divine relationships,

42. Ibid., 175.
43. Ibid., 176.

and to take men and women, with the whole of creation, into
the life-stream of the triune God: that is the meaning of creation,
reconciliation, and glorification.[44]

Moltmann continues with what is gradually becoming part of a
truly ecumenical set of arguments for the elimination of the *filioque* in
the Nicene Creed in the West. The last section of the book is on the
soteriological effects of the Trinity upon the redeemed creation; the participation of the faithful as they are taken into the life and mission of the
Trinity. The passion of God with which the book began, delineating the
inner trinitarian life in eternal relations and personal being, manifest in
the life of Christ, particularly the death of Christ and his resurrection
is the ground for the inclusion of creation in the perichoretic life of the
triune God. Throughout the work, Moltmann develops his reflection on
the overall contours of Scripture. His is not a highly exegetical method
but his total shaping in the revelatory narratives of Scripture along with
its didactic rigor is not lacking. Hardly can one imagine a more engaged
Scriptural reasoning.

Trinitarianly one observes the following *sine qua non*: the fundamental distinction between the Creator and the creature; and the distinctions among the persons of the Trinity, each as to their identity and
economic involvements with creation. Absent, refreshingly, are all references to necessary conditions for being Trinity, or one God, in relation
or creatively disposed to the temporal exteriority of creation. His reasoning, in classic Reformed fashion, is to consider all things in the life of
God according to his eternal decision to *be*, and thus there is no sense of
an openness that is elusive of his sovereignty or of his self-completeness.
And yet it is the divine passion in the perfection and the completeness
of divine love to include that which is not God and to create a boundless
creative love that would not exist apart from creation.

In Moltmann's proceeding to the implications of the Trinity, so
socially conceived, for the community, he enunciates his now famous
phrase: "The Trinity is our social program." What had been crucial in
dispensing with the metaphysics of monotheism now impacts anthropology and the errors of individualism—the monarchies of divinity and
humanity (authoritarian models of community). "The notion of a divine
monarchy in heaven and on earth, for its part, generally provides the

44. Ibid., 178.

justification for earthy domination—religious, moral, patriarchial, or political domination—and makes it a hierarchy, a 'holy rule.' The idea of the almighty ruler of the universe everywhere requires abject servitude, because it points to complete dependency in all spheres of life."[45] This would develop a personalist socialism and a socialist personalism. Where Christians are united and uniting they convey the truth of the triune identity and reconciling work.[46]

Once he has established trinitarian theology on the basis of eternal divine relations—something that was a *sine qua non* for Augustine as well—but without the transcending priority of monotheistic singularity, Moltmann can develop fully the implications of trinitarian soteriology. Beginning with trinitarian protology: the triune-will of the uncreated sociality of God in the *creatio ex nihilo*, he appropriates the *zimzum* (lit., "contraction") of Judaic reasoning about God's "withdrawal,"[47] the originating act for created sociality. This means that God has sovereignly limited himself in his triune nature: kenosis applies varying and yet fully to God. The result is a trinitarian ecclesiology. "The doctrine of the Trinity constitutes the church as 'a community free of dominion' . . . Authority and obedience are replaced by dialogue, consensus, and harmony. Therefore a presbyterial and synodal church order and the leadership based on brotherly advice are the forms of organization that best correspond to the doctrine of the social Trinity."[48]

Moltmann takes a cue from Joachim of Fiore's dispensationalism of three eras for the history of creation: Father, Son, and Holy Spirit.[49] Fiore's is "the trinitarian history of the kingdom of God as the history of humanity's progressive and growing liberty." Moltmann thinks simultaneously eschatologically and ecclesially through the kingdom of God. The triadic epochalism is trinitarianly informed but is definitely not proposed as an example of *vestigia trinitatis* (i.e., traces of the Trinity manifest in creation and conducive of analogizing and a virtual natural

---

45. Ibid., 192–92.

46. Cf. Moltmann, "The Reconciling Power of the Trinity in the Life of the Church and the World."

47. Cf., Konstantin Burmistrov, "He contracted Himself into Himself": Kabbalistic doctrine of self-withdrawal of God and its interpretations in European culture. *History of Philosophy*, Moscow. 14, 2009, http://eng.iph.ras.ru/page48910394.htm#

48. Moltmann, *Trinity and the Kingdom of God*, 198.

49. Ibid., 203–9.

trinitarian theology). It is however crucial that all three are historical epochs, mutually reinforcing one another as trinitarian history of salvation and in anticipation of the triune glory that shall be revealed in the eschaton and the participation of the redeemed creation in the consummation of the works of the Trinity: creation, liberation, glorification.[50]

In the first instance, liberation is liberation from necessity in order to pursue goodness at a level beyond the natural. Moltmann points to the perpetuation of feudal, princely freedom in the freedom liberalism offers to self-determining individuals only in the modern world. But what of freedom in community? The only answer can be the freedom of love and its full social implications in fellowship and the project of shared community and rule. God desires for his creation what he enjoys in his own eternal, triune relations such that "God is the inexhaustible freedom of those he has created."[51]

In this context, one last triad comes to the fore in Moltmann's theological reflections, based upon the use God makes of his creatures in relation to himself: servants, children, friends. As the Servant of God in Isaiah 53 and Philippians 2, Christ is the pattern of all believers as they come into the free relation that is giving and receiving of the self and community in God. At the same time, they are children, not merely servants, and thus belong fully to God and God to them, as in John 15. The bond of relation, of offspring and their Progenitor, entails a belonging that transcends the relation of servants to their Master. And yet this relation is transcended further to that of friend, beyond any entailment of subservience to that of the prophets like Abraham (e.g., Jas 2:23) who were drawn into greatest intimacy with the triune divine, in the acts and being of God's greatest intentions for creation. This is the relation of conversation; the life of prayer that is quintessentially friendship with God—sharing in the deepest desires of God for the world and for himself.

Each of these relations is its own stage of freedom on the road to the consummation of the kingdom of God as it develops historically and dynamically under the influence of the Holy Spirit, in Christ and to the glory of the Father. These are "strata in the concept of freedom" such that they are transitions "present in every experience of freedom."[52] The

50. Ibid., 212.
51. Ibid., 218.
52. Ibid., 221.

destiny of this historical freedom is the consummate freedom realized in the full revelation of the glory of God to and in creatures caught up in the redemption inclusive of them.

What shall we say then about the Trinity witnessed to us in Moltmann? He is clearly not dominated by any extra-biblical model, even while very well-versed in the Christian metaphysical tradition. He takes the Gospel narratives, particularly of John, as the source of the knowledge of the triune God. One of the primary burdens of this chapter has been to discern the degree to which his accusers have correctly identified tri-theistic tendencies. But at every turn, Moltmann is alert both to the intricacies of the tradition, both East and West, to the balances of emphasis, and since he is not interested in some sort of founding metaphor, but simply the biblical revelation of relations among Father, Son, and Holy Spirit, even his political sensitivities do not interfere with his basic receptivity that is the first duty of every theologian.[53] Ultimately, the trinitarian covenantal life of created/redeemed and therefore perichoretic relations are eschatological.[54]

Moltmann comes under criticism on at least two fronts: the rejection of monotheism and universalist soteriology. The rejection of monotheism is not a theological error but a rational one. All the matters that he finds alien to Scripture do not cancel the validity of the phenomenon—the intuition of a single cosmic agency (as in Rom 1:18–21; Jas 2; et al.). Monotheism, as J. Assmann points out, is at root a response to the truth of the one and only God who is to be worshiped.[55] It is in the first instance about human origins and obligations at the highest order.

The latter is obviously regarded as erroneous by the tradition, both historic and contemporary. There is no mention of the reserve expressed by von Balthasar, that with the proviso, one may hope for this outcome as a recipient of the pure grace of God in Christ. Indeed, given Moltmann's deep reflection upon the gospel of Jesus in all of its dimensions, the words of Jesus on this matter are not mentioned. Indeed, there are construals of Pauline material that can be taken this way along the lines of exchange: the righteous for the unrighteous, etc. Barth also expressed far more reserve on the matter. It is perhaps best understood on

53. Cf. McDougall, *Pilgrimage of Love.*

54. Cf. Moltmann, *The Coming of God.*

55. "The decisive moments of monotheism are accordingly situations of conversion." Jan Assmann. *The Price of Monotheism.* Stanford: University Press, 2010, p. 119

Moltmann's part as overreaching. Moving from the passion of God in solidarity with humanity, God trinitarianly suffers with and for them in their suffering and for their redemption—without exception. In contrast to the universalisms that do not take human sin, evil, and death seriously, Moltmann witnessed it up close (survivor of the last days of WWII, witness to Dresden, prisoner of war) from all sides. But the theological judgment entailed in his universalist formulations, while never facile, are monophonic and lack the attention he will pay to human eschatology later on.

3

Moltmann on Creation

Graham Buxton

FOR JÜRGEN MOLTMANN, THEOLOGY has always been an adventure, a creative open-ended enterprise that finds its origin not only in his wartime experiences but also in endless curiosity, "unbounded joy in the presence of God's Spirit,"[1] and a rich imagination for the kingdom of God. These fertile sources have given rise in Moltmann to constant wonder and a celebration of "the power of hope" that he first discovered when he was exposed to the gospel of Christ in the Protestant theologians' camp where he was imprisoned after the Second World War. This eschatological focus runs all the way through his theology, no more evidently than in his doctrine of creation.

It is not possible in one chapter to do justice to the wide range of themes that embody the extensive theological material that constitutes Moltmann's doctrine of creation. Many of these themes interact with one another, offering a rich kaleidoscope of ideas that can be subsumed under three main categories, identified by Moltmann in *The Coming of God*: "firstly, a trinitarian thinking about God, secondly . . . an ecological thinking about the community of creation; and thirdly . . . an eschatological thinking about the indwellings of God in his people, in his Christ, and in our hearts through his life-giving Spirit."[2] This chapter is specifically concerned with Moltmann's doctrine of creation, and it will become evident that these three lines of thought are integral to the

---

1. Moltmann, "A Lived Theology," 94.
2. Moltmann , *Coming of God*, xii.

development of that doctrine in Moltmann's own theological explorations. We will focus on a number of critical perspectives, addressing along the way some points of divergence with evangelical thinking, before concluding with a summary appraisal of the doctrine of creation from an evangelical perspective.

THE "ECOLOGICAL CRISIS"

Moltmann's *magnum opus* on creation, *God in Creation*, published in 1985 as the second in a series of six systematic contributions to theology—under the general rubric of "messianic theology"—is characterized by a number of critical perspectives that define his whole approach to the Christian doctrine of creation. The most obvious is that this is an *ecological* doctrine. Throughout his life, Moltmann has been profoundly influenced by significant turning points that have shaped him as a human being and as a theologian. The exploitation of nature was not something to which he had given much attention in his early theological output: his first major work, *Theology of Hope*, was published in 1964, a time when "the 'ecological crisis' had not yet penetrated my consciousness."[3] However, his volume on *The Trinity and the Kingdom of God* with its focus on community, mutuality, and *perichoresis* prompted him towards a deeper contemplation of the relationship between God, human beings, and creation. This reflection culminated in the 1984–85 Gifford Lectures that produced *God in Creation*.

If *The Trinity and the Kingdom of God* stimulated Moltmann's *theological* reflection about God's place in creation (and creation's place in God), then a growing awareness throughout the 1970s and into the next decade about humanity's exploitation of nature fuelled his determination to present a doctrine of creation that was also shaped by *anthropological* considerations. For Moltmann, the contemporary environmental crisis is not just an environmental crisis *per se* but a crisis in human beings themselves. It is not just an ecological crisis, but more fundamentally a *crisis of domination* that has to do with the total orientation of human beings towards the life system on which they depend:

> It is a crisis which human beings have brought on themselves and
> their natural environment, and into which they are driving both

3. Moltmann, *History and Triune God*, 170.

themselves and their environment more and more deeply . . . So
when we talk about the ecological crisis of modern civilization,
we can only mean the crisis of the whole system with all its part-
systems, from the dying of the forests to the spread of neuroses,
from the pollution of the seas and rivers to the nihilistic feeling
about life which dominates so many people in our mass cities. [4]

We notice here the essential symbiosis between humanity and nature that drives Moltmann's project. One gets the sense when reading
Moltmann that he *feels* the crisis himself, reflecting not only a liveliness
in his Christian faith but also a sensuous dimension in his own being
that is discernible in his writings, particularly his later works. For example, in his small book on the Holy Spirit, *The Source of Life*, he writes
of his awareness of the physicality of creation, an awareness that stirs all
of his senses, quickening them to life by what he has called elsewhere the
"sensuousness of the Holy Spirit." The Spirit who lures creation towards
its eschatological goal is also the quickening Spirit who awakens us to a
new love—a new love for God and all that finds its place in God: "When
I love God I love the beauty of bodies, the rhythm of movements, the
shining of eyes, the feelings, the scents, the sounds of all this protean
creation. When I love you, my God, I want to embrace it all for I love
you with all my senses in the creations of your love."[5] This emphasis on
entering into the reality of things rather than observing them analyti-
cally from a distance shapes Moltmann's doctrine of creation: it implies
an affirmation of life that is lived "wholly and without reserve."[6]

Ultimately, to live fully in God's image means to enjoy the experience of life in God, life with other human beings, and life in relationship to God's creation. Evangelical Christianity has given prominence
(rightly) to the first, acknowledged the second, but in large part given
only lip service to humanity's relationship with the natural world. What
Moltmann has achieved in *God in Creation*, and other subsequent writings, is to fire a comprehensive warning shot across the bows of evangelicalism in an attempt to correct a deficient theology that exalts humanity
as the ultimate crown of God's creation *at the expense of non-human
creation*. One particular schema that he endorses in this regard is the
controversial *Gaia* hypothesis, with which the scientist James Lovelock

4. Moltmann, *God in Creation*, 23.

5. Moltmann, *Source of Life*, 88.

6. Moltmann, *God in Creation*, 270.

is particularly associated.[7] According to *Gaia* thinking, planet Earth is a living self-regulating open system, and human beings have a symbiotic relationship with everything else that makes up the planet. Celia Deane-Drummond critiques Moltmann for not distancing himself sufficiently from the philosophical basis of Lovelock's thesis,[8] and argues that this is a weakness in presentation (a similar criticism might be made regarding Moltmann's rather speculative adoption of the concept of *zimsum*, to which we shall turn later). While the *Gaia* perspective is clearly one that Moltmann appreciates, he is careful to note in *God and Creation* the pantheism implicit in the "Mother Earth" concept, in which the distinction between transcendence and immanence is abolished.[9] In raising the question, "is humanity a gigantic *cancerous growth* in the comprehensive organism earth, or will the human civilization one day develop into something like the nerve-system of the comprehensive organism earth?"[10], it is possible to argue that Moltmann is skating close to an ecology that, in Deane-Drummond's estimation, is *anti-anthropological*, rather than *anti-anthropocentric*.

However, Moltmann has always interpreted theology as a provisional enterprise, and his engagement with the scientific community is one particular example of his willingness to dialogue with others in order to gain wisdom.[11] While he draws us back again and again in his writings to the central place of nature in God's history, a theme that has been long neglected in evangelical theology, it is misleading to suggest that his ecological theology veers towards being anti-anthropological. On the contrary, Moltmann's messianic vision exalts the dignity of human life in its invitation to all humanity to participate in the joy of the liberated new creation:

7. See especially Moltmann, "Destruction," 166–90, and Moltmann, "Ecological Crisis," 5–18.

8. Deane-Drummond , "Critique," 554–65.

9. Moltmann, *God in Creation*, 317; note also Moltmann's reservation about "the Mother Gaia who engenders and slays" in *Coming of God*, 279.

10. Moltmann, "Ecological Crisis," 18 (author's italics).

11. See, in particular, the collection of essays in Moltmann, *Science and Wisdom*. On this point, it is worth noting McPherson's criticism of Moltmann's "theological dictatorship over science" in that he "has taken the "open system" metaphor and transformed it so freely that it is difficult to relate his "open system" to its scientific counterpart. See McPherson, "Life, the Universe and Everything," 34–46.

With the rebirth of Christ from death to eternal life we also expect
the rebirth of the whole cosmos. Nothing that God has created is
lost. Everything returns in transfigured form. So we expect that
the Spirit of the new creation of all things will vanquish human
violence and cosmic chaos. More than that: we expect that the
power of time and the power of death will be vanquished, too.
Finally, we expect eternal consolation when "tears are wiped
away" from our eyes. We expect eternal joy in the dance of fellowship with all created being and with the triune God.[12]

The obviously spiritual overtones of *Gaia*—represented within
emerging expressions of ecologically-aware Christianity, in a wide range
of neo-pagan belief systems, such as Earth-goddess worship and New
Age consciousness, and in contemporary ecofeminist perspectives—is
"evidence of the shift in global consciousness from the subject/object
split to an awareness of the 'subjective'—or better, *personal*—nature of all
knowledge."[13] The epistemological framework developed by Moltmann
in *God in Creation* reflects this shift in perspective in its demand for a
new orientation towards a *participatory* knowledge of creation and away
from scientific knowledge and its inevitable objectification—and conse-
quent exploitation—of nature.

What Moltmann is offering in *God in Creation* is not, as Richard
Bauckham has rightly noted, a doctrine of creation that is oriented
explicitly towards *praxis*,[14] but a doctrine that needs to be received inwardly by human beings so that their *attitude* towards creation undergoes a revolutionary paradigm shift whereby the world is recognized
as *God's* creation. It is precisely because human beings "know more
and more about less and less"[15] that they need a new paradigm of seeing things-as-a-whole in order to live more sympathetically, and ultimately more humanly, within the creation of God's love. As Moltmann
points out, to speak of nature in terms of *our* environment is already
to diminish nature's integrity by making it part of the human world.
Nature will not—cannot—be saved that way.[16] A move away from
an anthropocentric understanding of creation towards a theocentric

12. Moltmann, *Source of Life*, 123.

13. Snyder, *EarthCurrents*, 182 (author's italics).

14. Bauckham , "Evolution and Creation," 74.

15. Moltmann, *God in Creation*, 2.

16. See Moltmann, *Source of Life*, 118–21.

perspective has the potential to transform humanity's relationship with nature from one of domination to one of communion. As expressed succinctly in a recent Anglican report, "We are not consumers of what God has made; we are in communion with it."[17] In *God in Creation* Moltmann is calling for a moral and ethical revolution in our hearts if we are to arrest the impoverishment of the earth caused by our exploitative abuse. Recognizing the world as God's creation may take us part of the way along the road. But there is a second revolution that needs to be experienced, a spiritual revolution that percolates deep within the human psyche: "The truly ecological task is to repair not just our damage in the outer world but also the deep splits in our psychological make-up and dualistic world view."[18]

In a lecture delivered at the University of Stirling in 1987, Moltmann declared that to live according to nature means "to live one's life in *agreement* with the laws and rhythms of the earth system from which we all exist."[19] In *God in Creation*, he quotes the poet and revolutionary Ernesto Cardenal, who once wrote that "God's signature is on the whole of nature. All creatures are love letters of God to us."[20] By calling us to pay attention to God's language in nature, which he distinguishes clearly from "natural theology," Moltmann is pointing us to a critical link between the transcendent beauty of creation and the realm of the sacred, leading us into a richer experience of transcendence, wonder, and divine glory. However, as Langdon Gilkey rightly reminds us, "What is known of God in nature by no means represents the center of the knowledge of God for the Christian"[21] In his distinction between natural theology and revealed theology Moltmann is thoroughly orthodox: "Natural knowledge of God certainly confers wisdom, but it does not confer salvation and blessedness. The knowledge of God that confers blessedness comes solely from the 'supernatural' revelation of God in Jesus Christ, because it is this which leads to perfect fellowship with God."[22]

But a concentration on the centre, which is the person of Jesus Christ as the sum and fulfillment of the Christian revelation of God,

17. Church of England, *Sharing God's Planet*, vii.

18. Tacey, *ReEnchantment*, 177.

19. Moltmann, "Ecological Crisis," 18 (author's italics).

20. Moltmann, *God in Creation*, 63–64.

21. Gilkey, *Nature, Reality, and Sacred*, 195.

22. Moltmann, *God in Creation*, 57.

should not devalue the sacramental significance of nature, for "to know nature truly is to know its mystery, its depth, and its ultimate value—it is to know nature as an image of the sacred, a visible sign of an invisible grace."[23]

THE MESSIANIC "COMMUNITY OF CREATION"

This emphasis on communion with God and with his creation is given expression in Moltmann's concept of the "community of creation," which is developed most fully in his chapter in *God in Creation* on "The Evolution of Creation," a motif that forms a central platform in his doctrine of creation. Drawing from the biblical account of creation in Genesis 2, he distinguishes between human beings as the *apex* of creation (the sixth day) and the Sabbath as the *crown* of creation (the seventh day). This leads into the development of his thesis that human beings are as much *imago mundi* as *imago Dei*. They are created *for the Sabbath*, in the sense that their ultimate destiny is the *creatio nova* in the coming kingdom of God, when "[h]eaven and earth are clasped and gathered into a whole, and in the all-embracing peace of Christ arrive at their open communication with one another."[24] The implications of this for human life on earth are profound, implying a universal way of life in this world that sanctifies the Sabbath by abstaining from productive work and resting, just as God himself blessed the Sabbath not through his activity but through his repose.[25] The ultimate goal and redemption of creation is not anthropocentric but theocentric—it is *God's* Sabbath, the goal for which human beings are created. The Sabbath is the "feast of creation," its completion, and its crown. This interpretation "distinguishes the view of the world as creation from the view of the world as nature"[26] and it is a theme that drives Moltmann's messianic ecological theology.

The priority in Moltmann's doctrine of creation is always the messianic future of God's glory. Drawing from Jewish and Christian sources, he traces the outlines of this *messianic* doctrine of creation, grounded in

23. Gilkey, *Nature, Reality, and Sacred*, 204.
24. Moltmann, *God in Creation*, 171.
25. Ibid., 281.
26. Ibid., 6.

eschatological hope. For Moltmann, the promise of the future has less to do with the *eschaton* as future event than with a total orientation in Christian theology. Eschatological hope, birthed in Moltmann's wartime experiences, is given cosmic significance in his first book, *Theology of Hope*, where "the promise of the kingdom of God shows us a universal eschatological future horizon spanning all things—'that God may be all in all.'"[27] This cosmic messianic perspective is presented in *God in Creation* in ecological terms, in which the coming of the kingdom of God is articulated not as the end of all things but the beginning of the new—*creatio nova*. Moltmann argues that there is no contradiction in principle between creation and evolution: within the tripartite schema of *creatio originalis*, *creatio continua*, and *creatio nova*, evolution finds its place in *creatio continua*, which—within the messianic orientation of his doctrine of creation—anticipates *creatio nova*. The original act of creation is theologically distinct from evolutionary processes within nature, but the two should not be regarded as separate from each other. If original creation speaks to us of the transcendence of God, continuous creation (involving the evolution of matter, life, and consciousness) speaks to us of the immanence of God in his creation. For Moltmann, transcendence and immanence are bound together in his trinitarian concept of creation, which, as we shall see later in this chapter, is grounded in a "mutual indwelling of God in the world and the world in God."

An important theme in Moltmann's theology is that of God's *friendship* with all that he has created. This is elaborated primarily at the human level as believers discover that "the friendship of the 'Wholly Other' God which comes to meet us makes open friendship with people who are 'other' not merely possible but also interesting, in a profoundly human sense."[28] There is an *ekstatic* dimension to this type of friendship, in which the doors are thrown wide open for others to enter in and participate in the joy of divine life. It is an "open friendship," a "vulnerable atmosphere of life," which is based on the virtues of affection and respect. "Friends throw open the free spaces of life for one another, and accompany one another in sympathy and immense interest."[29] Freedom in the kingdom of God is, for Moltmann, expressed supremely in this idea of friendship: human beings experience stages on the journey in the

27. Moltmann, *Theology of Hope*, 224.

28. Moltmann, *Spirit of Life*, 259.

29. Ibid., 256.

history of the kingdom of God, a trend from being a servant to being a child, and then to being a friend of God's (so John 15:15): "In friendship the distance enjoined by sovereignty ceases to exist."[30] In his doctrine of creation, Moltmann extends this friendship to the community of all creation: "if nature and humanity are to survive on this earth, they must find the way to a new community with each other. Human beings must integrate themselves once more into the earth's cosmic setting."[31] In *God in Creation*, the eschatological vision of the completion of creation finds expression in a new image: not power or dominion, grounded in sovereignty, but one shaped from the perspective of friendship, *delight*: "But on the Sabbath the resting God begins to 'experience' the beings he has created. The God who rests in face of his creation does not dominate the world on this day: he 'feels' the world; he allows himself to be affected, to be touched by each of his creatures. He adopts the community of creation as his own milieu. In his rest he is close to the movement of them all."[32]

Moltmann's orientation here is clearly towards a theology of "openness" which is not just an eschatological reality but also a present reality. In this regard, he is sympathetic to the insights of "openness" theologians like Clark Pinnock, who propose an understanding of God as one who desires "responsive relationship" with his creatures, challenging Augustinian and Thomist notions of divine immutability, impassibility, and foreknowledge: "God's perfection is not to be all-controlling or to exist in majestic solitude or to be infinitely egocentric. On the contrary, God's fair beauty, according to Scripture, is his own relationality as a triune community. It is God's gracious interactivity, not his hyper-transcendence and/or immobility, which makes him glorious."[33] Theologians have been deeply divided over "openness theology," leading at times to charges of heresy by conservative evangelicals who espouse the classical doctrines of God's sovereignty and immutability. The issue comes back to what Langdon Gilkey has called the central problem for the doctrine of God: how to unite intelligibly the *absoluteness* of God as the unconditioned source of our total being with the dynamic *relatedness* and the *reciprocal activity* of God as the ground, guide, dialogical partner, and

---

30. Moltmann, *Trinity and Kingdom*, 221.

31. Moltmann, "From the Closed World," 168–69.

32. Moltmann, *God in Creation*, 279.

33. Pinnock, *Most Moved Mover*, 5–6. See also Pinnock et al., *Openness of God*.

redeemer of our freedom.[34] Grenz and Olson suggest that somewhere along his theological journey Moltmann "became convinced that hierarchy and power are intrinsically evil and set about to erase all vestiges of lordship from his doctrine of God."[35] This leads them, along with other evangelical theologians, to criticize Moltmann's theological method on the basis that his doctrine of God is shaped by his aversion to all forms of social and political domination rather than by the biblical revelation of a sovereign and transcendent God. In other words, his theology is not sufficiently grounded in *Deus dixit*.

In acknowledging this theological *modus operandi*, it is probably fair to say in Moltmann's defense that his entire theological output is conditioned by his deep awareness of the contexts within which human beings experience life, with all its inherent contradictions, pain, and suffering. This leads him to set out his social doctrine of the Trinity as "the true theological doctrine of freedom," eschewing all hierarchy, servitude, and oppression. In this project, which really reflects his life's work, his *theologia viatorum*, he has drawn richly from many traditions. As he writes in *The Coming of God*, what interests him is the adventure of theological ideas, and their revision and innovation. But his theology is not personal opinion: he is acutely aware that he offers suggestions—not dogma—within the *communio sanctorum* "provided that the true saints are not merely justified sinners but accepted doubters too, thus belonging just as much to the world as to God."[36] While this assertion might make many evangelicals uneasy, he is clear in his own mind that theology is always *public* theology—not church dogmatics and not a doctrine of faith: "Some people think that I say too much theologically, and more about God than we can know. I feel profoundly humble in the face of the mystery that we cannot know, so I say everything I think I know."[37] This sets him apart from those in the evangelical community whose rallying cry is either Luther's "Here I stand!" or Barth's *Deus dixit!* Of course, while evangelicals have much to learn from his ecumenical engagement with those of other persuasions, whether Catholic or Pentecostal, liberationist or feminist, their criticism of Moltmann's approach to theology needs to be heard: Moltmann would expect nothing less. In the midst

34. Gilkey, "God," 108.

35. Grenz and Olson, *20th Century Theology*, 184.

36. Moltmann, *Coming of God*, xiv.

37. Moltmann, *Coming of God*, xiv.

of this tension, we do well to recall the words of Douglas John Hall that "theology was made for human beings, not human beings for theology."[38]

THE IMMANENCE OF THE SPIRIT

Moltmann's willingness—indeed eagerness—to engage with people from many different disciplines and persuasions has contributed to a winsome freshness in his theological output. In particular, his open dialogue with scientists has added new insights in his development of a *holistic* theology of the Spirit. He suggests that "God acts upon the world not so much through interventions or interactions, but rather through God's presence in all things and God's *perichoresis* with all things."[39] This perichoretic mutual indwelling of God in the world *and* the world in God is, for Moltmann, fundamentally pneumatological, in which the "self-organization of matter and the self-transcendence of all that lives are the divine Spirit's signs of life in the world."[40]

This understanding of God's immanence in the world is expressed by Moltmann in terms of the *preservation* of the world in preparation for its consummation. We shall discuss later his interpretation of God's self-limitation, or *kenosis*, in the context of *creatio ex nihilo*, but here we note his insistence that God is almighty not because of his power, but because of his love. This love is interpreted in terms of his *patience*: "Through the power of his patience God sustains this world with its contradictions and its conflicts."[41] Moltmann argues that God does not sustain and rule the world like an autocrat or dictator; rather, "God acts in the history of nature and human beings through his patient and silent presence, by way of which he gives those he has created space to unfold, time to develop, and power for their own movement."[42] So God respects *free natural processes* as well as human free will. He respects the unfolding of his universe with its own inbuilt laws, initial conditions, and potentialities, as well as respecting human beings as free agents created *imago Dei*. Moltmann's thinking here echoes that of Thomas F. Torrance, for

---

38. Hall, *Thinking the Faith*, 63.

39. Moltmann , "Reflections on Chaos," 208.

40. Ibid.

41. Moltmann, "God's Kenosis," 149.

42. Ibid.

whom God is immutable because of his constancy as the ever self-living and ever self-moving being. In ecstatic love he graces his creation with a reality and freedom of its own, authentic yet contingent upon God's own unlimited freedom. That authenticity is guaranteed by the activity of the Holy Spirit whereby creation is "creatively upheld and sustained in its existence beyond its own power in an *open-ended relation* toward God in whom its true end and purpose as creature are lodged."[43] The Spirit is therefore the eschatological "perfecting" Spirit who holds the whole created order—animate and inanimate, human and non-human, personal and non-personal—in the freedom of divine love. This view of divine omnipotence threatens classical evangelical interpretations of an immutable God who reigns on high, sovereign in power and dominion over his creation, intervening in special ways to accomplish his purposes throughout history. As we shall see later, the idea of a God who allows his creation to unfold, or emerge, according to an inherent capacity for self-organization points us towards a crucial relationship in Moltmann's thinking between *kenosis* and *perichoresis* in his doctrine of creation.

In his doctrine of the Trinity, Moltmann has frequently been criticized for emphasizing the immanence of God at the expense of his transcendence, exposing him to the charge of anti-monotheism. Though he acknowledges a distinction between the immanent and transcendent Trinity on doxological grounds in order not to conflate the two,[44] his critics are concerned that he gives too much ground to the notion of a social Trinity at the expense of divine unity. However, for Moltmann, as for Karl Barth, God's transcendence is the sum of his freedom, which incorporates *his freedom to be immanent.* This is spelled out by Moltmann in the context of his doctrine of creation: "*It is only if God remains God that his immanence in the world effects what is everywhere detectible: the self-transcendence of all open-life systems, their evolution, and their ever more complex warp and weft in relationships of community; for it is in this immanence that we find the 'more' which thrusts beyond every existing condition.*"[45] This "transcendent immanence of

43. Torrance, *Divine and Contingent Order*, 239 (footnote 16, author's italics).

44. Moltmann maintains that the "assertions of the immanent Trinity about eternal life and the eternal relationships of the triune God in himself have their *Sitz im Leben*, their situation in life, in the praise and worship of the church." So, the "'economic Trinity' is the object of kerygmatic and practical theology; the 'immanent Trinity' is the object of doxological theology" (Moltmann, *Trinity and Kingdom*, 152).

45. Moltmann, "From the Closed World," 170 (italics added).

God"—which Moltmann also understands as "immanent transcendence"—is expressed pneumatologically in Moltmann's exegesis of
the cosmic Spirit, whose presence in creation as "the fountain of life"
conditions its potentiality and realities, preserving and renewing it until
it reaches its eschatological goal in the messianic kingdom of the new
creation. Moltmann states that his doctrine of creation takes as its starting point the indwelling Spirit of creation, and he notes in his preface
to God in Creation that by this title he means God the Holy Spirit. The
Spirit is the immanence of God in creation, a cosmic Spirit who is "the
Spirit of the universe, its total cohesion, its structure, its information, its
energy,"[46] embodying an eschatological vision of hope for the whole of
creation. Moltmann's pneumatological framework contrasts noticeably
with Barth's christological approach to his doctrine of creation—Barth's
reluctance to concede a place for any form of "natural theology" as well
as his focus on the transcendence of God offered little room for a theology of immanence in which the Spirit is seen to be active in the world in
creative and energetic ways.[47]

But for Moltmann, the Spirit is the Spirit of creation as much as
he is the Spirit of redemption. His rejection of *filioque* reflects his desire to affirm the unity of God's work in the creation, redemption, and
sanctification of all things: "But if redemption is the resurrection of the
body and the new creation of all things, then the redeeming Spirit of
Christ cannot be any Spirit other than Yahweh's creative *ruach*. If Christ
is confessed as the reconciler and head of the whole cosmos, as he is in
the Epistle to the Colossians, then the Spirit is present wherever Christ
is present, and has to be understood as the divine energy of life animat-
ing the new creation of all things. "[48] Moltmann's doctrine of creation
explicitly correlates the redeeming Spirit of Christ and the creative, life-
giving Spirit of God so that the "community of creation" is at the same
time the fellowship of the Holy Spirit: "both experiences of the Spirit
bring the church today into solidarity with the cosmos, which is so mor-
tally threatened."[49] He interprets the "community of creation" as a web
of life embracing the human and the non-human, the material and the

---

46. Moltmann, *God in Creation*, 16.

47. For a full discussion of Barth's doctrine of creation, see Crisp, "Karl Barth on
Creation," 77–95.

48. Moltmann, *Spirit of Life*, 9.

49. Ibid., 10.

immaterial, all inhabited and energized by the Holy Spirit. The creative and re-creative Spirit is the vitalizing Spirit, active from the moment of the big bang, releasing life and possibility as creation unfolds and reaches towards its intended goal.[50] Because creation is not, in its *essential* nature, constituted by individual particles but by the life principle of symbiotic ecosystems, the goal of evolution is community. This corresponds to Moltmann's recurring messianic theme that the activity of the Spirit is the eschatological power of God at work in creation, enabling all that exists to fully and finally become itself in the freedom of divine love in the coming kingdom of glory. All humanity is caught up in this eschatological drive towards fulfillment in God, who, as trinitarian love, welcomes and draws all creation—human and non-human—to himself through his Spirit. From a charismatic perspective, Moltmann identifies God's Spirit as *vitalizing energy*, an "eroticizing energy" that "holds the world together and keeps it alive, anthropologically and cosmologically."[51] So life is always relational, or rather *communal*, because the trinitarian fellowship of the Holy Spirit is the full community of God with all created being. *All* that God has created—τὰ πάντα—is integral (that is, finds its integrity) in the eschatological community of creation: "Anyone who disparages this community of creation compared with the community of soul is quenching God's creative Spirit and denying him the fellowship which he seeks with all created being, so as to redeem them."[52]

THE TRINITARIAN SHAPE OF CREATION

Moltmann's accent on the energetic perichoretic life within the Trinity is conspicuous in his doctrine of creation, in which he offers what he defines as a paradigm shift from a hierarchical to a relational doctrine of creation:[53] "the levels of relationship in *perichoresis* and mutuality within the Trinity, rather than the levels of constitution within the Trinity, are normative for the relationship of God to creation and all

50. For a fuller development of this theme, see Buxton, *Trinity, Creation and Pastoral Ministry*, 247–87.

51. Moltmann, *Spirit of Life*, 196.

52. Ibid., 21.

53. See also Moltmann, *History and Triune God*, 125–42, in which he critiques Barth's insistence upon superiority and subordination as normative for all the conditions in creation that correspond to God.

the corresponding relationships in creation."[54] This shift towards dynamic perichoretic relationality as the fundamental hermeneutic of Moltmann's pneumatological doctrine of creation is made explicit in his movement away from the language of "order of creation" to "community of creation" in the "cosmic body and relationships of heaven and earth and the anthropological relationships of soul and man and woman."[55] Furthermore, he asks, "Why should not scientific descriptions also discover the complexes of life and thus also complexes of the Spirit?"[56] This idea of a cosmic *perichoresis* implicit in the writings of other trinitarian theologians, and articulated more precisely in Colin Gunton's 1992 Bampton Lectures,[57] represents the culmination of more than half a century of trinitarian reflection and debate since Karl Barth re-opened the door in his biblically-based presentation of the doctrine of the Trinity.

The seeds of the trinitarian shape of Moltmann's doctrine of creation had been sown well before his Gifford Lectures in the unfolding of his doctrine of the Trinity. First in *The Crucified God*, and subsequently in *The Trinity and the Kingdom of God*, Moltmann explores his understanding of an open and relational Trinity, contradicting the immutability, impassibility, and timelessness of classical theistic concepts of God. He critiques both Barth and Rahner, arguing that neither "does justice to the history which is played out between Jesus the Son, 'Abba' his Father, and the Spirit."[58] Moltmann's "salvation-historical" approach to his doctrine of the Trinity is therefore a project that explores the collaboration between the three triune subjects in the history of the world, and it is ultimately eschatological in its orientation. Believers are, in the language of *theosis*, caught up into the inner life of God himself, and this is a process that takes place through history, culminating in the consummation of God's unconditional love, which is full of hope: therefore, "the Trinity is no self-contained group in heaven, but an eschatological process open for men on earth, which stems from the cross of Christ."[59]

54. Moltmann, *History and Triune God*, 132.

55. Ibid., 135–40.

56. Ibid., 128.

57. Published in Gunton, *One, Three and Many*. See especially pages 155–79, in which Gunton proposes a theology of relatedness, presenting the concept of *perichoresis* as a helpful way to map the eternal dynamic of deity.

58. Moltmann, *History and Triune God*, 82.

59. Moltmann, *Crucified God*, 249.

But open too for all created reality. In his later works, Moltmann laments an exclusive preoccupation with the limited horizons of a "historical Christology," and directs us to a Christology that recapitulates the cosmic vision of Christ in Col 1:15–20:

> Anthropological Christology fitted the modern paradigm "history," and itself unintentionally became one factor in the modern destruction of nature; for the modern reduction of salvation to the salvation of the soul, or to authentic human existence, unconsciously abandoned nature to its disastrous exploitation by human beings. Only a growing awareness of the deadly ecological catastrophes in the world of nature leads to a recognition of the limitations of the modern paradigm "history" and makes us enquire again into the wisdom of ancient cosmic Christology and its physical doctrine of redemption.[60]

This leads him to propose a "cosmic Christology" that dispenses with the dualism between nature and grace, a dualism that excludes nature from the full redemptive power of the cross. For Moltmann, the cross is the centre of *all* Christian theology, including his doctrine of creation. "The nucleus of everything that Christian theology says about 'God' is to be found in this Christ event."[61] To think otherwise is to "speculate in heavenly riddles"![62] More specifically, Moltmann spells out a trinitarian interpretation of the cross within the framework of dynamic relationship. The cross is what transpires between Jesus and the Father in the realm of the Spirit: something of personal *and cosmic* significance happens between the triune persons that actually constitutes their unity as God. Moltmann's point of departure in his understanding of the Trinity is not the "One God" of philosophical enquiry but the three persons of biblical history, made explicit in *Heilsgeschichte*.[63] At the cross, there is no death *of* God, but death takes place *in* God: Moltmann's language about the dying of the Son and the grief of the Father as a God-event in trinitarian terms is replete with the dynamic reality of abandonment, surrender and suffering. For example, the Son "suffers in his love being

---

60. Moltmann, *Way of Jesus Christ*, 274.

61. Moltmann, *Crucified God*, 204.

62. Ibid., 207.

63. See Moltmann, *Trinity and Kingdom*, 148–50.

forsaken by the Father as he dies. The Father suffers in his love the grief of the death of the Son."[64]

Furthermore, Moltmann's trinitarian theology of the cross is given pneumatological shape—a *pneumatologia crucis*—in his discussion of the role of the Spirit as a "companion in suffering" in the *kenosis* and dying of Jesus: "The path the Son takes in his passion is then at the same time the path taken by the Spirit, whose strength will be proved in Jesus' weakness."[65] Just as the suffering of the Father is different from the suffering of the Son, so too is the suffering of the Spirit a different form of suffering, for he is Jesus' strength in Gethsemane and at Golgotha. So Moltmann outlines his trinitarian *theologia crucis*, in which the three persons of the Trinity participate in the historic outworking of cross and resurrection in dynamic perichoretic interdependency. This historic unfolding is given both ecological and eschatological focus in Moltmann's "twofold trinitarian order," in which the Spirit is vitally involved in the two historic movements of sending and gathering: "In *the first order* the divine Trinity throws itself open in the sending of the Spirit. It is open for the world, open for time, open for the renewal and unification of the whole creation. In *the second order* the movement is reversed: in the transfiguration of the world through the Spirit all men turn to God and, moved by the Spirit, come to the Father through Christ the Son. In the glorification of the Spirit, world and time, people and things are gathered to the Father in order to become *his world*."[66]

For Moltmann, the "second order" movement of gathering is a trinitarian move "inwards": in the glorification of the Spirit all creation is gathered to the Father in order to become *his world*, the glorification of all things, which is the messianic hope of the gospel of Jesus Christ. This *creatio nova* is the Sabbath "feast of creation," the eternal "dance of the redeemed," Dante's *riso dell'universo*, the cosmic Shekinah of God. "Just as the cross of the Son puts its impress on the inner life of the triune God, so the history of the Spirit moulds the inner life of the triune God through the joy of liberated creation when it is united with God."[67]

We will take a further look at Moltmann's ecological eschatology—which he also describes as eschatological ecology—later. Here we note

64. Moltmann, *Crucified God*, 245.

65. Moltmann, *Spirit of Life*, 62.

66. Moltmann, *Trinity and Kingdom*, 127 (author's italics).

67. Ibid., 161.

that his interpretation of *creatio originalis*, while open to the charge of speculation, is in fact thoroughly trinitarian in its grounding in a God who is at the same time inner-trinitarian perichoretic love, self-communicating love, and self-limiting love.[68] Creation is, in Moltmann's view, that which flows out of the depths of inner-trinitarian love. God creates because he is love, and he desires that all creation finds fellowship in the free kingdom of his Son. In LaCugna's words, the "God who *is* love (*Ipse Amore*) does not remain locked up in the 'splendid isolation' of self-love but spills over into what is other than God, giving birth to creation and history."[69] God, true to himself, is self-communicating love, causing to exist that which was not, *creatio ex nihilo*, or—more evocatively—*creatio ex amore Dei*.

ZIMSUM AND *KENOSIS*—SELF-LIMITING LOVE

But God is self-limiting love too. Here we need to distinguish between Moltmann's interpretation of self-limitation as it applies to the doctrine of *creatio ex nihilo*, and as a secondary consideration his understanding of how God acts within his creation. In both cases, he draws from the christological notion of *kenosis*, applying it to the creation of the world and its subsequent unfolding in *creatio continua*. The creation of the world is, firstly, the specific outcome of God's decision. God's self-determination to be Creator of a non-divine world is therefore an initial self-limitation on God's part since this decision implies the renunciation of all other possibilities in God. God has limited himself to this specific world, calling it into existence by his free will: "There is no external necessity which occasions his creativity, and no inner compulsion which could determine it."[70] In the freedom of his love God graces his creation with a reality and freedom of its own, authentic yet contingent upon God's own unlimited freedom. As an expression of his inner-trinitarian life, this creation is the contingent creation of his ecstatic love, "an unheard-of condescension, self-limitation and humiliation on the part of God who is without compare."[71]

---

68. For a succinct summary, see Moltmann, *Trinity and Kingdom*, 105–14.

69. LaCugna, *God for Us*, 353 (author's italics).

70. Moltmann, *God in Creation*, 74.

71. Ibid., 78.

In developing this thesis further, Moltmann distinguishes between an act of God *outwards* and an act of God *inwards*. Orthodox Christian theology presupposes that God brought creation into being by filling a space outside himself, requiring the existence of an *extra Deum*. But this presents for Moltmann a conundrum, leading him inexorably to the theological presupposition for his employment of the kabbalistic doctrine of *zimsum*: "If there were a realm outside God, God would not be omnipresent. This space 'outside' God would have to be co-eternal with God. But an 'outside God' of this kind would then have to be 'counter' to God."[72] The only way to resolve this enigma is to conceive of an inversion of God, whereby the infinite God "concentrated himself" in order to free the space into which he could act creatively. Divine self-limitation is thus expressed in terms of God making room *within himself* for creation: God, in trinitarian love, withdraws into himself in order to free the space into which he can act creatively.[73] The dynamic perichoretic freedom of the triune God *in se* therefore finds ecstatic, kenotic expression as a creation that "exists in the space God yielded up for it through his creative resolve."[74] This space, however, is not the vacuum or "empty space" of Lurian *zimsum*: it is "qualified and structured through the God who receives his creation."[75] What exactly Moltmann means by this is not altogether clear, except that something intentional and purposive happens in God by which the Creator becomes the *God who can be inhabited*, a phrase that is full of perichoretic and ecological significance, which Moltmann connects to Jesus' high-priestly prayer in John 17:21.[76] In his theology of space, which is, as we have noted, thoroughly ecological, every living thing has its own world in which to live, a world to which it is adapted and which suits it. Space, as created reality, is primarily *living space* for the richness and variety of different forms of life: "Every living thing has its space or home: *oikos*. Every living thing is a space for others: *perichoresis*."[77]

The major problem here, as others have pointed out, is that God's self-negation within himself must necessarily imply a dualistic

72. Ibid., 86.

73. Ibid., 86.

74. Ibid., 156.

75. Moltmann, *Coming of God*, 299.

76. Ibid.

77. Moltmann, "God and Space," 115.

prior condition before the act of creation in which Nothingness—*nihil*—emerges.[78] Anticipating this, Moltmann defends his position—not altogether satisfactorily—by defining this *nihil* as an "affirmative force" in a partial negation of the divine Being, and stating that "in a doctrine of Nothingness, a distinction has to be made between the non-being of a creature, the non-being of creation, and the non-being of the Creator. It is only in connection with the last of these that we can talk about Nothingness."[79] Moltmann's reliance here on Jewish mysticism has given rise to criticism amongst evangelicals in particular: where is the biblical justification for what is, in effect, mere speculation? There have been many attempts to work through the implications of Moltmann's employment of kabbalistic cosmology in his doctrine of creation. For example, Brian Walsh is troubled by the implication that if evil is ontologically constitutive of creation, then creation becomes a matter of ontological necessity rather than an act of free grace. He also poses the question that if the *nihil* in God was a necessary precondition to *creatio originalis* "then how can the God/creation distinction still be maintained when this *nihil* is vanquished and God is all in all?"[80] The inference here is that Moltmann's structure of a panentheistic interpretation of reality is threatened by a logically inevitable pantheism that dissolves the God/creation distinction. Of course, questions of this nature will always arise, presupposing as they do a finite capacity to understand the free actions of an infinite God in the ultimate glorification of all things, so we need to be wary of pushing them too far. But they do reflect a certain unease that evangelicals have with Moltmann's speculative thought here.

Notwithstanding these reservations, there are others who recognize positive elements in Moltmann's kenotic theories. Collapsing *zimsum* and *kenosis* into one in his doctrine of creation, Moltmann argues that in a profound sense God 'creates' by "letting-be, by making room, and by withdrawing himself."[81] This withdrawal, or "shrinkage," conveys the idea of a humble, self-restricting love that finds christological expression in the *kenosis* of the incarnation. For Alan Torrance, this kind of exposition highlights in a very appealing way the continuity between creation and incarnation: "The 'self-emptying of God in the incarna-

78. See, for example, Molnar, "Function of the Trinity," 686.

79. Moltmann, *God in Creation*, 88.

80. See Walsh, "Theology of Hope," 53–76.

81. Moltmann, *God in Creation*, 86.

tion is not now simply to be seen as an event which takes place 'out of the blue.' Rather, the divine 'contraction' in love at Bethlehem and on the cross is the culmination and fulfillment of precisely that dynamic which is constitutive of the very event of creation. Christian theology in its entirety may be seen, therefore, to be an integrated articulation of a divine *becoming* on the part of God . . . "[82] So for Moltmann, kenotic Christology—along with later ideas about the assumption of human nature by the eternal Logos—deepens what he calls "Shekinah theology," in which God will be all in all. Just as the new creation presupposes the old one, so the Shekinah presupposes the Sabbath in the order of promise and fulfillment: "the eschatological Shekinah is the perfected sabbath in the spaces of the world."[83] The great eschatological question has to do with the nature of the ultimate relationship between God and his creation: the world in God or God in the world? "But if we follow the Jewish teaching about the Shekinah, God's 'indwelling', and the Christian doctrine about the incarnation of the Son of God and the indwelling of God's Holy Spirit, then the infinite God can certainly 'indwell' his finite creation, its salvation history and its consummation, as once he indwelt Solomon's temple, and can interpenetrate everything human as in the God-human being Jesus Christ."[84]

In Moltmann's trinitarian theology of the eschatological glorification of all things, *kenosis* and *perichoresis* are brought together in the new world organism of the "deified universe," not in a pantheistic mutual absorption between God and creation, but in a—albeit ambiguous—panentheistic structure of ultimate reality. In a technical discussion about Moltmann's understanding of the nature of space and time, Alan Torrance notes these ambiguities, preferring "a rather less complicated Christian the-en-panism, that is, that by the Spirit, God is freely and ecstatically present in, to, and for the created order."[85] While panentheism maintains that God and the world are *not* identical (unlike pantheism, in which deity is *wholly* immanent), the term is, in fact, difficult to define with exactness, because the distinction between God as a *transcendent* being and the reality included in God is notoriously imprecise. In *The Crucified God*, Moltmann gives panentheism his own meaning, tying

---

82. Torrance, "*Creatio ex Nihilo*," 89–90.

83. Moltmann, *Coming of God*, 266.

84. Moltmann, "The World in God," 37.

85. Torrance, "*Creatio ex Nihilo*," 90–93.

his interpretation to a strongly trinitarian theology of the cross: "in the hidden mode of humiliation to the point of the cross, all being and all that annihilates has already been taken up in God and God begins to become 'all in all.'"[86] In this understanding of God, divine sovereignty is, for Moltmann, not infringed, but actually enhanced: at all times God remains the subject of his kenotic action in history.

It is clear that *kenosis* and *perichoresis* are integral to Moltmann's whole theological enterprise, reflecting the continuity of his thought from creation and incarnation through to cosmic consummation.[87] Both concepts involve God "making room" within himself:

1. As a way of understanding the Trinity as *unitas in trinitate* and *trinitas in unitate* in ontological *perichoresis*.

2. In the original act of creation via the kabbalistic doctrine of *zimsum*.

3. In the incarnation of Jesus Christ as kenotic self-humiliation involving at the same time the perichoretic structure of the two natures of Christ.

4. In the preservation of creation as a patient, kenotic God working immanently by his Spirit in perichoretic action in *creatio continua*.

5. In God's self-glorification in his cosmic Shekinah when all creation—human and non-human—will dwell in God in "mutual interpenetration," which "makes it possible to preserve both the unity and the difference of what is diverse in kind: God and human being, heaven and earth, person and nature, the spiritual and the sensuous."[88]

Kenosis and *perichoresis* are therefore complementary theological concepts that reflect Moltmann's presentation of an open, sensuous, self-giving God, unchangeable in his faithfulness and freedom.

---

86. Moltmann, *Crucified God*, 277.

87. It is interesting to note this correspondence in Alan Lewis's understanding of Christian vocation as that which takes place within a theology of the cross (*theologia crucis*), where the language of *kenosis*, of suffering and ecstatic love, is expressed in terms of trinitarian *perichoresis*: see Lewis, "Unmasking Idolatries," 110–28.

88. Moltmann, *Coming of God*, 278.

COSMIC ESCHATOLOGY

In *The Coming of God* Moltmann engages in what he calls "integrative eschatology," seeking to draw together perspectives that too often have been treated separately. These perspectives are personal eschatology (dealing with the theme of eternal life), the eschatology of history (relating to the kingdom of God), and cosmic eschatology (focusing on the new heaven and new earth), culminating in his vision of divine eschatology, or the glorification of God. We do not have the space here—nor is it appropriate in this chapter—to comment at length on Moltmann's treatment of personal eschatology. However, it is important to explore the link between the doctrine of universal salvation with which he identifies and his understanding of cosmic eschatology in order to avoid what he calls a "gnostic doctrine of redemption,"[89] which teaches a redemption *from* the world rather than the redemption *of* the world.

Citing especially God's resolve in Christ to "unite all things in him, things in heaven and things on earth" (Eph 1:10 and Col 1:20), Moltmann's starting point is that God will be "all in all": nothing will be lost. This eschatological perspective, of course, is not peculiar to Moltmann, and can be traced back to Origen, who followed Clement of Alexandria in teaching the doctrine of *apokatastasis*.[90] In this view, all creatures will participate in the glory and grace of salvation, although the unrepentant will endure an extended, but finite, purifying "eternity." Noting that evangelicals and fundamentalist theologians "reject the doctrine of universal salvation as speculative theology,"[91] Moltmann addresses a number of biblical passages, maintaining that the decision between universalism and a double outcome of judgment cannot be made "on the ground of Scripture" since both are well attested biblically.[92] Acknowledging the pros and cons of each position, he asks the critical question: "Who makes the decision about the salvation of lost men and women, and where is the decision made?"[93] To say that everything depends on human decision is, for Moltmann, consistent with the

89. Ibid., 259.

90. See especially Sachs, "Apocatastasis," 617–40. The doctrine was officially condemned as an anathema in 543 at the Council of Constantinople, although it has reappeared at different times in the history of the church.

91. Moltmann, *Coming of God*, 240.

92. See ibid., 240–41.

93. Ibid., 245.

modern egocentric age. Adopting a christological—as distinct from an anthropological—answer, he turns to Christ's descent into hell as "the ground for the confidence that nothing will be lost but that everything will be brought back again and gathered into the eternal kingdom of God."[94] God, who cannot be other than true to himself, "does not give up what he has once created and affirmed, or allow it to be lost."[95]

Moltmann's thesis understandably attracts extensive evangelical indignation, especially regarding his treatment of key passages in the Bible that deal with such important soteriological themes as the role of human faith and the reality of damnation. He concedes that there is indeed damnation, but then goes on to ask: is it eternal? His biblical exegesis leads him to the conclusion that "unbelievers are 'given up for lost' temporally and for the End-time, but not to all eternity."[96] Here we recognize an eschatological structure in Moltmann's theology that distinguishes between the penultimate (aeonic) and the ultimate (eternal). More poignantly, in the light of the literal future resurrection of individual human beings, Catherine Keller asks, "does Moltmann's universal salvation not come into conflict with those very longings for justice that gave rise to eschatology in the first place?"[97] But for Moltmann, the eschatological vision that so drives his theology has to do with the final transformation of all things, a transformation that offers no room for retaliatory justice: "This means that the eschatological Last Judgment is not a prototype for the courts of kingdoms and empires. This Judgment has to do with God and his creative justice, and is quite different from the forms our earthly justice takes. What we call the Last Judgment is nothing other than the universal revelation of Jesus Christ, and the consummation of his redemptive work . . . Judgment at the end is not an end at all; it is the beginning. Its goal is the restoration of all things for the building up of God's eternal kingdom."[98] In this new beginning a new order of reality comes into play, a "fullness of God" where "we are at liberty to leave moral and ontological concepts behind, and to avail ourselves of aesthetic dimensions."[99] In this new order, we experience a transfigura-

---

94. Ibid., 251.
95. Ibid., 255.
96. Ibid., 242.
97. Keller, "Last Laugh," 387.
98. Moltmann, *Coming of God*, 250–51.
99. Ibid., 336.

tion that transcends finite understanding: it is the triumph of grace, in which God's *charis* is more powerful than human sin. For Moltmann this is "no more than a small beginning of the transfiguration of the whole cosmos,"[100] precisely because individual salvation is inconceivable without a new heaven and a new earth.

God's self-restriction, by which he opened up space, time, and freedom for a world different from his own being reflects his action inwards on himself, restricting his omnipresence, eternity, and omniscience. In God's eschatological self-glorification (which is, in effect, God's de-restriction of himself), *creatio originalis* becomes *creatio nova*, a cosmic *perichoresis* of divine and cosmic attributes, in which God dwells in the world and the world dwells in God in panentheistic—though not pantheistic—glory. God will be "all in all." In his eternal Shekinah all that is temporal is transmuted into eternal and all that is spatial becomes omnipresent, participating in God's eternal *perichoresis* in the aeon of the new creation.

SUMMARY FROM AN EVANGELICAL PERSPECTIVE

Evangelicalism's distinctively high regard for Scripture has been interpreted by the more fundamentalist stream of evangelical theologians in narrow, biblicist terms. Much of mainline evangelicalism, however, is hermeneutically less restrictive, and many evangelicals are comfortable with Moltmann's respect for biblical authority. His theology is, for the most part, grounded in the biblical text, but he is no simple biblicist. David Gibson once wrote of Karl Barth that his exegesis of the biblical text is "a monument to refusing to treat the text in narrowly historicist or even biblicist terms, but rather as a unified testimony to Jesus Christ."[101] The same might be said of Moltmann, whose experimental approach to theology never loses sight of the biblical witness to the centrality of Jesus Christ. Gibson adds: "Would that more so-called 'evangelicals' read Scripture in order to find Christ!"

Moltmann's eschatological horizons reflect an ontic rather than a noetic order, which is at odds with the characteristically evangelical focus on personal salvation. This ontic framework is evident in the

---

100. Moltmann, *Coming of God*, 338.

101. Gibson, "The Day of God's Mercy," 165.

ecumenical, political, and liberationist orientation of his theology,[102] as well as in his doctrine of creation, in which the *shalom* of new creation is the overriding paradigm within which individual salvation finds its place in the community of creation. In his ecological passion, Moltmann at times leaves himself open to the charge of relegating human beings *below* nature, but, as noted at the beginning of this chapter, his theocentric emphasis on nature as God's creation serves to steer evangelical theology away from a lop-sided perspective that exalts humanity as the ultimate crown of God's creation at the expense of non-human creation. As Moltmann drolly observes, "One-sided human domination stupefies nature and makes human beings stupid!"[103]

We have seen how Moltmann's notion of God *in* creation supplants the evangelical tendency to locate God *over* creation. His orientation— not only in his doctrine of creation, but throughout his theological *oeuvre*—towards a theology of God's immanence, as well as his espousal of a theology of "openness," has irked those conservative evangelicals who prefer to speak about God in terms of his transcendent attributes. He has been criticized for shaping his theology around the human condition with all of its contradictions rather than the biblical revelation of a sovereign, omnipotent God. In what might be viewed as a rather harsh evaluation, Grenz and Olson conclude their brief review of Moltmann's theology as follows: "By linking God's innertrinitarian being so closely with historical events, the German theologian calls into question the deity of God."[104] This clearly demonstrates the hazard of doing theology "from below." However, Moltmann's passion for living, which includes

102. In an earlier work, Moltmann draws a distinction between two interpretations of the *theology of revolution*. One strand of thinking—specifically associated with the evangelical tradition—interprets revolution in an individualistic sense, in terms of personal repentance and regeneration. However, another way of understanding revolution, one which Moltmann clearly avows, has to do with the "political responsibility of Christianity . . . in the people, with the people and for the liberation of the people." See Moltmann, *Church in Power of Spirit*, 17. Moltmann is careful not to dismiss the personal dimension of revolution, proposing a comprehensive "open concept" of liberation which runs from the abolition of all forms of exploitation "down to faith's experience of liberation from the compulsion of sin and the eschatological hope of liberation from the power of death." What is noticeable is his ordering of the different dimension of suffering, *down to* freedom from sin and death (which would be the priority statement for evangelicals).

103. Moltmann, *Science and Wisdom*, 28.

104. Grenz and Olson, *20th Century Theology*, 186.

his love for people and his encounter with the whole breadth and depth of life, imbues his theology with a profound awareness of participating in the joy of God's presence in creation: "I smell a rose, and smell the kingdom of God"![105] Perhaps we might re-phrase Gibson, quoted earlier, "Would that more so-called 'evangelicals' smell the roses in order to discover the kingdom of God!"

Moltmann's exploration into Jewish mystical thought—especially in his use of the kabbalistic *zimsum* concept—and his endorsement of the *Gaia* hypothesis in his ecological theology have both given rise to concern amongst evangelicals that his doctrine of creation is excessively influenced by speculative and philosophical ideas that have insufficient grounding in Scripture. However, Moltmann's appeal to the mystical tradition may be viewed as one dimension of his theology of mystical experience, which, in Bauckham's words, reflects "his determination to speak of an intimacy with God which excludes no aspect of God's creation."[106] For Moltmann, mysticism is not doctrinal wisdom but experiential wisdom, earthed in the reality of living in *this* world, a way of knowing that is epistemologically suspect amongst many evangelicals. James B. Torrance once helpfully wrote that "more important than our experience of Christ is the Christ of our experience"[107], but that should not encourage us to throw the baby out with the bathwater by inserting an "evangelical wedge" between the two. As Bauckham notes, the fellowship of the crucified Christ and the hope of the coming of the kingdom are two recurring themes in Moltmann that "characterize Christian experience of God as participation in God's trinitarian history with the world and so not as flight from the world but as suffering solidarity with the world for the sake of its future."[108] Mysticism for Moltmann is defined not by a Platonic upward progression from the concrete to the abstract, nor by a narcissistic inward "transcendental meditation": it is "at its innermost heart *meditatio passionis et mortis Christi*"[109] as the believer is drawn into

105. Moltmann, "A Lived Theology," 89, referring to his encounter with the Dutch theologian Arnold van Ruler at a theological conference in 1956–57, where he became familiar with his kingdom of God theology.

106. Bauckham, *Theology of Moltmann*, 247.

107. See especially Torrance, *Worship, Community, and Triune God*, 6–31.

108. Bauckham, *Theology of Moltmann*, 223.

109. Moltmann, *Spirit of Life*, 203.

the history of Christ for the sake of the world—outward and forward, as summarized by Bauckham. This is given more mystical expression in Moltmann's theology in his proposal for a meditative experience of God that is "pre-eminently a way of sensory perception, of receiving, of absorbing and participating."[110] The French mystic and philosopher Simone Weil suggests that to see in this way is tantamount to prayer.[111] To praying we might add playing, since for Moltmann the kingdom of freedom is the kingdom of play: "The game of redemption perfects a unique feature of the creative play of human beings with the world."[112]

Perhaps the dimension of Moltmann's experimental theology that has caused greatest concern amongst evangelicals in recent years is his preference for universal salvation, grounded in his conviction that, in the final divine self-glorification, when God will be "all in all," nothing will be lost. While we do not need to rehearse the evident challenge to mainline evangelical interpretation of Scripture with regard to the role of faith in personal salvation and the biblical support for a "double out-come," it is evident that Moltmann's apocatastatic position is determined by his doctrine of the transcendent sovereignty of God: divine grace and human decision cannot be brought to the same level, for this means "hu-manizing God and deifying the human being."[113] This God, sovereign in choosing to affirm his love for *all* that he has made, has acted in Christ, whose resurrection is the "open plenitude" of God for the redemption of τὰ πάντα—human and non-human—within the new creation of his glory: "what God wants to do he can do, and will do."[114] In *The Coming of God* Moltmann asks: what do we really and truly hope for? To which he answers, the *kingdom of God*, which "embraces the *salvation* and eter-nal life of human beings, the *deliverance* of all created things, and the *peace* of the new creation."[115] When evangelical convictions place per-sonal salvation first in the eschatological horizon, the theological debate about universal salvation predominates. However, when the *shalom* of

110. Ibid., 200.

111. Weil suggests that when prayer is intense and pure enough for contact with God to be established, "the whole attention is turned towards God." See Weil, *Waiting on God*, 66.

112. Moltmann, *God in Creation*, 311.

113. Moltmann, *Coming of God*, 245.

114. Ibid., 244.

115. Ibid., xvi (author's italics).

God's new heaven and new earth becomes the principal horizon, a new way of seeing emerges, grounded in the restoration of all things. This ecologically-shaped messianic perspective of the glorious completion of creation is perhaps one of Moltmann's most profound legacies. It is one from which evangelical theology has much to learn.

4

Moltmann's Theological Anthropology

From Crisis to Kingdom

Lanier Burns

Today, the annihilation of the human race and the inhabitable earth is the real threat. So every country has the urgent task of restraining humanity's nuclear self-annihilation.[1]

What is at issue here is the liberation and redemption of human beings from their sinful godlessness and their deadly inhumanity, and thus also the realization of their original destiny through having been created in the image of God.[2]

INTRODUCTION

MIROSLAV VOLF INTRODUCED *The Future of Theology* with the following tribute: "Perhaps no single other theologian of the second half of our century has shaped theology so profoundly as has Jürgen Moltmann . . . In terms of fecundity, Moltmann's opus remains unmatched among his generation of theologians. Over 130 dissertations

---

1. Moltmann, "Progress and Abyss," 21.
2. Moltmann, *On Human Dignity*, 21.

written so far on his thought—most of them in the past decade—testify eloquently to its continued attractiveness."[3]

Moltmann's voluminous writings, his extensive dialogues, and his open-ended invitation to engage the world substantiate Volf's assessment. His bibliography includes his own 1,217 writings and 1,043 books and articles about his theology. His thinking resonates with major movements in academic theology, panentheism in process theology and various liberation theologies. His method attempts to synthesize a vast number of disparate sources, which causes his readers to search for their place in his theological system.

This chapter concerns Moltmann's view of "human nature." Its task is complicated by the fact that he does not develop a comprehensive theological anthropology: "Important anthropological insights arise from his theology either simply through an incidental comment, or as an implication of the larger theological point that he is at that time making."[4] This void has resulted in an abnormally large number of footnotes in an attempt to present his thought accurately. Our task is also complicated by Moltmann's sense of urgency about contemporary crises. He focused his thought and research on the potential annihilation of the world and called for a reformulation of Christian theology in view of the crisis. Most readers will struggle with his rejection of the past and his novel view of trinitarian history and its relevant future. They will constantly seek their equilibrium in his eschatological orientation of inhumanity becoming humanity. His *God in Creation* will be used as a unifying text for these disparate threads, since it represents his most complete statement of humanity in creation.

Moltmann develops his anthropology on the basis of "the ecological apocalypse" that threatens life on earth. This modern crisis was initiated by Western visions of "a new world order," which resulted in a scientific and technological seizure of power over nature. The nineteenth century was a period of remarkable progress. Triggered by hopes in chiliastic (Joachim of Fiore) and ethical (Kant) futures, revolutions in France (over democratic rights) and England (for industrial prosperity) generated an atmosphere of evolutionary progress. The twentieth century was an age of unprecedented catastrophes: world wars, ethnic holocausts, nuclear threats, and impending ecological disasters. Earlier

3. Volf, "A Queen and a Beggar," ix.
4. Cosden, *A Theology of* Work, 127.

messianic visions had tragic apocalyptic downsides. In our era, he emphasized, "we are globalizing the nineteenth century's world of progress, and at the same time all the weapons of mass destruction developed and employed in the twentieth century are still kept in readiness for mass extermination, which would provide the 'final solution' of the question of the human race."[5] Accumulations of power are matched by its misuse at every turn. We have trapped ourselves in addictions to compulsive progress and destructive powers, both of which have been divorced from humane goals. The crisis is catastrophic for nature and humanity. Moltmann introduced his *God in Creation* with his characteristic emphasis: "What we call the environmental crisis is not merely a crisis in the natural environment of human beings. It is nothing less than a crisis in human beings themselves. It is a crisis on this planet, a crisis so comprehensive and irreversible that it cannot unjustly be described as apocalyptic."[6] Today, these perversions against nature and humanity are marked by a transparently destructive lust for power.

His Thesis

Moltmann's clarion call for about fifty years has been a confrontation of crisis with hope through the recovery of an eschatological orientation of theology. This preoccupation with the future contains a structural openness to promote dialogue in a broad constituency concerning the church's mission of pointing modernity toward the promises of God's kingdom. Dialogue has been very important for Moltmann. He acknowledged the contingency of his positions and the need for mutual participation and unifying sympathy to incorporate the voices of oppressed populations. In his words, "Behind all this is the conviction that, humanly speaking, truth is to be found in unhindered dialogue . . . But it is only in free dialogue that truth can be accepted as the only right and proper reason—namely, that it illuminates and convinces *as* truth."[7] In

---

5. Moltmann, "Progress and Abyss," 4. Cf. Moltmann, *Man*, 28–30.

6. Moltmann, *God in Creation*, xiii. The crises are spelled out in terms of science, industry, and anthropology's "crisis of domination" in *ibid.*, chap. 2. Also, Moltmann, *Creating a Just Future*, 51–55.

7. Moltmann, *The Trinity and the Kingdom*, xiii. In a later volume Moltmann states: "Theology is a community affair. Consequently theological truth takes the form of dialogue, and does so *essentially*, not just for the purposes of entertainment," *The Coming of God*, xiv.

such freedom, he believed, Christians could be the source of an impulse for change, dialogical agents who are charged with promoting the mission of life on earth.

From his first trilogy he built eschatological hope with a christological center.[8] The cross and resurrection, in his interpretation, were dialectical opposites; the resurrection constituted God's promise of his presence for all of humanity and creation (*Theology of Hope*), while the cross demonstrated God's solidarity with the godlessness of the world (*The Crucified God*). The cross must be interpreted with themes of divine love and fellow-suffering. The outcast Son of Man, who died between two oppressed wretches, cried in death, "My God, My God, why have you forsaken me?" So, God was dialectically present in his own contradiction to lovingly deliver his creation from sin and suffering as well as to express love within himself. The cross was not meant to solve the problem of suffering but to embrace it with voluntary fellow-suffering. On the other hand, in Moltmann's view, "The distinctive element of the Christian possibility of hope rests in the fact that it is born of the memory of the raising up of the crucified Son of Man. The fact that the future of really human man began with this rejected and outcast Son of Man can well be called the 'impossible possibility' of hope in this world."[9] The contradiction between hope and despair, life and death respectively, was reconciled in the single person of Christ. Also, the contradiction formed Moltmann's "dialectic of reconciliation," a methodological device that sought to demonstrate the interdependence of the relevance (suffering) and identity (hope) of his theological enterprise. Through the dialectic the hope of the person is "embedded" in the comprehensive hope of the cosmos in its Creator. The cross pointed to a trinitarian and messianic history in which God has reciprocally related to the world, being both affecting and affected as a community of divine persons who have included creation within their love. The Spirit has resolved the dialectic by indwelling creation and transformatively moving it in resurrectional hope toward the new creation, when God's glorious presence will fully indwell all of reality. Moltmann has described this central theme of his trinitarian history as "immanent transcendence," a concept that is

---

8. *Theology of Hope* (*Theologie der Hoffnung*, 1964), *The Crucified God* (*Der gekreuzigte Gott*, 1972), and *The Church in the Power of the Spirit* (*Kirche in der Kraft des Geistes*, 1975). Also, Moltmann, *Jesus Christ for Today's World*, chaps. 5–6.

9. Moltmann, *Man*, 117.

akin to Schleiermacher's "common spirit" that coheres reality.[10] People, therefore, discover who they are at the boundary of transcendence in their immanent historical realities. The new creation will not merely be a fulfillment of present possibilities but also a radically new life, righteousness, and glory.

Moltmann's eschatological orientation, Christological center, and trinitarian mission replaced a traditional ontology of humanity as the framework of his theology. In other words, the foundational "proofs" for God are mere anthropological shadows, while true humanity has as its goal a universal human nature that is in the process of realizing God's promises for creation.[11] God's liberating future is the basis for our hope in every historical present: 'Man attains to knowledge of himself by discovering the discrepancy between the divine mission and his own being, by learning what he is, and what he is yet to be, and yet himself cannot be."[12] A personal search for self exposes a hoping being, whose possibilities in the divine mission are mediated through bodily presences. The difference between experience and hope, in his view, is historical motivation, which defines anthropology. Thus, like trinitarianism the study of humanity is not concerned with an immutable ontology but rather with an awareness of our present journey with a view to whom we will become.[13]

His Method

Moltmann's thesis of an eschatological hope in God's indwelling all of reality necessitated a theological method in which traditional language could be redefined to express new concepts. He advanced a symbolic, non-analytical way of thinking to formulate his view of the future, an approach that embodied "post-critical scientific methods and ways of thinking."[14] His *Theology of Hope* presented the historical symbol of hope in the kingdom of God. It lacked the natural symbol of hope in the

10. Moltmann, *The Spirit of Life*, 31–38.

11. Thiselton, *Interpreting God*, 153, refers to the divine promises as Moltmann's "promissory perspective."

12. Moltmann, *Theology of Hope*, 285.

13. Moltmann, *The Way of Jesus Christ*, 55–63, discusses at length the notion of the modern alienated self ("Modern Jesuology") that he addressed under the heading "Anthropological Christology."

14. Moltmann, *God in Creation*, 4.

new creation of all things. So, in *God in Creation* "I have eschatologized nature by seeing nature at this point in time as the true symbol of its new creation in God."[15] And, to counter the particularizing language of modern science, we "must try to get away from analytical thinking with its distinctions between subject and object, and must strive to learn a new, communicative and integrating way of thought."[16] He continued: "Integrating, and integral, thinking moves purposefully in this social direction towards the goal of an inclusiveness that is many-sided, and ultimately fully comprehensive . . . We no longer desire to know in order to dominate or analyze and reduce in order to reconstruct. Our purpose is now to perceive in order to participate, and to enter into the mutual relationships of the living thing."[17]

Accordingly, the cross and resurrection focus the meaning of "time" to the future. Since the past represents death, the present in hope and promise takes its definition from the future resurrection of creation in God's life. "No human future," Moltmann stated, "can make good the crimes of the past," so creation must be interpreted from its eschatological future.[18] Space, by the same token, is the created space of God's world-presence: "The space of the world corresponds to God's world presence, which initiates this space, limits it, and interpenetrates it."[19] Hence, space and its history is homogenous and divine, abolishing the artificial distinction between sacred and profane.

Moltmann addressed "the ecological crisis' with his theological priority.[20] He explains his approach in two important statements. First, since God's indwelling of creation is the theological side of the ecological doctrine, the anthropological side must correspond to it. Existence

---

15. Ibid., xi.

16. Ibid., 2. Moltmann does not intend for us to understand chronological time in his eschatology, since the future already has been present from the beginning and in messianic resurrection.

17. Ibid., 3.

18. Moltmann, "Progress and Abyss," 17.

19. Moltmann, *God in Creation*, 157.

20. Moltmann offers an insightful comment on his theological method in a response to Richard Bauckham, *God Will Be All in All*, 36: "Once a pastor, always a pastor, and once politically involved, always politically interested. Someone who, ultimately speaking, lives consciously in his own time never does theology in the form of abstractions for all times; he pursues it as a contemporary for contemporaries, specifically, contextually, and in relation to its *kairos*."

can only become a home if the relationship between nature and human beings is without stresses and strains—if it can be described in terms of reconciliation, peace, and a viable symbiosis. The indwelling of human beings in the natural system of the earth corresponds, for its part, to the indwelling of the Spirit in the soul and body of the human being, which puts and end to the alienation of human beings from themselves.[21]

Second, in the same introductory context, he states: "I have not followed the common practice of dividing the doctrine of creation from anthropology. This means that the anthropology has had to be curtailed. The sections on the individual an society, societies and humanity, and humanity and nature, have deliberately been omitted."[22] The implication of these statements is that his anthropology must be accessed through his distinctive emphases on the Trinity and cosmology. In other words, his view of humanity flows from his trinitarian history of nature.[23]

The apocalyptic need also guided his selection of diverse sources. His wartime imprisonment (1945–48) introduced him to the power of hope and the comfort of God's presence in suffering.[24] They encompass a broad range of expertise around the midpoint of the twentieth century, which should be seen through the lens of his roots in German Idealism. His research surfaced in his extensive body of work: von Balthasar, Barth, Bloch, Bonhoeffer, Iwand, Metz, von Rad, Käsemann, Liberation theologians, Weber, Wolf, van Ruler, Hoekendijk, and Whitehead among others. Glimmers of Barth can be seen in his emphasis on incarnational Christology, though their anthropologies differed sharply. With von Balthasar he affirmed the intrinsic beauty of divine creation. Arnold van Ruler and J. C. Hoekendijk through Otto Weber and others introduced him to an eschatological perspective of the church's mission in God's kingdom.[25] From Dietrich Bonhoeffer and Ernst Wolf he developed a concern for the church's social imperative.

21. Moltmann, *God in Creation*, xv.

22. Ibid., xvi.

23. Ibid., 1: "With this doctrine of creation I am taking a further step along the road on which I started out with *The Trinity and the Kingdom of God* (1980; ET, 1981). In that book I developed a social doctrine of the Trinity. Here my subject is the corresponding ecological doctrine of creation." He had similarly stated earlier, "Accordingly a book about 'Man' will inevitably slip into being a book about God," *Man*, x, cf. 105–8.

24. See Moltmann, *Experiences of God*, 1–18. Also, Moltmann, *A Broad Place*, chap. 3.

25. Meeks, *Origins of the Theology of Hope*, 2, states, "But, as we shall see, [con-

Hegel through Iwand contributed to his "dialectic of reconciliation" between cross and resurrection as well as his view of history as a movement of Spirit. Johann Baptist Metz aided his adoption of an antithesis between the cross and oppressive political structures. Moltmann's long-term dialogue with Ernst Bloch matured his appreciation of a transcendent messianic hope.[26] With Whitehead he developed a panentheism in the bipolarity of God's immanence and transcendence. He referred to his method as "ecumenical" dialogue, embracing Protestant, Catholic, Orthodox, Jewish, and Eastern sources in transhistorical perspective. Perhaps "eclectic" would be a better description, since he was convinced that science, technology, and economics determine the relationships between people, machines, and nature in the world. He wrote at a time when European theology was profoundly depressed, and he used every source at his disposal to restore a relevant hope to his dying world.

HUMANITY IN CREATION

Moltmann's desire to write a new approach to creation had been on his agenda since *Theology of Hope* in 1964. *God in Creation* was the result and appeared in his second trilogy between *The Trinity and the Kingdom of God* (1980, ET 1981) and *The Way of Jesus Christ* (1989, ET 1990).[27] It represents the substance of his Gifford Lectures in 1984–85, and the series formed his trinitarian history of God into an over-arching "messianic theology." His secondary emphasis on anthropology can be traced over time from his *Man* (1974) through *On Human Dignity* (1984) to *God in Creation* (1985). Thus, the Christological center in his first trilogy became the trinitarian model for his thinking about humanity in his second trilogy.

cern for eschatology] is true of almost all mainline German theologies of the twentieth century. In fact, Moltmann's theology on the most fundamental level is radically from all of the other recent eschatological theologies." Its "newness" lies in his "dialectic of reconciliation," juxtaposing the relevance of biblical themes and the negative dimensions of the post-Enlightenment world. Anthropologically, humanity was starved for hope out of despair.

26. Bauckham, *Theology of Moltmann*, 1–2. Cf. Moltmann, ed., *How I Have Changed*, 15–20.

27. *Gott in der Schöpfung: Ökologische Schöpfungslehre*, which was published in 1985. The reader may note the English translation, p. xi, for Moltmann's intent.

Rejection of the Past

His "ecological theology of nature" is a rejection of "the biblicist misunderstanding of the biblical testimonies to think that they are laying down once and for all particular findings about nature, and render all further research superfluous."[28] Biblicism disregarded the wealth of mutual relationships in the world in its static cosmos. Its error was the theological perversion of the church's medieval cosmology based on Genesis 1 and the Ptolemaic tradition. It was a one-sided monotheistic view with a transcendent Creator, who distinguished himself from nature and subjected it to oppressive bondage under humanity as its ruler. This anthropocentric emphasis objectified nature and dominated it as an object to be exploited: "God is the Creator, Lord and owner of the world; and in the same way the human being had to endeavor to become the lord and owner of the earth. This was the idea behind the centralistic theologies, and the foundation of the hierarchical doctrines of sovereignty . . . Creation is certainly not the world which human beings are supposed to 'subdue.'"[29] The ideological distinction between God and the world was maintained by modern apologetics, which used the language of divine causation to counter the secularizing process of modern Europe.

In light of this unfortunate emphasis, Moltmann mandates that theology must:

> start again . . . if it to comprehend creation and God's activity in the world in a new way, in the framework of today's knowledge about nature and evolution, and if it is to make the world as creation—and it's history as God's activity—comprehensible to scientific reason also. If this is to be our purpose, we must first of all be critical, and must get rid of the bias and narrowness which have taken root in the Christian doctrine of creation in the wake of polemic against the theory of evolution.[30]

The problem was that evolution had demoted Christians and Europeans alike, who in the name of God had understood themselves

---

28. Ibid., 192. Later he similarly expressed a need to reformulate biblical testimonies: "So it is not merely possible to relate the biblical testimonies about creation and God's history with his creation, to new insights about nature, and new theories about the interpretation of these insights; it is actually necessary to make this connection and to reformulate the biblical testimonies in the light of these things," ibid., 193.

29. Ibid., 1–2.

30. Ibid., 192. Cf. page 186 as well.

as the masters of nature. The theory undermined the anthropocentric view of the world by reducing it to a small link in a sequence whose end could not be determined. Churches and civic communities over-reacted because evolution threatened their justification for conquest of the world and exploitation of nature. The ideology, he asserts, is neither biblical nor Christian.[31]

The rise of the modern sciences led to the rejection of ancient and medieval cosmologies, and historical criticism dismissed biblical narratives about origins as myths. Conflicts between science and the church were severe as evidenced by the trials of Bruno and Galilei and subsequent reactions against Darwin and Freud. Moltmann refers to this era as "peaceful co-existence on the basis of mutual irrelevance."[32] There could be no reconciliation, he held, when the sciences naturalized the world and neutralized theology's anthropocentrism.

One of science's lingering problems, on the other hand, is that it cannot be separated from pantheism.[33] Terminology like "self-ordering" and "self-transcendence" regarding matter gravitates to a lack of urgency, in which nature exists *ex se* with divine attributes: "The exponents of evolution do not always realize clearly enough that the ideological application of their theoretical concepts hinders their scientific work rather than promotes it."[34] In addition, the "social Darwinism" of T. H. Huxley politicized evolution to justify European colonialism, racism, patriarchalism, and class conflict.

Reconciliation toward the Future

Moltmann argues for a rapprochement between theology and the sciences in behalf of survival on earth, "Science and theology cannot afford to divide up the one, single reality."[35] We have noted earlier that he sets forth an open, dialogical theology with eschatological hope in the

31. Ibid., 194.

32. Ibid., 33. Elsewhere, he described the coexistence as the "new bond" between faith and science, in which "faith does not get in the way of reason and reason does not dissolve faith," *Theology Today*, 9.

33. Interestingly, Moltmann defined evolution as "a basic concept of the self-movement of the divine Spirit of creation," *God in Creation*, 19.

34. Ibid., 194.

35. Ibid., 34. Cf. pp. 13, 19, where he states, "What we are seeking is a *community* of scientific and theological insights," and we must "stop thinking of creation and evolution as opposing concepts, and instead link them with one another as complements."

culmination of trinitarian and messianic history. Creation, he asserts, must be defined by its future in which the Spirit creates a universal, sabbatarian community in divine love. To develop this thesis of creational transformation toward resurrectional glory, he advances three corrective themes to replace the one-sided perversions of the past: from biblicism to *zimsum*, from monotheistic causation to panentheistic trinitarianism, and from anthropological dominance to communitarian indwelling.

First, in place of the biblical account in Genesis 1–2, Moltmann used the kabbalistic doctrine of *zimsum* as "the only serious attempt ever made to think through the idea of 'creation out of nothing' [*creatio ex nihilo*] in a truly theological way."[36] The *zimsum* principle is that God must act inwardly before he can act outwardly: "It is only as *causa sui* that God can be *causa mundi*."[37] So, God self-determined to concentrate and contract himself (=*zimsum*), a withdrawal into himself "in a shrinking process," to create a Nothingness for creation: "In der Selbstverschränkung des göttlichen Wesens, das, anstatt in seinem ersten Akt mach außen zu wirken, sich vielmehr zu sich selbst, wendet, tritt das Nichts zutage. Hier haben wir einen Akt, in dem has Nichts hervorgerufen, wird. Es ist die affirmative Kraft der Selbsnegation Gottes, die zur schöpferischen Kraft in Schöpfung und Heil wird."[38]

---

36. He cites Gershom Scholem's account of Isaac Luria and Jacob Emden *Major Trends in Jewish Mysticism*, 244 ff. and 411. Kabbalah in Jewish mysticism is a "way of transformation." Readers who are interested in comparing Luria and Moltmann on the theme of transformation may consult Eliahu Klein, *Kabbalah of Creation*.

37. Moltmann, *Trinity and Kingdom*, 108. Elsewhere, "in order to create a world 'outside' himself [in creation, incarnation, and redemption], the infinite God must have made room beforehand for a finitude in himself," *God in Creation*, 86. On pages 298–302 of *God in Creation*, Moltmann uses the symbols of "Great World Mother" and "Mother Earth" to support his principle of nurturing life: "The interpretation of the world which emerges right down the line, from the symbol of the World Mother to the symbol of the redeeming cosmic human being, Christ, is the panentheistic understanding of the world as the sheltering and nurturing divine environment for everything living," 300.

38. Moltmann, *Gott in der Schöpfung*, 100. His German captures Moltmann's nuances in this foundational statement of his position. His inclusion of creation and salvation in a single process means that "every act outwards is preceded by an act inwards which makes the 'outwards' possible. God, that is to say, continually creates inwards and outwards simultaneously," *Trinity and Kingdom*, 110. Also, *creatio ex nihilo* in the beginning is the preparation and promise of the redeeming *annihilatio nihili*, from which the eternal being of creation proceeds," ibid., 90. The kabbalistic analog for this self-limitation is the presence of God in the temple, the Shekinah. He doesn't engage the awkward fact that this confuses covenantal with cosmological presences and implies

The *nihil* as negation of divine being, is literally "God-forsakenness, hell, absolute death."[39] Moltmann believes that in sin it becomes annihilating Nothingness (*verniehtanden Nichts*). This act of self-humiliating, creative love is the initiation of God's *kenotic* interrelationship with the world, which Philippians continues as the mystery of Messiah: "Through his self-emptying, he creates liberation, through his self-humiliation he exalts, and through his vicarious suffering, the redemption of sinners is achieved."[40] Accordingly, "creative making" in masculine terms can be changed to a loving process in feminine terms: "Creation as God's act in Nothingness and as God's order in chaos is a male, an engendering notion. Creation as God's act in God and out of God must rather be called a feminine concept, a bringing forth. God creates the world by letting his world become and be in *himself*: Let it be!"[41]

Through the Son on the cross, God enters the annihilating Nothingness and "becomes omnipresent," gathering *nihil* into his being and giving creation a part of his eternal life. The crucified Son, in turn, becomes the foundation of the kingdom of glory, which begins with his resurrection and glorification. In light of the cross, *creatio ex nihilo* eschatologically means forgiveness of sins, justification of the godless, and the resurrection of the dead: "The cross is the mystery of creation and the promise of its future . . . The hope of resurrection brings the living and the dead into a single fellowship of hope."[42] A consequence of the creational process is that eschatology can be redefined as faith in the Creator and faithfulness to life on earth.[43]

---

that God's omnipresence can be confined in a space.

39. Moltmann, *God in Creation*, 87.

40. Ibid., 89. "Liberation," for him, is a central concept in his anthropology and soteriology and is broader than egalitarian movements in the mid-twentieth century, though it includes them. It refers instead to freedom from situations that alienate and oppress people as well as freedom to take responsibility for their world. It is a gift that is experienced when God invites a person into his "broad place" of perichoretic living.

41. Moltmann, *Trinity and Kingdom*, 109. God's self-limitation involved his "pathos" for his image, a concept that he attributed to Abraham Joshua Heschel, "who perceived for the first time that the divine pathos is the appropriate hermeneutical point of reference for the anthropomorphic utterances of God in the Old Testament," ibid., 26. Cf. Heschel, *The Prophets*, 2.1–47.

42. Moltmann, *God in Creation*, 91–92.

43. In his perspective, "eschatology is nothing other than faith in the Creator with eyes toward the future," ibid., 93.

Second, the feminine process means that panentheistic trinitarianism must replace monotheistic causation. Monotheism, Moltmann
maintains, has led to differentiation within the Trinity, distinction
between God and the world, and human domination over nature. He
decries the monotheistic tradition, which has placed God the Father
over against creation as its Lord. God's transcendence objectified nature
as his immanent domain; as a consequence, "nature is stripped of her
divinity, politics become profane, history is divested of fate."[44] We must
"eliminate the concept of causality from the doctrine of creation, and
indeed we also have to stop thinking in terms of cause at all . . . creating the world is something different from causing it."[45] Instead, we must
think of an intricate web of interrelationships, a cosmic community of
being between God the Spirit and all of his created beings. Finally, we
also must cease to understand God monotheistically as the one absolute
subject, but instead see him in a trinitarian sense as the perichoretic
unity of the Father, the Son, and the Spirit. Therefore, we can no longer
conceive his relationship to the world he has created as a one-sided relationship of dominion.

Moltmann portrays the Trinity as the Father affecting reality out
of his overflowing love; the Son creating, reconciling, and redeeming
all things; and the Spirit as divine presence in reconciliation and redemption. In his "pneumatological doctrine of creation," the Spirit is the
transforming agent who brings trinitarian history to its goal: "In the life
giving operations of the Spirit and in his indwelling influence the whole
trinitarian efficacy of God finds full expression. In the operation and
indwelling of the Spirit, the creation of the Father through the Son, and
the reconciliation of the world with God through Christ, arrive at their
goal. The presence and efficacy of the Spirit is the eschatological goal of
creation and reconciliation. All the works of God end in the presence of
the Spirit."[46]

Ecology and pneumatology converge in the symbolism of creation
as home, the Spirit's indwelling according to the kabbalistic view of

44. Ibid., 13.

45. Ibid., 14. Also, Moltmann, *Creating a Just Future*, 55–61.

46. Ibid., 96. Moltmann offers a lengthy description of God's changing trinitarian
relationships in himself as he experientially changes with the world. In turn, when we
experience God's love, we also experience the intertrinitarian love.

Shekinah.[47] The Creator dwells in his creation as a whole, maintaining life in every creature in mutual suffering and joy. Through this commitment to his home, the indwelling Spirit transfigures creation into the eternal heaven and earth.[48] The emphasis means that creation is an evolving openness toward the future sabbatical world community. This concept involves a finitude that embraces infinity (*finitum capax infiniti*), in which "everything will not be in God, but God will be in everything."[49]

Moltmann identifies his "new kind of thinking about God" with panentheistic theology.[50] Its center is the recognition of the presence of God in the world and the presence of the world in God. In his words, God creates the world and manifests himself through its being. "Everything," he states holistically, "exists, lives, and moves *in others* . . . in the cosmic interrelationships of the divine Spirit."[51] The Creator of the world is the Spirit of the universe, "its total cohesion, its structure, its information, its energy . . . The evolution and the catastrophes of the universe are also the movements and experiences of the Spirit of creation."[52] This identification of Spirit with creation is a progression in his eschatological dialectic to an inclusion of the whole creation and history within the divine experience. Accordingly, spirit becomes the organizing principle of the symbiotic ecosystem of creation, involving synchronic integration and diachronic self-transcendence. The human spirit is largely unconscious as a complex, multi-layered life system: "Spirit is the quintessence of the human being's self-organization, and his self-transcendence, his inner and his outward symbioses."[53] We are thus concerned with a spirit-soul

47. In his "Progress and Abyss," 24–25, Moltmann states: "The 'housekeeping' of this earth requires the keeping of a dwelling place fit for human beings; while, for their part, human beings should be prepared to live in the ecosystem, and no longer stand against or apart from nature as hostile aliens." He concludes in a footnote, "If this is correct, then a new ecological anthropology is required . . . In the new ecological anthropology, the insights of modern feminist anthropology must be taken into account."

48. Moltmann defines heaven as "the openness to God of the world he has created," *God in Creation*, 165. And he noted, "The symbol of heaven signifies the inner relative transcendence of creation," ibid., 174.

49. Moltmann, "The World in God or God in the World?," in *God Will Be All in All*, edited by Bauckham, 37, 40.

50. Moltmann, *God in Creation*, xi.

51. Ibid., 11.

52. Ibid., 16.

53. Ibid., 18.

and a spirit-body and their unity in the spirit. Through the spirit people are bound together socially and culturally with humanity and the natural environment in a "spiritual ecosystem." In the process, the Spirit of creation (the cosmic Spirit) must be distinguished from the Holy Spirit who accomplishes redemption and sanctification. The latter is the Holy Spirit of Christ, who forms human beings in a fellowship of love.

However, the two concepts merge in the transformation of humanity: "The Holy Spirit does not supersede the Spirit of creation but transforms it. The Holy Spirit therefore lays hold of the whole human being, embracing his feelings and his body as well as his soul and reason."[54] His principle of "mutual interpenetration" implies that "all relationships which are analogous to God and reflect the primal, reciprocal indwelling and interpenetration of the trinitarian perichoresis: God *in* the world and the world *in* God."[55] The imperative, therefore, is to expand personal consciousness to embrace integration and self-transcendence to social, ecological, cosmic, and divine realms.

Perhaps we should not be surprised that Moltmann seeks to distinguish his panentheism from pantheism. He notes that a philosophical root of evolution is Neoplatonic pantheism, and he quotes Ernst Haekel as saying, "Pantheism is *the world-system of the modern scientist*."[56] He also cites Heinrich Heine's rejection of pantheism because it translates into indifference.[57] The indifference refers to the inevitable consequence of equating God and the godlessness of the present world. In that case, future glory would be transformed into a perpetually hopeless chaos. He rejects Heine's "differentiated panentheism," because it cannot link God's immanence in the world with his transcendent relation to it. Instead, his "creation as a dynamic web of interconnected processes" advances a cosmic openness to God's future: "Without the difference between Creator and creature, creation cannot be conceived of at all; that this difference is embraced and comprehended by the greater truth . . . the truth that God is all in all. This does not imply a pantheistic dissolution

54. Ibid., 263.

55. Ibid., 17. In his *Science and Wisdom*, 123, Moltmann explains the mutual indwelling as follows: "This is a reciprocal indwelling of the unlike, not the like. The world lives in God in a world-like way, and God lives in the world in a God-like way. They interpenetrate each other mutually without destroying each other." Also, Moltmann, Nicholas Wolterstorff, and Ellen Charry, *A Passion for God's Reign*, 2.

56. Ibid., 194, 341.

57. Ibid., 103, 336.

of creation in God; it means that the final form which creation is to find in God."[58] In effect, Moltmann presses God's initial self-limitation to a future delimited "pantheistic" oneness.[59]

Third, the feminine process of panentheistic trinitarianism means that communitarian equality must replace anthropological dominance. Moltmann blames the "ecological crisis" on the fact that "modern European anthropology uncritically took the modern anthropocentric world picture as its premise,"[60] which necessarily entailed the modern abuse of nature. The modern crisis stemmed from theological traditions that presented creation as six days of labor with humanity as its crowning achievement. However, "the crown of creation is not the human being; it is the Sabbath."[61] The weekly rest and the year of jubilees point to the anticipation of the world's redemption: "The Sabbath is the prefiguration of the world to come. So when we present creation in the light of the future—'the glory of God,' 'existence as home,' and 'the general sympathy of all things'—then we are developing *a sabbath doctrine of creation . . .*"[62] In other words, when God is all in all, then all of creation becomes an egalitarian community in the Spirit.

The Sabbath doctrine of dethroned humanity introduces us to Moltmann's creational anthropology *per se*. "If we are to understand what it means to be human in the widest sense," he observes, "we must start with the complexes and milieus in which human beings appear and from which they live."[63] From global to individual meanings, people are on an evolving quest in an "unintelligible hall of a thousand mirrors and masks," being known more by their drive for humane living than

58. Ibid., 203. However, if difference is comprehended by universal divinity, then difference would seem to be dissolved.

59. Sensing the danger of an ultimate pantheism, Moltmann disclaimed the inference, ibid., 64: "The Creator's distance from those he has created will be ended through his own indwelling in his creation: though the difference between Creator and creature will not disappear." Elsewhere, his equivocation was expressed as "everything is not God: God is everything," ibid., 103. See as well, his *Trinity and Kingdom*, 110. In describing the parousia, he returned to Luria's kabbalistic thought to say that "God de-restricts himself and manifests his glory so that in the transfigured creation he may be 'all in all,'" *The Way of Jesus Christ*, 329.

60. Ibid., 185.

61. Ibid., 31.

62. Ibid., 6.

63. Moltmann, *God in Creation*, 186.

by self-knowledge.[64] Thus, for him, "It is more appropriate to practice theology in action, related to the experiences and life of man in contemporary industrial society, and to explore ways for this man to become man. This is indeed the starting point for all anthropology."[65]

Anthropology always involves comparisons that should never be analyzed in the abstract, any more than man occurs in isolation, both modes being unacceptable in his thinking. He describes four dimensions in ascending order: biological, cultural, religious, and Christian. From a biological comparison of humanity with animals, we can see ourselves as educated creatures with a conscious capacity for change. He explained the importance of biology as a proper foundation: "Before we interpret [humanity] as *imago Dei*, we shall see him as *imago mundi*—as a microcosm in which all previous creatures are to be found again, a being that can only exist in community with other created beings and which can only understand itself in that community."[66] From cultural comparisons we learn that we have harbored ethnocentric hostilities toward strangers, even as we share a common history and destiny: "Man as he appears in different cultures (*homo hominatas*) is an historical figure, but the creative germ-cell in man (*homo hominans*) is eternal."[67] From comparisons between religions, we discern a perpetual human unrest that flows from creaturely limitations and flaws. Finally, in biblical anthropology we are confronted with a history of specific calls in which God's promise leads to the future. Specifically, the promises point to the universal "*Ecce Homo*," who in crucifixion is "the Son of Man who identifies with those who are below the mean of humanness, in order to call them human . . . The deepest grounds of Christian universalism do not lie in monotheism, 'one God, so one humanity,' but in belief in the crucified Lord: the 'crucified God' accepts men in their lack of full humanness."[68] In this way, Christian anthropology absorbs the mirrors and masks of biological, cultural, and religious anthropology in the reality of the crucified Messiah.

The fundamental concept behind the anthropological comparisons is the *imago Dei*: "The nature of human beings springs from their

64. Moltmann, *Man*, 2.

65. Ibid., x.

66. Moltmann, *God in Creation*, 186.

67. Moltmann, *Man*, 11.

68. Ibid., 19–20.

relationship to God. It is this relationship which gives human nature its definition—not some characteristic or other which sets human beings apart from other living beings."[69] He emphasized that the relationship means humanity in its whole existence: "The whole person, not merely his soul; the true human community, not only the individual; humanity as it is bound up with nature, not simply human beings in their confrontation with nature—it is these which are the image of God and his glory."[70] The wholeness of humanity, in turn, encompasses three dimensions: the original designation (*imago Dei*), the messianic calling (*imago Christi*), and the eschatological glorification (*gloria Dei est homo*). In these dimensions Moltmann's anthropology is eschatologically framed. The original divine resolve was the culminating work that honored humanity in community with stewardship in creation and that pointed to Christ as the promise of creation's kingdom.

First, the original designation of humanity was the final work of creation, which was accomplished by God's special resolve to manifest himself kenotically in human community. The image of God (singular) corresponds to the internal plural of God. Self-resolving God is a plural in the singular of his being, while his image on earth is a singular in the plural. Accordingly, humanity is *imago trinitatis*: "The one God, who is differentiated in himself and is at one with himself, then finds his correspondence in a community of human beings, female and male, who unite with one another and are one."[71] Sexually differentiated humanity brings community to the forefront and means that people are social beings in a perichoretic sense. He notes, "The isolated individual and the solitary subject are deficient modes of being human, because they fall short of likeness to God."[72] The *imago trinitatis* means that the Trinity is "the archetype of true human community."[73] Thus, the Augustinian-Thomist view of one divine being with sovereignty must be changed in the direction of the Orthodox understanding of the social doctrine of

69. Moltmann, *God in Creation*, 220. Gunnlaugur Jónsson. *The Image of God*, 179 and 221, helpfully relates Moltmann's view to a growing scholarly response to the environmental crisis.

70. Ibid., 221.

71. Ibid., 218.

72. Ibid., 223.

73. Ibid., 234. On page 241 he similarly states, "In their various communities, human beings are to be understood not merely as the image of God's rule over creation, but also as the image of his inward nature."

human likeness in a theology of the open Trinity to the extent that the human family becomes a community of generations over space and time. Contrary to Augustine's emphasis on humanity's image of the "closed" Trinity, people are fashioned according to the openness of the Son alone, the foundational image through whom "the Father creates, redeems, and perfects human beings through the Spirit."[74]

Second, the original designation called humanity to be God's image in the forward-looking direction of Christ (*imago Christi*): "Then the christology is understood as the fulfillment of the anthropology, and the anthropology becomes the preparation for the christology." [75] The perfect reflection of the image is Christ, so the *imago Dei* is both *imago* and *similitude*: "The first of these terms is used for the concrete representation, the second for the similarity. The first expresses more the outward representation, the second rather the reflexive inward relationship."[76] Using royal theology, in which kingship represented the divine presence on earth, the biblical account "democratized" the role to the extent that all people and every human being reflects and represents divine presence in creation.[77] Humanity's transformation into the image of Christ is a reciprocal identity in cross and resurrection, an open dialectic of reconciliation in God's freedom to love, which can be resolved only in the eschaton of all things. True humanity, therefore, is identity with Christ's solidarity with the broken world in opposition to its power structures. The designation placed humanity in an irrevocable relationship with the Creator, which assured creation of his promised future: "Likeness to God means God's relationship to human beings first of all, and only then, as a consequence of that, the human beings relationship to God."[78]

The present dilemma is that we have to consider human beings as God's image and sinners at the same time. Moltmann reviews the ecclesial impasse over whether sin is *substantia* or *accidentia*. He concludes that we must abandon an anthropology of substance and define *imago Dei* as God's relationship to humanity. Human sin may certainly pervert human beings' relationship to God, but not

---

74. Ibid., 243. Also, Moltmann, *Trinity and Kingdom*, 21–22.

75. Ibid., 218.

76. Moltmann, *God in Creation*, 218–19.

77. Cf. Moltmann, *Man*, 110. Also, Moltmann, *On Human Dignity*, 23–24.

78. Moltmann, *God in Creation*, 220.

God's relationship to human beings. That relationship was resolved by God, and was created by him, and can therefore never
be abrogated or withdrawn except by God himself. Consequently
the sinner is subjectively speaking wholly and entirely a sinner
and godless. But he remains at the same time wholly and entirely
God's image, and does not lose this designation as long as God
adheres to it and remains faithful to him. The presence of God
makes the human being undeprivably and inescapably God's
image.[79]

Thus, the original designation of humanity as image must be viewed
as the grace of God, which will be completed at the end of trinitarian
history with human beings. Sin is the perversion of humanity's relationship to God, but not its loss, so that even idolatry is a form of the image.

The point is crucial for his anthropology, which, as noted previously, has a secondary place in his panentheistic history of nature. As a
consequence, people rule over other creatures as God's representatives;
they are his counterparts in perichoretic relationships; and they reflect
his glorious appearance on earth. They "mirror the face of his presence" until all of creation eschatologically beholds him "face to face":
"Whatever else may be called 'the seat' of the divine likeness, whether it
be the soul or the upright posture, domination or community, it is expressed in concentrated form in the person's face."[80] Therefore, the image
and likeness of humanity through Christ reflects his glorious kingdom
to come.

Third, the original designation was that humanity was distinctively
honored with the stewardship of creation. The original resolve was both
promise and destiny: "The first promise which we hear from the Bible
about man is his creation in the image of God . . . The world is the good
creation of God, but is not his image. Man in his destiny to be the image of God cannot be represented by anything else."[81] Moltmann's anthropology is aligned to a futuristic understanding of the present, and
we should understand the beginning in light of the *gloria Dei est homo*.
In the meantime, "a strong eschatological drive pervades the messianic
present."[82] Image is God's claim upon humanity to promote rights in life.

---

79. Ibid., 233.

80. Ibid., 221–22.

81. Moltmann, *Man*, 108–10.

82. Moltmann, *God in Creation*, 228.

Humanity's perversion of the divine mandate is the source of domination over nature, his focus of various evils in the world. Stewardship of the earth must be distinguished from the subjugation of creation. By implication, vegetarian nourishment meant that the intended human function was to be little more than a "justice of the peace." Traditional theological doctrine lost the distinction with disastrous consequences: "It is only as God's image that human beings exercise divinely legitimated rule; and in the context of creation that means; only as whole human beings, only as equal human beings, and only in the community of human beings—not at the price of dividing the human person into spirit and body—not at the price of dividing human beings into ruler and ruled—not at the price of dividing mankind into different classes."[83]

Moltmann proposed that the honor of the *imago Dei* placed humanity between our greatest loves and fears. People love the honor of responsible freedom in creation and even their fragile place in the world. But they become wretched when they forget the trust and usurp divinity in earthly relationships by using their position to accumulate power and destroy nature. Human beings are not divine, so the prohibition against images in the Law is designed to protect the special responsibility of all people. The *imago Dei*, properly understood, "cuts the ground from under the feet of the self-deification of man, of national politics, of nationalism, and of the fetishism of goods."[84]

The wholeness of humanity has been compromised in the tradition of anthropological domination; the soul has been differentiated and separated from the body in the interests of power and exploitation: "The whole trend toward a 'spiritualizing' of the soul and a 'materialization' of the body also unconsciously dominates the whole of Western anthropological theory."[85] Patristic theology generally followed the Platonic idea of the liberation of the soul from the body. The Platonic *meditatio mortis* used the immortality of the soul to separate death from personal existence beyond mortality. Medieval theology was influenced by the Aristotelian view that the body is formed by the soul. Modern European anthropology has given the conscious mind instrumental power over the body as exemplified by Descartes, who posited a superior soul as

83. Ibid., 225.

84. Moltmann, *Man*, 108. In his later writings, the sharpness of the prohibition seemed to fade.

85. Moltmann, *God in Creation*, 244.

a thinking self that dominates its machine-like body as its extended property. Karl Barth theologized the Aristotelian-Thomist tradition with analogous relationships of sovereignty: the ruling Father over the obedient Son and Spirit, the ruling God as Lord of the world, heaven over earth in cosmology, soul over body in theology, and man over woman in anthropology. According to Barth, the *imago Dei* is evidenced in the soul's control over the body in correspondence to the hierarchy of God's grace. The older traditions used the hierarchical pattern to preserve ordered relationships. Modern developments discarded the "higher-lower" dichotomy as irrelevant for a scientific, technological civilization. Besides, Moltmann concludes, "A world with an 'order' of this kind can hardly be called a peaceful one."[86]

We too should discard the self-alienated person; we must restore the oneness of body and soul. To do this, Moltmann reconstructs anthropology on the basis of the Old Testament, which in covenantal community and divine promise does not analyze soul and body as component parts: "The person thinks with his body. The brain and the bodily organs instruct one another . . . This surely indicates that in this anthropology soul and body, the core of the inner life, and the outward mental horizon are seen as existing in reciprocal relation and mutual interpenetration."[87] On this foundation he developed his contemporary anthropology according to the trinitarian analogy, a perichoretic relationship between the differentiations in human beings and their societies. He bridged the past exemplar, present perversion, and future kingdom with a process of embodiment. Ultimately, all of God's works in humanity lead to the embodiment of his promises for all living things in his kingdom, a reversal of the traditional emphasis on the dominance of the soul.

The process involves social trust and identity and occurs in the comprehensive work of the Spirit in forming the human Gestalt, "the configuration or total pattern—of the lived life."[88] That is, the Gestalt is the whole human organism as formed by different environments like genetics, geography, ethnography, background circumstances, and religious values: "But the Spirit whose efficacy forms body, soul and their living Gestalt is not merely the creative Spirit: he is at the same time the

86. Ibid., 255.
87. Ibid., 257.
88. Ibid., 259.

cosmic Spirit: for body, soul and their Gestalt can only exist in exchange with other living beings in nature and in human society."[89]

This holistic perspective means, in turn, that "human life is dependent on natural and social communication and only exists in such communication . . . Human life is necessarily life in community. It is communication in communion."[90] Presently, the living Gestalt is a fragmentary unity in which bodily and verbal languages experience centrations (a consentual equilibrium) and decentrations (dissonance from disequilibrium). Centrations reflect shared concerns that concretely merge and form a healthy human community.[91] These can even be experienced as "ecstatic moments in doxology," intense awarenesses of rest that interrupt the transience of time and remind us of the sabbatical rest to come.[92] The Spirit is the directional character of human beings, so healthy communication is the alignment of existence and the harmonization of who we are into what we will become. Human communication centers in promises, like the divine analogue, which promotes social dependability and trust. Through a continuity of promise-keeping, a person acquires a trustworthy name: "This identity of the person in his life-history is denoted through *his name*. Living together socially consists of a dense web of promises and fulfillments, compacts and dependabilities, and cannot exist without these structures of trust . . . The process whereby a person becomes a configuration or Gestalt is both inwardly and outwardly to be seen as a process of dependability and faithfulness."[93] In other words, in the process of building healthy communities, people construct complex forms of organization which allows them freedom and opportunity to shape their entitled lives. He concludes, "So every 'spirited' and 'inspirited' human society will develop

---

89. Ibid., 263.

90. Ibid., 266. In his *Man*, 81–86, Moltmann embraces Martin Buber's I-Thou relationship as necessary for "life in dialogue."

91. Moltmann defines healthy human living as the shared acceptance and love of mortal life; because death is merely a transition into a different Gestalt in view of the resurrection of the body and life everlasting, *God in Creation*, 275.

92. Moltmann, *Spirit of Life*, 302–3.

93. Ibid., 262. By "structures of trust" Moltmann again has a larger perspective in view, in which societies are free to live in a "broad place" without cultural, social, and religious coercion.

into a democracy that is both anticipatory and participatory. The future literally belongs to social forms of this kind."[94]

Central to the evolving process is an inalienable human dignity, which is God's creational claim on humanity as his image and is expressed in human rights: "Human dignity requires human rights for its embodiment, protection, and full flowering. Human rights are the concrete, indefeasible claim of human dignity."[95] This is the foundation of his political theology, which "does not want to 'politicize' the churches, but to make the churches aware of their political ties and 'Christianize' their political existence."[96] His emphasis on human rights added specificity to his call for ecclesial activism but also connected his political theology with non-Christian activities and goals to facilitate a common struggle for human liberation. Theologically, human beings were given responsibility to maintain creational life by promoting four dimensions of human rights: individual, social, rights to self-determination, and the rights of future generations.[97] In a word, humanity has a right to God's future: "The specific task of Christian theology in these matters is grounding fundamental human rights in God's right to—that is, his claim upon—human beings, their human dignity, their fellowship, their

94. Ibid., 268.

95. Douglas Meeks, "Introduction," in Moltmann, *On Human Dignity*, xi. Human rights emerged in the mid-twentieth century as the "concrete" focus of ecumenical dialogue, in which Moltmann was deeply involved. It corresponded to the collaborative dialogue surrounding the "Universal Declaration of Human Rights" (1948). Liberal ideology had asserted the rights of individuals over the state; Marxists emphasized the rights of society; and Third-World liberationists advanced the rights of oppressed peoples to self-determination. The deadly struggle among power elites threatened the rights of humanity in general.

96. Moltmann, *Creating a Just Future*, 27. On page 29 he notes, "Since the middle of the 1970s, the political theology which we began in the 1960s in the awareness of the Jewish holocaust in Auschwitz has increasingly become a theology of peace in the face of the nuclear holocaust which threatens all mankind." European theologians are more concerned with social performance than the confessional polemics of their American counterparts. His eschatological emphasis seeks to mediate Lutheranism's apocalyptic two-kingdoms doctrine and the Barmen Confession's call for the lordship of Christ (1934). Moltmann's messianism has sought to avoid utopian alternatives by placing hope in the suffering of God at the cross.

97. Moltmann's arguments can be found in two position papers, "Theological Basis of Human Rights and the Liberation of Man" and "A Christian Declaration on Human Rights."

rule over the earth, and their future."[98] Negatively, he advocated "the *right to resistance* and the *duty to resistance* against illegal, illegitimate, and inhuman regimes in favor of the right of the neighbor."[99] These rights free humanity from religious and political domination that keeps them from giving their lives to others as God has done through Christ. They are the duties of daily labor, for the human being has the right and duty to participate in reconciling communities that point to the approach of God's kingdom.

In summary, we have seen how Moltmann has confronted crises with hope by developing a christological center and an eschatological orientation in his theology. The center is the cross of God's solidarity with his godless world, and the resurrection is his promise of eschatological presence with his creation. The indwelling Spirit has been resolving the dialectic by transforming present darkness toward a radically new face-to-face presence in God's kingdom. In his development of this thesis he advanced three themes as corrections to traditional Christianity; *zimsum*, panentheism, and communitarian equality. Through his kenotic self-limitations God liberates, exalts, and redeems creation into a single fellowship of hope. The process is feminine in which God births creation by letting it become eternal in his omnipresence. Consequently, eschatology is redefined as faith in the Creator as we serve his future in the intricate web of interrelationships of his cosmic community. The s(S)pirit is the panentheistic presence who energizes the universe and symbiotically directs humanity's ecosystem toward its transformation.

The fundamental basis for Moltmann's theological anthropology is the *imago Dei*, which is human community in creation; namely, perichoretic relationships that are accepted kenotically by the crucified God (*imago Christi*) for his eschatological glory (*gloria Dei est homo*). Christ is the perfect reflection of the image, making anthropology the preparation for Christology. But how do we view humanity as image and sinner at the same time? His answer is that the image is God's original resolve to be inescapably present in humanity. Thus, sin is human beings' "usurped divinity" in the accumulation of power to oppress people and to destroy nature. It has separated a dominant soul and its enslaved body, which has corrupted Western anthropological ideology. The s(S)pirit will

---

98. Moltmann, *On Human Dignity*, 20. In eschatological terms, he refers to this as "*life in anticipation* of the Coming One," *The Way of Jesus Christ*, 340.

99. Ibid., 24.

form people into a living Gestalt as embodied in God's kingdom. In the meantime, reconciling communities in a anticipatory and participatory democracies should be formed by a "communication in communion" that builds "structures of trust," which promote human rights and resist inhuman regimes.

CRITIQUE OF MOLTMANN'S ANTHROPOLOGY

Moltmann has been recognized as one of the most prolific, seminal theologians of the last century, one of its outstanding scholars according to some of his peers. In support of the assessment, his work is a veritable encyclopedia of modern European scholarship, educating his readers in behalf of his "new thinking." His eclectic approach tangents several theological movements, which provides insightful glimpses into the fault lines of the theologians as they have sought to address compounding crises. His background gave him "a vivid awareness of the significance for Christian faith of the cries from the depth of human misery and of Jesus' abandonment on the cross."[100] Almost all of his critics have been impressed by his profound understanding of the problems of the century and his passion about their urgency. Among other examples are his analysis of power structures and rampant injustices. Biblically, he correctly formed a nexus of covenant, promise, messianic kingdom, the presence of the Spirit, and eschatological hope.

While scholars have appreciated his contributions, they have criticized his lack of conceptual rigor, his spotty engagement with traditions, and his uneven treatment of sources according to their usefulness for his agenda. He clearly rejected traditional, analytical thinking, but his imaginative, post-critical ways of thinking have been problematic: "For me theology is not church dogmatics, and not a doctrine of faith. It is *imagination for the kingdom of God* in the world."[101] His reaction to Christian traditions is undercut by his selection of classical biblical themes to express his new theology, which is a testimony to their enduring power rather than his creativity.

In this section we will apply the general criticisms to several biblical and theological issues that have an anthropological bearing. First, his

---

100. Charles and Marjorie McCoy, "Foreward," in *Humanity in God*, xi.
101. Moltmann, *The Coming of God*, xiv.

anthropology will be examined methodologically in terms of his uneven use of the Scriptures. Second, his use of the *imago Dei* summarily dismisses the distinctiveness of humanity as presented in biblical aspects that set human beings apart from other living things. Third, the impact of his panentheism on his anthropology will be criticized. Did he cross the line to pantheism in spite of his disclaimers? Fourth, is his view of sin consistent with his presentations of contemporary depravity? Finally, does Moltmann offer hope to the modern world?

First, how should we respond to Moltmann's methodological emphases? He pictured a world in apocalyptic crisis and a human threat. On occasion he described the crisis as comprehensive and irreversible, yet he proposed the radical reform and renewal of an indistinct church to herald the coming kingdom. He has confronted the crisis with a christological hope, whose "impossible possibility" will reconcile God's messianic solidarity with the godforsaken world and his creational promise to fully indwell all of reality through resurrection. Accordingly, he began with an evolving present, projected to an open future, and found support in an eclectic use of the past to buttress his thesis. In a word, he worked backward from his contemporary starting point. For him, the *kairos* required a fresh start with new concepts and language. Through his post-critical, non-analytical, symbolic way of thinking, he has sought to dismantle theological monotheism, creational causality, and anthropological dominance that underlie the ecological crisis. He reconfigured space and time in terms of his conception of God's future world presence. So, the Trinity, anthropology, and creation converge in a trinitarian archetype with anthropology reduced to a subordinate, relational subtheme in his trinitarian history of nature. In the process he subsumed salvation history and special revelation into universal history and general revelation: "The distinction between 'natural' theology and 'revealed theology' is misleading. There are not two different theologies. There is only one, because God is one."[102]

His theological revisions were directed against traditional Christian methods, which analyze the present and anticipate the future only after a careful consideration of biblical authority and ecclesial traditions. That is, the methods have analyzed the possibility of hope based on time-tested systems of belief in spite of the perennial violence through world history. In this perspective, He is cavalier to jettison a one-sided,

102. *God in Creation*, 59.

anthropocentric monotheism with a transcendent Creator, who distinguished himself from nature. Is monotheism to blame for stripping nature of her divinity, profaning politics, and divesting history of its fate? Perhaps its perversion in monarchical and colonial situations was a contributing factor, but that does not warrant a generalized condemnation of the doctrine. Ton van Prooijen is correct:

> Although Moltmann would probably deny that he claims that he as a theologian can grasp the totality of our society and even the whole world intellectually, his approach suggests that he understands modernity better than it does itself and that it needs Christian theology to move in the right direction again . . . However, we must go beyond a simplistic distinction between (anthropocentric) modernity and the ("theocentric" and nature friendly) Christian faith and view both as multilayered, complex and open traditions which, moreover, have influenced each other.[103]

Moltmann decries the European anthropocentrism of his modern peers, but, in the end, he embraces them in seeking a rapprochement between theology and the sciences in behalf of survival on earth. As a consequence, his panentheism is expressed in equivocal language that is neither distinctively Christian nor biblically precise.

In view of the worldwide crisis, Moltmann's eclectic sources embrace every discipline, because science, technology, and economics determine human relationships. Through his theological sources he sought to build a broad constituency to match his participation in international dialogues. Perhaps his most interesting anthropological selection was the kabbalists' *zimsum* as a Jewish alternative to Western Christianity's view of creation. The concept of divine self-limitation and mutability was suitable not only for his ecumenical method but also for his need for a theological basis for panentheism and God's kenotic interrelationship with creation. In the end, through *zimsum* God becomes omnipresent through the cross and negates all godlessness, wrath, judgment, hell, and death in his all-consuming love. Naturally, his desire to expunge causality and pervasive domination from creation made the switch inevitable.

His use of the Bible is uneven. At times, he used "biblical testimonies" to support his views.[104] However, he opposed the biased narrow-

---

103. Ton van Prooijen, *Limping but Blessed*, 333–34.

104. For example, Moltmann, *Human Dignity*, 16; *Man*, 13–14; and his lengthy

ness of biblical authority. On other occasions, he equivocated as follows: "For a *biblical* doctrine of creation we have to draw on the whole testimony of Scripture, not merely Genesis 1 and 2. By 'biblical', we mean here Jewish and Christian, not fundamentalist. The starting point for a *Christian* doctrine of creation can only be an interpretation of the biblical creation narratives in the light of the gospel of Christ. This means that a Christian doctrine of creation cannot be biblicist."[105]

Certainly we can agree that the whole testimony of Scripture and the bearing of Christ are necessary. Then we must deal with Christ as causative Creator (Col 1:16–20, John 1:1–2), the preaching of Paul (Acts 14:15–18; 17:24–28), and the heavenly anthem (Rev 4:11). In fact, biblical causation in Acts 17:24–27 is the basis for one of Moltmann's oft-cited verses, "For in him we live and move and have our being" (17:28). One can only conclude that labels like "biblicist" represented some kind of threat to dialogical openness and eschatological synthesis.

The Bible portrays humanity as "fearfully and wonderfully made" for worship and fellowship in covenant and promise.[106] Theologians in general would affirm that its foundational concept is the *imago Dei*, even with a holistic focus on the person rather than a particular aspect of personhood. But the richness of biblical anthropology in general and the image concept in particular should not be dismissed with "some characteristic or other which sets human beings apart from other living beings." In fact, people have distinctive qualities among living creatures, including the image as Moltmann recognizes. Why, then, does he bother with "biblical testimonies," when he rejects their mythologies except for his favored themes and passages? Is he not speaking to himself, when he argues, "It always causes misunderstanding when biblical texts are torn out of their proper context in the biblical tradition, and are used to legitimate other concerns."[107] The answer lies in his own background and Christianity's indispensable contribution to his theological agenda; its suffering Savior who attacked the oppressions of sin, its ethic of love, and its "pregnant ideas for revolution in our attitude to nature which is

---

discussion in *God in Creation*, chap. 9.

105. Moltmann, *God in Creation*, 52–54.

106. For example, Hans Walter Wolff, *Anthropology of the Old Testament*.

107. *God in Creation*, 30.

so vitally necessary today."[108] In other words, biblical Christianity is still applicable to the global challenges that humanity faces today.

Second, how should we assess Moltmann's view of the *imago Dei* and its role in the destiny of humanity? We recall that he bypasses traditional discussions of the nature of a human person in his definition of the image as God's relationship with humanity. The image is "social likeness." [109] The imaged relationship involved in human community with nature. His governing assumption is that faith in modernity requires experiential self-consciousness: "What it does mean is that experience of the self has to be integrated into the experience of God, and that experience of God has to be integrated into the trinitarian history of God with the world. God is no longer related to the narrow limits of a fore-given, individual self. On the contrary, the individual self will be discovered in the over-riding history of God, and only finds its meaning in that context."[110]

Through the *imago Christi* we find our meaning in trinitarian history, and Christianity becomes universal, because "the 'crucified God' accepts men in their shared lack of full humanness."[111] In other words, the human "condition" rather than the human "being" defines image, which is an extraordinary shift in the history of biblical interpretation.

Third, Moltmann's panentheism significantly affected his anthropology. In *Man* he strongly opposed divinization, anthropotheism, or excessive claims for *theosis*.[112] Later in *God in Creation* he panentheistically introduced humanity into the "mutual interpenetrations" of the Trinity. The result of the development is a "new thinking" toward pantheism that he consistently resisted. He expressed an aspect of this change in messianic terms with panentheistic implications:

108. Ibid., xv. Moltmann stated in *Man*, 20, "The cross is therefore the point of difference between Christianity and world religions."

109. The phrase is found in Moltmann, *God in Creation*, 234–43. The phrase seems to bypass his distinction between the "concreteness" of image and the reflexivity of *similitude*.

110. Moltmann, *Trinity and Kingdom*, 5.

111. Moltmann, *Man*, 20.

112. The customary boundary between acceptable and excessive *theosis* has been conformity to the character of God, while preserving the distinction between personal identity and the divine being. Cf. Stephen Finlan and Vladimir Kharlamov, eds., *Theosis; Deification in Christian Theology*. His view can be found in *Man* is found on pages 108–11.

Whereas in the ancient church the dispute about the relationship of the two natures in the person of Christ was always a dispute about physical redemption as well, and the idea of the real incarnation of God was always associated with the deification of man (*theosis*) which it made possible, the dispute at the present time about the true humanity of Jesus, his awareness of God, his "inner life" and his freedom finds its basis in the demand for true humanity, authentic life, inner identity, and liberation. The point of reference and the purpose of the questions have changed, and Jesus is accordingly manifested in a different way and must supply a different answer.[113]

Moltmann expressed "true humanity" in terms of panentheistic spirit, and he developed his view of panentheistic spirit from his assumption of bipolarity in God, whereby the Spirit became totally present in creation on the basis of Messiah's resurrection.[114] "Everything," we have noted, "exists, lives, and moves *in others . . .* in the cosmic interrelations of the divine Spirit." The Spirit is "the total cohesion, structure, information, and energy" of the universe "to the extent that its movements and experiences" are his as well."[115] Spirit is the "quintessence of the human being's self-organization, and his self-transcendence, his inner and his outward symbioses." God is in the world, and the world is in God."[116] The imperative, therefore, is to expand our personal consciousness to embrace integration and self-transcendence to cosmic and divine realms. Has human finitude seems to have disappeared into the infinity of spirit? Interestingly, Moltmann explicitly denies pantheism whenever he seems to blend man into God or vice versa.[117] We noted his claim that "without the difference between Creator and creature, creation cannot be conceived at all." However, his difference is "comprehended by the greater truth which is what the

---

113. Moltmann, *Crucified God*, 93.

114. Moltmann, *Trinity in Kingdom*, 27.

115. Moltmann, *God in Creation*, 16. Also, *Spirit of Life*, 274–78, on the "formative metaphors."

116. Ibid., 17; *Spirit of Life*, 211–12, 285.

117. For examples, *God in Creation*, 64; *Man*, 35; *Trinity and Kingdom*, 110; and *Spirit of Life*, 35. Elsewhere, he criticizes pantheism as a hindrance to scientific work, *God in Creation*, 194.

creation narrative really comes down to, because it is the truth from which it springs: the truth that God is all in all."[118]

He feared pantheism for at least three crucial reasons. First, it would affirm the *status quo* by equating a godless world with a "godless god." It would void his trinitarian history and human hope in its purpose and goal, "all possible experiences would have to be turned into the same thing and pantheistically made a matter of indifference."[119] Second, it would dissolve theological hope in the "internal ambivalence" of an enclosed world without transcendence: "Everything is dependent on everything else, and all men are dependent on other men."[120] That is, the openness of hope in God's trinitarian future would be lost. Third, humanity would be divine, and dialectics would be resolved only in God. There would be no anthropology.

He attempted to meliorate the dilemma by affirming "the personhood of the Holy Spirit," "The nature of the Holy Spirit is perceived only in his relationships to the other persons of the Trinity, who are 'of like nature.'"[121] We have noted his categorical rejection of the monarchical Trinity. It its place he substituted the eucharistic relationships of the "triunity" in which doxology proceeds from the Spirit to the Son and Father in reverse of the traditional order. In other words, the Godhead is to be understood as persons only in their perichoretic relationships with each other. However, his disclaimers tend to irritate his readers. We wonder with the irony of *Hamlet's* Queen Gertrude, "Methinks he doth protest too much."

Fourth, the juxtaposition of worldly godlessness and panentheistic presence necessitates a brief discussion of Moltmann's view of the human condition, an apocalyptic abyss that threatened human existence. Few contemporary scholars described the evils of the twentieth century more vividly. The dissonance is critical for his "impossible possibility" of hope out of despair. How does he understand sin and what is its source? The origin of evil, for him, is shrouded in the mystery of humanity's self-isolating response to *zimsum*, when the Creator partially withdrew his presence to form Nothingness, so that he could "outwardly" form his eschatological Sabbath for his creation.

---

118. Moltmann, *God in Creation*, 89.
119. Moltmann, *Spirit of Life*, 35.
120. Moltmann, *Man*, 35.
121. Ibid., 289.

The agents of evil are created beings, who have self-isolated themselves in sin and godlessness (*die Sünde und Gottlosigkeit*), creating an annihilating Nothingness that threatens both creation and God. Since God's resolve is to accomplish creation, he will absorb this outward alienation in himself. He does this through the God-forsakenness (*Gottverlassenheit*) of intertrinitarian relationships on the cross.[122] He defines sin as living in the annihilating Nothingness of the dominating powers of death, a wretched existence that is haunted by a symbolic, primordial knowledge of paradise.[123] In social terms, evil relates to "the practical and specific personal and social conflicts of people who have never received justice, and people who are themselves unjust."[124]

In his scattered descriptions of the "fallen" human condition, Moltmann clearly exhibits his selective use of Scripture. The "real history of human sin begins with Cain's fratricide (Gen 4) and with the spread of wickedness on earth through violence (Gen 6)." [125] Genesis 3 belongs to myth, "which offers a mythological interpretation of the physical history of the world."[126] But had he not already argued extensively for image as relationships based on Gen 1:26–28? Did he not use Old Testament narratives as a prelude to "the mystery of man"?[127] In his view, the weakness of "universal sin" as the basis of the Pauline and Protestant doctrine of justification is "that collective guilt of this kind makes people blind to specific, practical guilt. Indeed it can actually be used as an excuse for specific, practical guilt. The universality of sin leads to a universal night in which everything is equally black, and even to use weapons of mass extermination is no longer special."[128] This type of accusation may apply to instances of perversion and abuse of the doctrine, but Moltmann is wrong to dismiss it in principal. Can we connect the war crimes of the twentieth century with the fallenness of the world in any sense other

---

122. Moltmann, *God in Creation*, 87–88; Moltmann, *The Crucified God*, 145–53.

123. Moltmann, *Man*, 94; *God in Creation*, 57–59. Elsewhere, he similarly defines evil as "the perversion of good, the annihilation of what exists, the negation of the affirmation of life," *God in Creation*, 168–69. In the same context "demons" and the "rule of Satan" refer to non-human potencies which hinder or destroy living processes.

124. Moltmann, *Spirit of Life*, 128.

125. Ibid., 125–26.

126. Ibid.

127. Moltmann, *Man*, 13–14.

128. Moltmann, *Spirit of Life*, 126.

than explanation? "Collective guilt" does not excuse any "specific sin," regardless of how horrible it may be, not does it trivialize or obscure the degrees of evil in the world. Instead, the world wars and unspeakable horrors of the century should remind us of our need for divine grace and faith in God's promises for salvation. Why should Moltmann emphasize his interpretation of Romans 8 and 1 Corinthians 15 and fail to consider the life-and-death, righteousness-and-sin, and justification-and-condemnation through Christ and Adam respectively in the same contexts? The answer is that he reduces Scripture to his thesis, using modern criteria to dismiss or misinterpret objectionable texts. In place of biblical atonement, he substituted God's solidarity with his inhumane humanity and enslaved creation.

Finally, in view of our criticisms, does Moltmann offer the modern world hope? Biblical hope resonates with confident expectation, "being sure of what we hope for . . . a city whose architect and builder is God" (Heb 11:1, 10). By faith believers through millennia have lived in light of God's promises without receiving them (v. 39). Hebrews 11 is about believers' faith in trials and challenges rather than their universal calling to "real humanity." It is about faith in God's revelatory word as well as truths that are exposed through human dialogues. With him we can grieve about the world's injustices and catastrophes, and we can dialogue with a variety of people as opportunities present themselves. But we search Moltmann's writings in vain for the divine providence that brings comfort in contemporary struggles and provides substance for thought and practice. Are we supposed to hope that people who have created the problems are going to correct their addictions to power and exploitation? Are we to hope that the agents of mass destruction are going to change their elemental fears and violent behavior in behalf of "an intricate web of interrelationships," as desirable as that might be? Hebrews 12 points to "the author and perfecter of our faith, who is the same yesterday, and today and forever" as the object of our hope (vv. 2, 13:8). Instead, Moltmann offers us hope in a God, who "because of the restriction of his omniscience cannot foresee how those he has created will decide, and how they will develop. He leaves them time, and opens for them an unforeseeable future . . . He is curious about the path they will take, for they are his future. He learns from them."[129] He has traded the parousia of the biblical Messiah for

129. Moltmann, *Science and Wisdom*, 120.

an anthropological process that has been mired in sin for millennia under creation's struggling god. Has he given us hope or exposed an embedded hopelessness?

5

Moltmann on Jesus Christ

Stephen N. Williams

THERE IS NOTHING DISTINCTIVE about evangelical Christology. Its norms are those of Scripture in principle and Chalcedon in practice. Any evangelicalism credibly rooted in the Reformation will accord a measure of theological weight to the authority of tradition, for *sola Scriptura* relativized but did not obliterate the guiding role of creedal or confessional tradition in Luther and Calvin. Yet it remains the case that Chalcedon only retains a normative authority in evangelical theology so long as it is not demonstrably at odds with Scripture.

These truisms provide a logical point of entry into an evangelical evaluation of Moltmann's Christology. Moltmann's most sustained christological exploration, *The Way of Jesus Christ*, was published as the third in a series of systematic theological contributions that began with *The Trinity and the Kingdom of God*.[1] The very first page of its preface makes clear that its ambition is not to expound the great ecumenical creeds. "I am trying to think of Christ no longer statically, as one person in two natures or as a historical personality. . . In a liturgical doxology of Christ we contemplate in wonder the God who has become human, and the human Christ who is deified, and we formulate the christological dogma as they did in Nicaea and Chalcedon. But men and women who

---

1. *The Way of Jesus Christ: Christology in Messianic Dimensions*. From now on, titles of Moltmann's volumes will usually be abbreviated in the text of the essay once the full reference to the English translation has been given.

are living in the exile of history, and who are searching for life, need a Christology for pilgrims (*christologia viatorum*)."

Evangelical thought should have no difficulty in principle with a pilgrim Christology and an ethical orientation of the kind to which Moltmann aspires. In fact, it should welcome the approach as a counter-balance to the consuming interest in doctrinal standards that has frequently marked evangelicalism at the expense of theological engagement with the nature of Christian discipleship. In *WJC*, there is much that is commendable in the detail of Moltmann's discussion. His orientation to the poor, the suffering, the outcast, and needy—familiar to those acquainted with the main lines of his authorship all the way from *Theology of Hope* to *Experiences in Theology*—is edifying in this as in other volumes, as long as we try to practice what he preaches. *WJC* does not purchase praxis at the price of theological reductionism in that it does not sacrifice theology on the altar of practice. While it gears theology to practice, it consistently expends energy on the former in order to secure the right theological framework for the latter. This is what Moltmann is always about—a bland reminder worth uttering lest those who worry that "Chalcedon" and "praxis" signal contrasting worlds in modern theology and fear that the specter of theological displacement hovers over Moltmann's christological essay.

By not attending, in what follows, to the ethical and practical dimensions of discipleship which Moltmann explores, I risk confirming the suspicion that evangelicals want to worry mainly about doctrine or, if about ethics, only within limited parameters, circumscribed by the concerns of personal morality or national and political self-interest. My inattention to issues of discipleship should not fuel that suspicion. What my studied neglect signifies is respect for the substantive remit in this particular volume, which is designed to present a specifically evangelical response to Moltmann. The lack of a distinctively evangelical Christology in relation to the Chalcedonian inheritance has already been confessed; examining the particulars of ethical, pilgrim discipleship will not advance the cause of picking out evangelical distinctives. So we loop back to Moltmann's prefatory remarks in relation to Chalcedon in *WJC*. To start our discussion by attending to Moltmann's attitude to Chalcedon may appear to augur a mundane and predictable investigation, but it seems logical to do so. After all, Moltmann himself purposefully draws

our attention to Chalcedon (and to Nicea) at the beginning of his christological exploration.

The reader familiar with Moltmann's works from *Theology of Hope*
onwards will recognize the accent and interests that mark the launch
of *WJC*. The christological eschatology of *Theology of Hope* is more
fundamentally characterized by reversing the terms and describing the
theological centre of the work as an eschatological Christology.[2] To Jesus
Christ we should ascribe an eschatological identity[3] and the account of
this, later on in the volume, takes us to its heart. In criticizing theological
eschatologies that bear no relation to the cross and resurrection of Jesus
Christ, Moltmann indicated that the cross and resurrection were the
pivot of theology, which is to say that Christology is the pivot of theology. "Christianity is eschatology . . . Christian faith lives from the raising
of the crucified Christ, and strains after the promises of the universal
future of Christ. Eschatology is the passionate suffering and passionate
longing kindled by the Messiah."[4] A sound theological method for the
elaboration of eschatology will turn out to be christologically founded:
"Statements about the future are grounded in the person and history of
Jesus Christ."[5] The dominating chapter in this volume is the chapter on
"The Resurrection and the Future of Jesus Christ," in which Moltmann
argues that the future of Christ is a constitutive element in Christology.[6]
And what is Christian eschatology but "the study of this tendency of the
resurrection and future of Christ" which, he adds, "leads immediately to
the practical knowledge of mission?"[7] Statements about Jesus' identity
are embedded in a scheme of eschatological description and this scheme
is rooted in the supposition that cross and resurrection disclose the fact
that Jesus possesses his identity in infinite contradiction.[8] It is an "enig-
matic, dialectical identity."[9]

2. Moltmann, *Theology of Hope: On the Ground and the Implications of a Christian
Eschatology*.

3. Ibid., 40.

4. Ibid., 16.

5. Ibid., 16.

6. Ibid., 140.

7. Ibid., 195. "This tendency" refers to a form of historical process which is quite
technically understood by Moltmann against a specific intellectual background.
Hudson, *The Marxist Philosophy of Ernst Bloch* is helpful here.

8. Ibid., 85, 200.

9. Ibid., 220.

We encounter here a christological claim that merits examination in its own theological right.[10] However, *TH* is not altogether representative of the main drift of Moltmann's subsequent thought in terms of what we might describe as its metaphysical structure. Twice near the beginning of the book, we encounter under favorable conditions the claim that God has "future as his essential nature," but it is a claim later disowned.[11] Whatever relation this idea bears to his subsequent thought, it is the trinitarian framework elaborated in the next work, *The Crucified God*, which turns out to find an abiding place in Moltmann's thought and this is a work where Christology is tackled in specific relation to the Chalcedonian tradition.[12] Accordingly it is here that we begin a proper enquiry into Moltmann's christological thought.[13]

A CRUCIFIED GOD

"All Christian theology and all Christian life is basically an answer to the question which Jesus asked as he died: 'My God, why hast thou forsaken me?'"[14] It is a question that we shall never answer aright so long as we entertain a mistaken notion of God. And, according to Moltmann, Christian theology has blundered at this point. Its God has been a Greek immutable and impassible presence. But a trinitarian account, which is to say, an authentically Christian account, provides the desiderated alternative: God is dynamic and not static, capable of suffering and not impassible, containing within his life and being the godforsaken, aban-

---

10. Moltmann connects the notions of identity and identification, a connection which survives the modification, in subsequent works, of some of the conceptuality which informed *TH*. See, e.g., *The Church in the Power of the Spirit*, 125 on identity and identification.

11. These words, found on pages 16 and 30, were taken from the work of Ernst Bloch. A reader of *WJC* who was unfamiliar with *TH* would scarcely guess that Moltmann's later dismissal of this notion stood in contrast to his espousal of it in the earlier work: see *Way of Jesus Christ*, 321 and 380 n.13. But see what, in the light of all this, looks like a non-committal reference in Moltmann, *The Coming God: Christian Eschatology*, 23.

12. Moltmann, *The Crucified God: The Cross of Christ as the Foundation and Criticism of Christian Theology*.

13. Like *WJC*, *CG* has a practical-ethical orientation rooted in attention to the identity and relevance of its subject-matter. "The model of identity and relevance" persists: see Moltmann, *God in Creation*, 22.

14. Moltmann, *The Crucified God*, 4.

doned pain, misery and suffering of the world. The doctrine of God must be reconceived so that our relation to God may be reconceived. If that requires radical theological surgery, so be it. Having talked of history in God, Moltmann follows Braun in calling God himself an "event".[15] More specifically, "I think that the unity of the dialectical history of Father and Son and Spirit in the cross on Golgotha, full of tension as it is, can be described so to speak retrospectively as 'God'".[16] The whole of creation is in God. Prayer is in God; prayer viewed as being merely *to* God posits God as an almighty other. And it is this concept of God as personalized, transcendent, and discrete power against which Moltmann battles with particular determination and ferocity in this, as in later, work. This battle is a major phase in the campaign to rescue Christianity from atheistic disavowal. If we speak of divine power, we must speak of the cross and, so speaking, we describe a God who is no alien other. He is truly God with us.

Moltmann's Christology is not an *implication* of his doctrine of God; it is its *ground*. How does his Christology stand in relation to the Chalcedonian tradition? If, to all appearances, evangelical theology has tended in the past to exhibit a particular interest in the deity of Jesus Christ, it is not on account of a lack of interest or belief in the humanity (at least, not in principle) but because it is the deity rather than the humanity of Christ that has typically been the object of disbelief in recent Western centuries, whether within or outside the churches. Moltmann's avowed intention to revise the doctrine of God immediately invites the question of what fate befalls the Chalcedonian conception of deity in his proposals. The longest chapter in *The Crucified God*, the chapter that bears the title of the book, includes a discussion of the relationship between the author's christological outlook and that of the classical tradition. To speak of God being crucified unto death is a paradoxical impossibility on traditional premises, which ascribe to God (and hence to the divine nature of Jesus Christ) immutable immortality and to humanity (and hence the human nature of Jesus Christ) passible mortality. Methodologically, this impossibility is the function of a failure to construct a doctrine of God from a biblical and staurocentric point of view. Speaking biblically, the cross *is* God in action; it is not the external

15. Ibid., 247.
16. Ibid., 247.

manifestation of the action of an immanently immutable and untouchable being. So Moltmann maintains.

In the context of the traditional terms of the debate, what Moltmann wished to do was to take up the element of truth in kenotic Christology.[17] Kenotic Christology sought to affirm a mutable historical self-humbling on the part of God. In its principle, it led in the direction of predicating suffering and death to the *person* of Christ and not to one out of two natures (i.e., the human) anhypostatically assumed into unity with the person of the Son and his divine nature.[18] In that respect, as far as it went, Moltmann believed that kenoticism was travelling in the right theological direction. The Chalcedonian separation of natures leads to a Christology that is in its own way functional but not convincingly ontological. Luther was significantly closer to the truth of the matter here than was either Zwingli or Calvin.[19]

For myself, I believe that it behooves evangelicalism not to dismiss—indeed, to respond favorably to—the kenotic Christology to whose instincts Moltmann appeals on the point of personhood and nature. Kenoticism takes a wide variety of forms and it is unfortunate that the one word "kenotic" has been applied to all the christologies that have gone under that name, for it may tar a worthy theology with unworthy associations. The following argument seems to me to be in perfectly evangelical order. Our belief that God is Trinity derives from the New Testament witness to Jesus Christ. This witness should play a pivotal, if not determinative, role in the formulation of our beliefs about God's mutability or immutability, passibility or impassibility. It most naturally

17. Ibid., 201–7.

18. Ibid., 231.

19. These discussions are all found in the chapter on "The Crucified God," but Luther is more generally an inspiration for Moltmann in this volume. See too the positive remarks made in *CG* about Zinzendorf, starting with the prefatory "In Explanation of the Theme." Zinzendorf, who features quite prominently in Moltmann's *The Spirit of Life*, 167–71 (but see too, e.g., ibid., 159) is a figure who certainly deserves theological attention in "systematic," "ecclesial" or "missiological" contexts. Barth remarked of Zinzendorf that "in his preaching and poetry and dogmatics (so far as he had any)" he "was perhaps the only genuine Christocentric of the modern age" and "perhaps. . .the first genuine ecumenicist, i.e., the first really to speak and think wholly in terms of the matter itself," particularly in relation to Christ and community: *Church Dogmatics* IV/1, 683. In connection with Moltmann's *CG*, note Barth's remark, in the same volume, that he "has not really been trying to avoid" Zinzendorf's "theology of blood." Barth, *Church Dogmatics* IV/1, 275.

suggests that the Son who became incarnate is subject to a specific kind of mutability in his *person*. The New Testament altogether impresses on us the unity of the person of Jesus Christ as much as it does the unity of any other person who appears in its pages.[20] What it ascribes to Jesus Christ—including eating, sleeping, nescience, and death—it ascribes to his person in its incarnate state; that seems to be the most natural reading of the data. If, for formal theological purposes, we exchange the biblical *modus loquendi* for an account that strictly favors a division of predications between the two natures, we must have compelling reasons for doing so. Of course, such are alleged, but they rely on the supposition that it is metaphysically absurd to ascribe essential mutability to one of the persons of the Trinity. This supposition trumps the confession of Jesus, for example, that he was ignorant of the detail of the Father's eschatological timetable (Matt 24:36; Mark 13:32). In turn, kenotic theorists do not necessarily find the metaphysical difficulties in their account greater than those in the classical account.

A kenotic interpretation of the incarnation need not imply any denial of the deity of Christ, unless deity is defined as including the essential immutability of the second person of the Trinity, which is precisely what the kenotic view challenges on biblical and christological grounds. But do kenotic views obviously deny Chalcedon? It depends on what we regard as constitutive of Chalcedon. They deny the metaphysical framework and, to the extent that the framework is inevitably reflected in the Chalcedonian definition, they must be at odds with Chalcedon. However, if the significance of Chalcedon for the christological confession of the church is viewed principally in terms of the fact that it affirms

---

20. I have shifted here from the classical sense of the word "person" to what might be called an "ordinary language" sense. In any extended account, it would be important to distinguish here between ordinary-language, classically theological, and philosophical notions of "person." In ordinary language, I think that we should be inclined to say that the NT witness, taken as a whole, depicts Jesus Christ as a divine-human person, although I think that a conceptual distinction between "person" and "nature" can be mapped onto this in principle. However this may be, classical christological thought deriving from Chalcedon has applied the person/nature distinction to the Jesus Christ who appears in the Gospels in such a way that we are supposed to predicate of one of his two natures that which is ascribed to the person (in the ordinary-language sense) who meets us in the Gospels. This appears to me both artificial and implausible along lines which the best defences of kenoticism have spotted. These defences include Forsyth, *The Person and Place of Jesus Christ*; Mackintosh, *The Doctrine of the Person of Jesus Christ* and Evans, ed., *Exploring Kenotic Christology: The Self-Emptying of God*.

unequivocally that the one and the same Word, who is the second person of the Trinity, became incarnate and assumed to himself our humanity without divesting himself of anything essential to his deity, then there are kenotic views which can be regarded rather as modifications of than contrary to Chalcedon. Certainly, a kenotic move along these lines should be open to any tradition that affirms *sola Scriptura*, as does the evangelical tradition. Obviously, I cannot properly expound, let alone defend, a kenotic position in this essay; nor, in fact, am I unreservedly convinced of it. I only register the impression that, in one of its appropriate forms, it need cause no evangelical consternation. So, as far as that goes, we can have sympathy for Moltmann.

However, Moltmann's Christology goes considerably further than the polemical preference for a version of kenosis over classical Chalcedonianism. His references to "event" and "dialectical history" in connection with God in *CG* have obviously invited the question of the relation of his thought to that of Hegel. It is a question which we leave aside here to focus rather more specifically and simply on his christological position.[21] Moltmann's bugbear in this work, as in *TH*, was the notion of divine presence, the theological deposit of a static deity and an order of reality of Greek inspiration, standing in dismal contrast with the dynamic biblical view of God, history and the world, a view which, of course, embraces an eschatological Christology. But not everything in the Bible conforms to the biblical view that Moltmann wants to promote. Colossians falls under his axe here, along with post-biblical tradition: "'He is the image of the invisible God' (Col 1:15). 'In him all the fullness of God was pleased to dwell' (Col 1:19). He is of one substance with God . . . as the Nicene Creed says . . . The mystery of Jesus here is the incarnation of God, the incarnation of eternal, original, unchangeable being in the sphere of temporal, decaying, transitory existence, in

---

21. It may be argued that the decisive thing to be said here is precisely that Moltmann's Christology is Hegelian or altogether too close to it. What are we to make of the statement that "the incarnate God is present, and can be experienced, in the humanity of every man, and in full human corporeality" (Moltmann, *Crucified God*, 276)? Well, this is surely patient of more than one interpretation in relation to Hegel. But it may be said that, however it is related to Hegel, it is an eloquent statement of a cardinal feature of Moltmann's Christology which ought to attract critical evangelical attention and clear reproval. I do not really wish to dispute this, but neither do I want to get caught up in what might amount to a controversial exegesis of Moltmann's earlier Christology.

which men live and die."[22] This is lamentable, according to Moltmann.[23] However, this cryptic association with Nicene Christology, of particular interest to evangelicals in light of their positive view of the place of all the New Testament writings in the construction of doctrine, is not warranted. And it displays a characteristic feature of Moltmann's authorship: the persistent failure to make, and the habit of glossing over, distinctions.[24] It is possible to challenge the notion of God as eternal and as immutable in the classical sense and yet retain the christological teaching of Colossians as something integral to a healthy and well-orbed Christian theology. Colossians simply does not require the raft of metaphysical commitments that Moltmann apparently implies that it does and which he substantively rejects. To pursue this further in terms of an evangelical critique would take us into the domain of differences in the way Moltmann and evangelicals regard Scripture and this would lead us into an area too christologically non-specific in our present context.[25] But his remarks on and in association with Colossians open a window onto a steady tendency in Moltmann's literature to proceed theologically in terms of antitheses exclusive of a third (or fourth, etc.) way. It takes its toll on his Christology. It is true that Moltmann frequently positions his own thought as a third way. We frequently encounter in his literature a form of argument along the lines of: "Neither A nor B" (standard theological alternatives) "but C" (which either negates both or incorporates

22. Moltmann, *The Crucified God*, 88.

23. Colossians fares a little better in *WJC*, chapter 6 although (being regarded as non-Pauline) it still runs into conflict with Paul (Moltmann, *Way of Jesus Christ*, 285–86).

24. For documentation of this general claim, I take the liberty of referring to my essays: Williams, "Jürgen Moltmann: a critical introduction" in P. Duce and D. Strange, eds., *Getting Your Bearings: Engaging with Contemporary Theologians,* and Williams, "The Problem with Moltmann." I apologize for the appearance of self-advertisement in making reference here and later to various contributions; it is done simply in order to indicate a documentary basis for claims made in this essay which, as they stand, might seem too general and impressionistic.

25. Moltmann alludes to the fact that some "have ironically criticized my use of the Bible as a 'use *à la carte,*'" *Experiences in Theology: Ways and Forms of Christian Theology,* xxi. In response, Moltmann avers that he takes "Scripture as a stimulus to my own theological thinking, not as an authoritative blueprint and confining boundary" and he explains what this involves (Moltmann, *Experiences in Theology,* xxii). For a sharp criticism which, I believe, holds good despite Moltmann's response to it, see Bauckham, "Time and Eternity," 174–83 and Moltmann's response, "The Bible, the Exegete and the Theologian."

elements of truth in them into a higher synthesis). But sometimes he produces false antitheses, subsequently plumping for one rather than the other position that he is describing. And the worry about traditional notions of divine presence and power leads him to deploy Christology in the service of this move.

Thus, in *The Trinity and the Kingdom of God*, when he is dwelling on Jesus' proclamation, Moltmann insists that "God is not the Lord; he is the merciful Father" and we are not servants, only children; we love in freedom; we do not submit to rule.[26] This is highly irresponsible talk for anyone who aspires to integrate Christology into the fullness of the biblical witness, even when we look charitably beyond the words to judge fairly according to meaning. Lordship, almightiness, love, fatherhood, servanthood, friendship, freedom, and obedience must be integrated in a christologically-grounded theology and not pressed into antithetical combat.

It is not denied that questions surrounding the power and weakness of God, or his sovereignty and friendship, are demanding from a christological point of view and in the midst of a suffering world. We do not have to read the incomparable Dostoevsky to appreciate the force of Moltmann's comment: "It is in suffering that the whole human question about God arises; for incomprehensible suffering calls the God of men and women in question. The suffering of a single innocent child is an irrefutable rebuttal of the notion of the almighty and kindly God in heaven."[27] But, alongside the bewildering and agonizing scene of human suffering, there is another datum, as far as faith is concerned: the resurrection of Jesus from the dead. And the form of power there displayed warns us against the temptation to evict from the scheme of dogmatic theology an aspect of the biblical presentation, namely, the portrayal of transcendent divine power.[28] Moltmann justly admires Dietrich Bonhoeffer, whose celebrated dictum that "only the suffering God can help" was preceded by the claim that God "is weak and powerless in the world, and that is precisely the way, the only way, in which he is with us and helps us. Matthew 8.17 makes it quite clear that Christ helps

26. Moltmann, *The Trinity and the Kingdom of God*, 70–71.

27. Ibid., 47.

28. For the record, I have also criticised, alongside Moltmann, the representative of a standpoint more or less diametrically to his on this point: see my comments on John Frame in Williams, "The Sovereignty of God," 175–78.

us, not by virtue of his omnipotence, but by virtue of his weakness and suffering."[29] But is this quite right? Matthew 8:17 is a comment about the fulfillment of prophecy in Jesus' ministry of exorcism and healing. It is by no means only the weakness and suffering of Jesus Christ that we are led to see at this point of the Gospel; we are also in the presence of those signs and wonders that persist into the account of the early church in the book of Acts. There is Pentecostal power as well as the power of the cross and the resurrection displays a power akin to that of Pentecost while undoubtedly leading the church of Jesus Christ to suffer under the cross.

And so we are conducted to the question of the resurrection. At the heart of Moltmann's theology, and at the heart of any theology worthy of the name "Christian," is an affirmation of the resurrection of Jesus Christ from the dead. If we revert to Colossians for a moment, we find that the epistle integrates talk of the presence of God in Jesus Christ across the phases of Christ's "career," from pre-existence or co-existence with God to the risen Christ who is lord of the Church in his present and ours. Moltmann's remarks on Colossians in particular and presence and power in general lead us to enquire how resurrection fares in his theology in light of what he is resisting. The exaltation of Jesus Christ is something of which Moltmann is wary, to put it mildly (e.g., TH 158; CG 179). But at this point, we are well advised to rejoin The Way of Jesus Christ.[30]

29. Bonhoeffer, Letters and Papers from Prison, 360–61. Moltmann offers good brief discussions of and allusions to Bonhoeffer in more places than one (e.g., Moltmann, Church in the Power of the Spirit, 282–84) but he also published an early essay on Bonhoeffer in Moltmann and Weissbach, Two Studies in the Theology of Bonhoeffer, 1967.

30. Arguably, I should have included in discussion of CG what we should expect to be of unsurpassed evangelical interest, namely, the question of Moltmann's attitude towards the atonement. For some remarks, see S. Williams, "On Giving Hope in a Suffering World: Response to Moltmann," 13–14. A claim such as "[t]he real history of human sin begins with Cain's fratricide" (Moltmann, Spirit of Life, 125) is perilously close to denial of the theological significance of "the fall" and so of the atonement. For Moltmann's remark is surely less evidence that he does not wish to regard the fall as "history" as indicative of the fact that he wishes to avoid a portrayal of God as an "other" against whom one can meaningfully sin outside the context of regular inter-human social relationships. As far as Christology is concerned, the person and work of Jesus Christ are thought through together in Moltmann's theology and this is welcome. However, within the confines of an essay, I have sought to take Chalcedon as a point of departure and proceed to resurrection when turning now to WJC. Rightly or wrongly, christological issues arising in Moltmann's work have seemed to me more tractable by adopting the policy that I have in this present context.

A QUESTION OF RESURRECTION

Evangelical theology has always insisted on the need to affirm unequivocally the orthodox position of the church on the resurrection of Jesus Christ, embracing belief in an empty tomb and the bodily continuity between the crucified Jesus and the subject of the resurrection appearances. One of the gravest dangers to which theology is exposed, one of the deepest pitfalls into which is has stumbled, one of the most consistent features of its practice, is treatment of its subject matter as an idea or a set of ideas. This is true *par excellence* in relation to God, to all appearances discussed and written upon, with all the combination of mental curiosity but existential dispassion that we experience towards Jupiter (whether god or planet). At least, we male Westerners are guilty here. Christology enjoys no immunity in this respect. Argument in favor of the historicity of the bodily resurrection of Jesus is prey to at least two hazards. Firstly, its process and outcome invite an accusation of more or less pre-critical naïveté. Secondly, and more dismaying, is an engulfing sense of weariness. Are there not more exciting things in theology and life to think about than whether or not the tomb was empty and whether or not Jesus appeared bodily to assorted disciples in living objectivity?

The latter problematic is well illustrated by remarks in the brief essay "Coleridge's Dream" by that marvelous writer, Jorge Luis Borges.[31] Borges recalls that Coleridge's "Kubla Khan" was reputedly the result of a dream (interrupted and banished, we may add, to the consternation of all true lovers of literature) in the course of which he dreamed a poem about a palace. What Coleridge could not possibly have known was that the palace that figured in the dream was itself only built because the emperor (Kublai Khan) himself, in the thirteenth century, dreamed a palace whose construction he subsequently transferred from the land of dream onto hard empirical soil, building it in precise accordance with the architecture displayed in the dream. This fascinated Borges: "Compared with this symmetry of souls of sleeping men who span continents and centuries, the levitations, resurrections, and apparitions in the sacred books seem to me quite little, or nothing at all." "Resurrections in sacred books": this includes the resurrection of Jesus. Coleridge's dream world fascinates, intrigues, and absorbs; the waking world of the company

---

31. See Borges, *The Total Library: Non-Fiction 1922–1986*, 369–72.

allegedly at the tomb is relatively dull and boring.[32] As an *intellectual* fact, it should be said that there is nothing naïve about an affirmation of the historicity of the resurrection.[33] Weariness, however, is a *spiritual* condition. Anyone who takes seriously for a moment the possibility that Jesus rose from the dead is existentially affected to the core of his or her being; anyone who believes it seriously is transformed in one and the same being. Neither the fear of naïveté nor the prospect of weariness should stymie evangelical persistence in pursuing the question of what exactly is maintained and what denied in an affirmation of the resurrection of Jesus Christ.

It has been rightly said that Moltmann's *TH* could, with equal propriety, have been called a "theology of the resurrection."[34] We noted earlier that its central third chapter dealt with the resurrection (and future) of Jesus Christ. In this work, Moltmann, raising the question of how we approach the purportedly historical nature of the resurrection, quite rightly warned us against using *a priori* concepts of history and historicity and attempting to fit the biblical material into this preconceived framework rather than allowing biblical testimony to provide the appropriate framework. Whatever we make of the resultant treatment in *TH*, Moltmann returned to the question of resurrection in *WJC*. And a superficial survey of the material brings to light a problem which deeper digging does not seem to eliminate. Moltmann's language leaves the reader unclear about what he is trying to say.

From early in his theological career, Moltmann was subject to conflicting interpretations of his thought on account of the fact that he neither explained in principle nor clearly indicated in practice how he was using theological language.[35] The fact that he deliberately postponed discussion of theological method until the end of his series in dogmatics

32. I cannot resist apostrophising that what was interesting and what mattered must have looked quite different to Borges at the very end of his life: see Edwin Williamson, *Borges: A Life*.

33. For an extremely thorough and impressive study, see Wright, *The Resurrection of the Son of God*. As this essay goes to press, Licona's detailed *The Resurrection of Jesus: A New Historiographical Approach* has appeared.

34. So Bauckham, for example, right at the beginning of his introduction to *Moltmann: Messianic Theology in the Making: An Appreciation*, 3.

35. The interpretive hesitations and uncertainties encountered in what we might gnomically describe as an impartial representative reader of Moltmann like Stephen Travis, e.g., in *Christian Hope and the Future of Man*, 59 and 94, appear to me to be justified.

does not actually warrant this, for clarity and intelligibility are requirements that do not await the full explication of methodological or epistemological tenets.[36] To many of us who have read his work over the years,
it is frequently not clear (and not just because undeclared by Moltmann)
whether language is being used literally, univocally, symbolically, ana-
logically, metaphorically, not quite any of the above, or some of the
above in some combination. The difficulty plagues *WJC*.

The exact impact of this on Christology is doubtless moot, but the
fact that it is moot is of itself a cause for concern. Moltmann devoted
a chapter to "The Eschatological Resurrection of Christ" but, before
getting there, he offered a brief discussion of "The Community of the
Living and the Dead."[37] "In the community of Christ the dead are not
forgotten; they are present." "Like the living, they can draw hope from
the gospel." These sound like clear enough statements that, as far as we
are concerned here, draw in their train that which is their theological
presupposition, namely, the status of the risen Christ. In that same discussion, "the resurrection of the dead," like "the judgment of God" is
said to describe a "symbol," but "symbol" here apparently does not mean
"mere symbol" in a way that excludes ontologically realistic language in
respect of the dead.[38] The later reiteration of the remark that the "raising
of the dead" is a symbol and, moreover, one which "excludes ideas about
a "life after death," may cause an immediate and momentary twinge of
consternation. However, it should probably be no more than a twinge,
for it seems clear from what follows that Moltmann is thinking here of
characteristically Greek (or other non-Hebraic) forms of belief in such
phenomena as the immortality of the soul.[39] "Christ's resurrection is
bodily"[40] would seem to banish all conservative worries on the matter.

But a nonplussed perplexity nevertheless sets in, fomenting rather significant confusion. "All life . . . endures death with pain,"[41] says
Moltmann. This sentiment is applied to the whole of nature, something
that only makes good sense if we abandon the attempt to interpret it
literally, short of unadulterated panpassibilist panpsychism. The resur-

36. The final work in the series was *Experiences in Theology*.

37. Moltmann, *The Way of Jesus Christ*, 189–92.

38. For further reference to symbols, see Moltmann, *The Coming of God*, 131f.

39. Moltmann, *The Way of Jesus Christ*, 222.

40. Ibid., 256.

41. Ibid., 253.

rection of Christ may appear to be immediately untouched at this point. However, we proceed to read that "[t]he transition of Christ has more than merely historical significance. It has cosmic meaning too. Through this transition resurrection has become the universal 'law' of creation, not merely for human beings, but for animals, plants, stones and all cosmic life systems as well."[42]

Difficulties with this statement are not obviated by the fact that "law" appears to bear a rigorously contextual sense. It looks as though the tombstone whose removal disclosed the resurrection of Christ is itself destined for resurrection. Everything seems to be. Now the line of questioning or of potential objection to Moltmann which I am introducing here may appear plain silly, easily met by referring to the poetic status of his language with impeccable antecedents in Scripture.[43] So be it. But then, in light of the fact that the resurrection of Christ and the history of the cosmos are bound together, how are we to guard against a loosening of the literal reference for the resurrection of Christ? Is Moltmann's language used in an analogical fashion or were we wrong ever to take Moltmann "literally" on the resurrection of Jesus Christ? If Christology is set "in the framework of nature" and not just of history, what is the effect on our reading of Moltmann's view of the resurrection of our forced demythologizing of his description of the future of nature?[44] The notion of resurrection is attached to both the resurrection of Christ and the resurrection of non-human nature. What are we to make of the assertion that "what is eschatological is the raising of the body *and the whole of nature*?[45] Difficulty in understanding what Moltmann means in relation to nature entails that our question cannot easily be prevented from shading into some uncertainty about what he means by "the raising of the body" and, thus, the raising of Christ.[46]

---

42. Ibid., 258.

43. Self-accusation of silliness is, in fact, unduly self-deprecating; see the discussion of a sympathetic commentator on Moltmann, Bauckham, in *The Theology of Jürgen Moltmann*, 210. However, I confess that I find his attempt to alleviate the problem no less obscure than anything that Moltmann himself says on the matter.

44. Moltmann, *The Way of Jesus Christ*, 247.

45. Ibid., 303. My Italics.

46. See too the discussion in Moltmann, *Crucified God*, 166–77. Actually, I do not myself believe that the biblical or conceptual connection between the risen body of Christ and our risen bodies is as close and tight as is often assumed. Our concern here is with the former; the latter is only touched on inasmuch as it introduces questions about

Evangelical theology is doubtless often trite and wooden. But it must risk and bear the charge of wooden weariness as it ploddingly asks for some clarification of what Moltmann means by "resurrection." Evangelical theology is doubtless often unimaginative and lacking in subtlety. But it must risk and bear the charge of drab uni-dimensionality in pressing for clarity, for justification, for conceptual cleanness. It is in this area, in my view, that Moltmann's christological thinking is so unsatisfactory. The substance of what he wants to contend for christologically is obscured by modes of assertion and of argumentation that are general features of his writing taken as a whole and without necessary reference to Christology. That being the case, it can be hard to know what to make of the christological substance of his thought.

This is further illustrated by the opening discussions in *WJC*, which are geared to showing why some theological themes deserve a high profile in connection with Christology. *WJC* contends for the importance of grounding christological discussion in the context of Christian-Jewish dialogue and so fuses the needs of the present with the summons intrinsic to biblical thought, which is to think in Jewish terms about Jesus Christ. Let us grant that this particular contextualization is permissible and the principled recapturing of the Jewish roots of Christology mandatory. But, early on, Moltmann's failure to make distinctions or offer justifications is very discouraging for readers eager to appreciate the theological force and gain of a christological treatment which keeps the question of Israel in mind. I quote a passage at length because it illustrates how, in this volume, the kind of problems we encounter in other volumes are illustrated and compounded, here impinging damagingly on the contextual christological inquiry that Moltmann undertakes.

> If the Jewish "no" to Jesus' messiahship is due to inability, as Buber said, and not to unwillingness or ill-will, then there is no reason for Christians to deplore this "no" or to make it a reproach. Israel's "no" is not the same as the "no" of unbelievers, which is to be found everywhere. It is a special "no" and must be respected as such. In his Israel chapters, Romans 9 to 11, Paul saw God's will in Israel's "no." It is not because it says "no" that Israel's heart has been hardened. It is because God hardened its

---

the interpretation of Moltmann's Christology. It is important to add that, in the second part of his most recent book, *Sun of Righteousness, Arise! God's Future for Humanity and the Earth*, Moltmann does appear to take a very "conservative" position on the resurrection of Jesus—unequivocally so, if the book is considered independently.

heart that it cannot do anything but say "no." Hardness of heart
is not the same thing as rejection, and has nothing whatsoever to
do with a moral judgment . . .[47]

There is not a single sentence here that does not throw up serious
questions. Why should a Jewish "no" be treated as a single entity? Why
is it not accounted for in some cases by inability, in others by unwilling-
ness or ill-will? Christians may have no business reproaching and may
not deplore, but why can and should they not be dismayed? If Paul's
reasoning in Romans 9–11 is brought into play to support constructive
Christian theology in the present, what warrants our judging, on its peculiar basis, Israelite rejection in terms of tolerant respect? Paul may see
God's will in Israel's "no," but does it not break his heart? Does not the
entire Old Testament history testify to the fact that divine hardening is
the consequence of self-hardening? If Paul's account of the history of
Israel, grafted onto the Old Testament narrative, does not embrace elements of moral judgment, what on earth *does* constitute moral judgment
in Scripture?

Now, from all that Moltmann says in the pages preceding the words
which I have quoted, it would seem that questions such as I have put,
open or rhetorical as they may be, would be regarded as overt or covert
expressions of a disreputable point of view, one that is, indeed, laden
with anti-Semitism.[48] In fact, they are no such thing; but the prospect
of dialogue with him on the matter would portend a round of weary-
ing explanation in self-defense. No, it is neither said nor implied that
the churches are securely triumphant over unbelieving Israel: Paul specifically warns Gentile Christians, in the chapters Moltmann cites, to
beware of that presumption. No, it is neither said nor implied that God's
rejection of unbelieving Israel is eschatologically final. And so forth.
Moltmann sails assertorically past the obvious difficulties with his own
account. *Tertium datur* is one of the milder responses that must consistently cross the mind of conscientious readers faced with his explicit
or implicit alternatives. So I confess that I find that Moltmann all too

47. Moltmann, *The Way of Jesus Christ*, 34.

48. Moltmann can also rapidly describe as "anti-Jewish" (close enough to "anti-Se-
mitic" for my present purposes) biblical texts which deserve careful consideration, not
only in their own exegetical right, but against the background of prophetic declamation
in the Hebrew Scriptures which is capable of fiercely castigating the people of Israel.
See his remarks on assorted texts in the book of Revelation in Moltmann, *The Coming
God*, 198.

often frustrates. Some readers of this essay may enter a demurral to the effect that my objections constitute one evangelical's evaluation of selected features of Moltmann's Christology in the light of his theological style, rather than an evangelical evaluation of Moltmann's Christology. However, I can but hope that both the trail that I have followed and the reason that I have followed it are alike clear.[49]

AT THE END

"If I have a theological virtue at all, then it is one that has never hitherto been recognized as such: curiosity."[50] This statement is doubtless meant provocatively; announcing the discovery of a new theological virtue at the close of the second millennium is not something that we should expect to be done without a touch of self-parody. However, the force of the statement lies in the element of sober truth that it contains. So does its danger. We do not have to be awash with Schopenhauerean pessimism to recognize in the global phenomena of evil and suffering forces that arrest, search, and meticulously interrogate the guest "Curiosity" before he or she enters the gate marked "Theological Enquiry." And, of course, Moltmann's theology, influenced by his wartime and post-war experiences, testifies to the dark and dire background to theological exploration.

If that curiosity which Moltmann judges appropriate has an outlet in his theological enterprise, it is probably in the sphere of imagination. "Theology springs out of a passion for God's kingdom and its righteousness and justice, and this passion grows up in the community of Christ. In that passion, theology becomes imagination for the kingdom of God

---

49. At the end of the previous section, I noted the possibility that I had been culpable in omitting discussion of Moltmann on the atonement (n.17). So let a symmetrical consideration be flagged up here. Discussion of the question of justification has been neglected here in connection with Moltmann's theology of the resurrection of Christ. The significance of Moltmann's various treatments of justification throughout his corpus (including in volumes which do not belong to the formal series in dogmatics and which have been left aside in this essay, e.g., *The Future of Creation*, chapter 10) is highlighted in the comment in *ET*: "This event of justification, understood as new creation and new birth, is the actual hermeneutical category of Christ's resurrection" (Moltmann, *Experiences in Theology*, 108). So Moltmann's Christology could have been approached from the standpoint of its soteriological drive.

50. Moltmann, *The Coming of God*, xiv.

in the world, and for the world in God's kingdom."[51] "Imagination" is a word less provocative but no less plastic than "curiosity" and if, in turn, the imagination which Moltmann judges appropriate has a constantly prominent outlet in his theological enterprise, it is probably in his depiction of the drama of history. From *TH* onwards, Moltmann's theological orientation has been eschatological and christological; from *CG* onwards, it has been eschatological and trinitarian, the trinitarianism, of course, formally embracing and materially rooted in the Christology.

Moltmann's trinitarian, christological, and eschatological theological orientation seems to me admirable in principle. He trains our eyes in the direction in which the biblical witness trains our eyes and biblical and dogmatic theology are thus prepared for felicitous fusion. This is a strength in all his works, including the methodological path of christological exposition taken in *WJC*. What is disturbing and dismaying is the way in which theological conclusions are extrapolated from Christology. Moltmann confidently derives theological conclusions from a cross and resurrection-centered christological vantage-point, showing few qualms about brushing aside or riding roughshod over both biblical and theological considerations which challenge his construction. Having said something about cross and resurrection, I close with a note on the eschatology.

Moltmann concludes his Christology with an account of "the parousia of Christ." "It is only more recent, eschatologically orientated theology which has brought back the expectation of the parousia into Christology, historically and theologically . . . Because the eschatological 'person' of Christ is always defined in the light of the parousia, the parousia also belongs to the doctrine about Christ's person, not merely to the doctrine about his work."[52]

Of all the themes that cluster around parousia and eschatology, the most disputed of all, according to Moltmann, is universalism.[53] He sets himself to solve the problem unsolved since Origen and Augustine. But the exegesis and the reasoning fail him yet again. The conclusion that "universal salvation *and* a double outcome of judgment are *therefore* [my italics] both well attested biblically"[54] is actually wrapped up before

---

51. Moltmann, *Experiences in Theology*, xx.

52. Moltmann, *The Way of Jesus Christ*, 316.

53. Moltmann, *The Coming of God*, 237.

54. Ibid., 241.

any sustained reasoning gets under way. The reasoning that *is* offered is characteristically skewed. "If salvation or damnation depends on a person's faith and righteousness, is God then not making his Judgment dependent on the will of human beings, thus really making himself dispensible [sic.]?"[55] It is a rhetorical question expecting the answer "yes"; in fact, the answer is: "Not necessarily at all," but no space is allocated by Moltmann for reasoning this question out.

Methodologically, Moltmann wants, at this point as elsewhere, to derive his conclusions from the cross (and resurrection) of Jesus Christ, so that eschatological beliefs or hopes are co-coordinated theologically within the lines of a consistent eschatological Christology. That is a contribution that *WJC* makes. What happens there when Moltmann applies this method? "The crucified One will judge according to his gospel of the saving righteousness of God, and according to no other law. He will not judge in order to punish the wicked and reward the good, but so as to make the saving righteousness of God prevail among them all."[56] Isaiah makes the case in his exposition of righteousness in chapters 9–11: "It is quite clear that the divine righteousness which is under discussion here has nothing to do with rewards and punishments."[57] Now supposing that one brought forth a barrage of biblical texts in a protest that, at best, Moltmann is guilty of irresponsible one-sidedness. Moltmann is aware of the texts, of course. He acknowledges tension, divergence, and inconsistency in the biblical witness and, in this respect, mulls particularly over the question of apocalyptic. But a *theological* alternative to his position is apparently consigned to futility. What we must avoid, Moltmann tells us, is belief in the Last Judgment that is "the projection of suppressed guilty fears, as a way of satisfying a masochistic lust for self-punishment."[58] What we must remember is that Jesus will not "judge according to the penal law of retaliation."[59] What we must not imagine is that the "purpose of Jesus' judgment" is "retaliation in all directions."[60] "Indeed," we may assent to all these warnings; "but how does all this

55. Ibid., 239–40.
56. Moltmann, *The Way of Jesus Christ*, 315.
57. Ibid., 335.
58. Ibid., 315.
59. Ibid., 337.
60. Ibid., 338.

even tend to overthrow theological positions opposed to Moltmann's own or to establish his own position?"[61]

In conclusion, it may sound demeaning, but it is meant to do no more than accept and moderate the consequences of theological disagreement, when I say that it seems to me that the positive value of his Christology for evangelicals (and all others) lies in the signpost that Moltmann constructs. He indicates and sketches out for us the contours of a promising path. But we must surely walk it differently. An evangelical reading Moltmann may be conscious of reacting to him less from a specifically evangelical point of view than from the point of view of an *ex professo* theological neutral who wants clarity and fairness in exposition. There is a habit of conceptual analysis deep in the tradition of Anglo-American philosophy and theology that is logically sophisticated, but barren in its yield of religious insight. Yet, it is a tradition that does introduce a certain discipline into theology. To mention it might give the impression of succumbing to high provincial arrogance. I mention it only because "cultural" elements may appear to have impinged on my critique of Moltmann. If that is so, I confess that I do not see how these elements can be regarded as theologically optional or negotiable. The theological culture pleaded for here is not an evangelical theological culture in particular or, for that matter, an Anglo-Saxon one.[62] It is for one that is wary of sweeping judgments. I admit that I find these in Moltmann, including in his Christology.

Having said that, Moltmann in some ways does convict and does inspire. Everything in his theology is related to its centre and its centre is the centre of Christian witness itself, Jesus Christ. It is surely right that Christ, especially in his cross and resurrection, should be the hinge of Christian theology and surely right that our ears should be constantly attuned to the groans of a suffering world and our eyes constantly trained on the fullness of the kingdom which will banish it. Evangelicals will

---

61. Moltmann indulges in some even more culpably extreme and illogical remarks in *Sun of Righteousness, Arise!*, e.g., ibid., 144.

62. In this connection, let us give all praise to Gottfried Wilhelm Leibniz, who surely got it right, not in aspiring to a deductive system, but in advancing the cause of Platonic dialogue in the service of following up his realisation that there were habits of antithetical thought deeply ingrained in Western philosophy and needing to be uprooted. For the baldest of summaries, see Ross, *Leibniz*, 73–76. An excellent account of Leibniz' philosophy and philosophical style is that of Antognazza, *Leibniz: An Intellectual Biography*.

quarrel with Moltmann's execution of his theological program. But they will not come up with a much worthier one.[63]

---

63. One strong qualification, however, to this statement concerns the way in which evangelicals think of evangelism. This will make for significant differences between their and Moltmann's theological "programs."

6

The Spirit of Life

Moltmann's Pneumatology

Veli-Matti Kärkkäinen

INTRODUCTION

IN KEEPING WITH JÜRGEN Moltmann's stated theological approach which, rather than following any prescribed methodology, is elusive and open-ended,[1] I attempt to present an outline of his doctrine of the Holy Spirit in two movements. First, I will look at the ways this Tübingen systematician's pneumatology has emerged and taken shape during the three decades of constructive theological work, which culminated in his pneumatological magnum opus, *The Spirit of Life*.[2] It seems to me that

---

1. Moltmann describes the development of his evolving theological method particularly in prefaces or introductions to his several writings and in a more focused way in his book on theological method: "For me, theology was, and still is, an adventure of ideas. It is an open, inviting path . . . *The road emerged only as I walked it.*" Moltmann, *Experiences in Theology*, xv. In this respect, the difference of approach from, say, the methodologically rigorous Wolfhart Pannenberg, couldn't be more dramatic. Whereas Pannenberg devoted most of his theological prime time to honing the method, to the point that his *magnum opus*, the three-volume *Systematic Theology*, only appeared towards the end of his career, Moltmann set out to write constructive theology without any defined method and let the approach develop as he went along.

2. On the other hand, what makes the separate volume on pneumatology significant and somewhat unexpected in Moltmann's evolving theological path is that that volume

a number of significant themes are coming to the surface long before he presents them in a more focused form in that 1992 masterpiece. Furthermore, in light of the fact that Moltmann does not always repeat in later writings what he has developed earlier, it is necessary to walk the path that led to the formulation of his mature presentation of the doctrine of the Spirit.

In the second movement, again taking a clue from his own methodological comments—according to which in the context of any given topic, say the Trinity, Moltmann not only discusses that particular theme but also looks at the whole theological task from the perspective of that single locus[3]—I will seek to present his pneumatology against the context of his overall theological vision. In the final part of the essay, I will engage Moltmann from the perspective of evangelical theology by first looking at other evangelicals' assessments of *The Spirit of Life* and then offering my own reflections.

EVOLVING SPIRIT THEMES

Whereas *Theology of Hope* is built on christological (and *theo*-logical) foundations, *The Crucified God* for the first time opens up the pneumatological orientation in a fully trinitarian framework. The trinitarian grounding of theology becomes *the* defining framework for all of Moltmann's theology. It is highly significant that the place the Spirit is introduced in this trinitarian framework has to do with the cross. The Spirit emerges out of the dialectic of the cross and resurrection: "In the cross, Father and Son are most deeply separated in forsakenness and at the same time are most inwardly one in their surrender. What proceeds from this event between Father and Son is the Spirit which justified the

---

is not mentioned in the tentative plan of the six-volume "Contributions to Theology" beginning from his monograph on creation of 1985; Moltmann, *God in Creation: A New Theology of Creation and the Spirit of God*, xv.

3. This "method" emerges as early as in his first major work, originally published in 1964: *Theology of Hope: On the Ground and the Implications of a Christian Eschatology*, 11; in his "Preface to the New Paperback Edition [1990]," Moltmann reminiscences in hindsight: "With *Theology of Hope* I evolved a theological method, though more by chance than intention. I tried to see *the whole of theology in a single* focus. This was the method I used in writing the books that followed: *The Crucified* God in 1972 and *The Church in the Power of the Spirit* in 1975." See also *The Crucified God: The Cross of Christ as the Foundation and Criticism of Christian Theology*, x.

godless, fills the forsaken with love and even brings the dead alive, since even the fact that they are dead cannot exclude them from this event of the cross; the death in God also includes them." [4]

In his 1975 contribution to ecclesiology, the title of which has an explicit pneumatological orientation, *The Church in the Power of the Spirit*, Moltmann both continues the trinitarian shaping of his pneumatology and also makes a robust contribution to the doctrine of the Spirit. That "messianic ecclesiology" is structured around the trinitarian doctrine.[5] The author himself notes the close connection between this book and the two earlier ones: "having started from Easter and the foundation of the Christian hope and travelled by way of Good Friday and the exploration of God's suffering," he has now "arrived theologically at Pentecost and the sending of the Spirit." This, however, he hastens to remind his readers, does not mean in any sense leaving behind the suffering and hope, but rather means that the theological discussions of these movements in salvation history "dovetail into one another and their subject-matter overlaps."[6]

Indicative of a pneumatology much wider and more inclusive than a traditional church-based doctrine of the Spirit is the programmatic statement in the preface: "The Spirit fills the church with the power of the new creation, its liberty and its peace."[7] The eschatological and creation-oriented inclusive view of the Spirit is thus introduced as the backdrop of the discussion of a pneumatological ecclesiology. It is through the Spirit that the church of Jesus Christ becomes an eschatological community, an anticipation of the future of the kingdom. It is the work of the Holy Spirit to make possible the passing of history into eschatology and eschatology into history. This is because the "new life" experienced in the church is "life in the Spirit." "For through the Spirit the believer is determined by the divine future."[8] Not only that, but also the final

---

4. Moltmann, *The Crucified God*, 244. For Moltmann, "the cross of the Son stands from eternity in the centre of the Trinity." *The Trinity and the Kingdom: The Doctrine of God*, xvi.

5. "The Church of Jesus Christ, "The Church of the Kingdom of God," "The Church in the Presence of the Spirit," and "The Church in the Power of the Spirit," parts III, IV, V, and VI respectively in Moltmann, *The Church in the Power of the Spirit: A Contribution to Messianic Ecclesiology*.

6. Moltmann, *Church in the Power of the Spirit*, xvi.

7. Ibid., xiv.

8. Ibid., 33–34. Or to put it this way: "In the longer-range history of the Spirit the

eschatological glorification of the Father and the Son happens through the Spirit.[9]

When looking at the inner life of the church, Moltmann first develops the traditional ecclesiological topics such as proclamation, sacraments, and liturgy in a pneumatological context. Here is an example of his pneumatological sacramentology: "When it [the church] listens to the language of the messianic era and celebrates the signs of dawn and hope in baptism and the Lord's Supper, the church sees itself in the presence of the Holy Spirit as the messianic people destined for the coming kingdom. In the messianic feast it becomes conscious of its freedom and its charge. In the power of the Holy Spirit the church experiences itself as the messianic fellowship of service for the kingdom of God in the world."[10]

In addition to sacraments and proclamation, Moltmann also considers widely another aspect of church life, often either lacking or marginalized in Protestant theology, namely charismata, the energies of the Spirit. For Moltmann, the New Testament church, particularly the Pauline community, "is the place where the Spirit manifests itself (1 Cor 14) in an overflowing wealth of spiritual powers (charismata),"[11] and therefore, "[E]very member of the messianic community is a charismatic . . . "[12]

The trinitarian approach to the doctrine of the Spirit is further clarified and deepened in Moltmann's main work on the Trinity, *The Trinity and the Kingdom*. Crucial to a proper understanding of this trinitarian pneumatology is the continuing emphasis on "The Passion of God."[13] This is engaging, suffering, vulnerable love. This kind of God is relational. "The New Testament talks about God by proclaiming in narrative the relationships of the Father, the Son, and the Spirit, which are relationships of fellowship and are open to the world."[14] In keeping with current turn to relationality, Moltmann explains the meaning of "person[ality]"

---

church is a way and a transition to the kingdom of God. It lives in the experience and practice of the Spirit from the eschatological anticipation of the kingdom" (ibid., 35).

9. Ibid., 57–60.

10. Ibid., 289.

11. Ibid., 294.

12. Ibid., 296.

13. Title for chap. 2 in Moltmann, *The Trinity and the Kingdom*.

14. Moltmann, *The Trinity and the Kingdom*, 64.

in the context of relationships: "The three divine Persons exist in their particular, unique natures as Father, Son, and Spirit in their relationships to one another, and are determined through these relationships. It is in these relationships that they are persons. Being a person in this respect means existing-in-relationship." While the relation "constitutes the persons," it is also true that there is a genuine reciprocal relationship between "person" and "relation": there "are no persons without relations, but there are no relations without persons either."[15]

As explained already in the *Crucified God*, the Spirit emerges out of the "pain of God," from the mutually shared suffering of Father and Son. Further reflection on this mystery leads Moltmann to the development of a profound Spirit-Christology, which he takes up again in his work on Christology. In this context, he reflects on the mutual relationship between the Son and the Spirit through the lens of Christ's resurrection, taking his lead from the Pauline saying that the risen and ascended Christ is the "life-giving spirit" (1 Cor 15:45): "Whereas in the sending, in the surrender and in the resurrection, the Spirit acts on Christ, and Christ lives from the works of the creative Spirit, now the relationship is reversed: the risen Christ sends the Spirit; he is himself present in the life-giving Spirit; and through the Spirit's energies—charismata—he acts on men and women. The Spirit witnesses to Christ, and whoever confesses Christ as his Lord does so in the power of the Spirit who creates life from the dead."[16]

This "sent out Spirit" by Christ makes the Trinity "an open Trinity. Through the sending of the creative Spirit, the trinitarian history of God becomes a history that is open to the world, open to men and women, and open to the future." This means nothing less than that through faith and baptism, men and women "also become at the same time participants in the trinitarian history of God himself" through and in the agency of the Holy Spirit.[17] Part of this emerging emphasis on the mutually conditioning relationship between the Triune God and creation—which Moltmann names "Christian panentheism"[18]—is the role of the Spirit as the agent of creation,[19] an idea which will be fully developed in his work

15. Ibid., 172.
16. Ibid., 89.
17. Ibid., 90.
18. See, e.g., ibid., 106.
19. For first programmatic references, see Moltmann, *The Trinity and the Kingdom*,

on creation. In his main work on pneumatology he further clarifies that key idea. Similarly, in his eschatological work, Moltmann brings that train of thought to culmination by speaking of the final mutual indwelling of God and his people as well as the whole of creation.

Having spoken of the Spirit in terms of creative force, charismatic energy, and similar non-personal expressions,[20] Moltmann also wants to remind us that the Spirit is more than that: the Spirit "is a subject from whose activity the Son and the Father receive their glory and their union, as well as their glorification through the whole creation, and their world as their eternal home." In other words, not only the Father and Son, but also the Spirit is "person"[21] and "subject."[22] Moltmann will take up the challenge of defining more carefully the personhood of the Spirit in his main pneumatological work. Overall, his desire to affirm the personhood of each of the members of the Trinity is in keeping with Moltmann's basic orientation, which begins from the threeness and then works toward unity rather than the other way (the way of Christian tradition). Naming it a "Social Trinity," Moltmann resists all notions of subordinationism, even with regard to the Spirit.[23] The rejection of the *filioque* clause thus follows.[24]

Significantly enough, Moltmann's *God in Creation* is subtitled *A New Theology of Creation and the Spirit of God*. The intensifying of the panentheistic turn is heralded already in the preface, which states as the purpose of the theology of creation to "discover God *in* all the beings he has created and to find his life-giving Spirit *in* the community of creation that they share."[25] To accomplish this, the typical Protestant "christological concentration" has to be matched by "an extension of theology's horizon to cosmic breath" of the Spirit and the acknowledgment of the "indwelling divine Spirit of creation."[26] This is because in

---

113.

20. Moltmann (*The Trinity and the Kingdom*, 143) criticizes Karl Barth, among others, for failing to affirm the real personhood of the Spirit.

21. Ibid., 126; see also, e.g., Moltmann, *God in Creation*, 97.

22. Subtitle in Moltmann, *The Trinity and the Kingdom*, 125; see 125–26.

23. See, e.g., ibid., 174–75.

24. For details, see ibid., 178–87.

25. Moltmann, *God in Creation*, xi; for programmatic statement, see also pp. 13–17 under the subheadings "God's Immanence in the World" and "The Principle of Mutual Interpenetration."

26. Ibid., xiv; for the "Cosmic Spirit," see further 98–103.

biblical traditions, the German theologian notes, "all divine activity is pneumatic in its efficacy."[27] A trinitarian pneumatological "ecological doctrine of creation"[28] thus emerges.

While the Spirit of Yahweh is clearly presented as the agent of creation in the Old Testament, for a *Christian* theology of creation, Moltmann surmises, the christological "resurrection kerygma" and the "experience of the Holy Spirit" are necessary. A *Christian* theology of creation is less interested in the "protological creation" and much more focused on the "eschatological creation," which on the basis of Christ's resurrection looks forward to the final redemption of not only spiritual but also bodily life. In expositing this theme, Moltmann gives reference to key pneumatological texts in Rom 8:11, Joel 2:28, and Rom 8:19ff.[29] He summarizes the relation of original creation to the outpouring of the Spirit at Pentecost all the way to the eschatological consummation in this way:

> According to the New Testament testimonies, the outpouring of the Spirit and the experience of the energies of the Holy Spirit in the community of Christ belongs to the eschatological experience of salvation. The gift of the Spirit is the guarantee or "earnest"—the advance payment—of glory (2 Cor 1:22; 5:5; Eph 1:14). The powers of the Spirit are the powers of the new creation. They therefore possess men and women, soul and body, They are the powers of the resurrection of the dead which proceed from the risen Christ and are testified to the world through the church, which is charismatically wakened to external life . . . The power of the Spirit is the creative power of God, which justifies sinners and gives life to the dead. The gift of the Holy Spirit is therefore eternal life.[30]

The last major contribution to theology by Moltmann prior to the 1992 pneumatological work is on Christology, titled *The Way of Jesus Christ*—illustrating its dynamic and narrative nature in contrast to the traditional "static" two-nature approach;[31] it brings to fulfillment the

27. Ibid., 9; see further pp. 9–13 for an exposition of the role of the Spirit in creation, including the connection to the Nicene (Constantinopolitan) Creed's reference to the Holy Spirit as the Giver of Life, usually connected only with the "new life" in Christ.

28. Ibid., 1.

29. Ibid., 65–69.

30. Ibid., 95.

31. Moltmann, *The Way of Jesus Christ: Christology in Messianic Dimensions*, xiii;

previously announced Spirit-Christology or what he also calls a "pneumatological Christology":

> Jesus' history as the Christ does not begin with Jesus himself. It begins with the *ruach*/the Holy Spirit. It is the coming of the Spirit, the creative breath of God: in this Jesus comes forward as "the anointed one" *(masiah, christos)*, proclaims the gospel of the kingdom with power, and convinces many with the signs of the new creation. It is the power of the creative Spirit: through this he brings health and liberty for enslaved men and women into this sick world. It is in the presence of the Spirit that God reveals himself to him with the name "Abba," that Jesus discovers that he is the "Son" of this Father, and that he lives out this intimate relationship in his community of prayer with God. The Spirit "leads" him into the temptations in the desert. The Spirit thrusts him along the path from Galilee to Jerusalem. "Through the eternal Spirit" (Heb 9:14) he surrenders himself to death on the Roman cross. By the power of the Spirit, who gives new birth and new creation, God raises him from the dead . . . When we are considering the New Testament testimony about the theological history of Jesus, it is impossible to talk about Jesus without talking about the workings of the Spirit in him, and about his relationship to the God whom he called "Abba," my Father . . . [32]

After his earthly life and resurrection, Jesus is no longer with us—except for his presence through the Spirit: "If Christ is present now in the eternal Spirit of God, then his history must have been determined by this Spirit from the very beginning."[33] Consequently, following the "way" of the Messiah in the biblical record, Moltmann reflects on the implications of Christ's birth in the Spirit, his baptism with the Spirit, his proclamation of the Good News to the poor in the power of the Spirit, as well as healings and exorcisms.[34] An example of his pneumatological focus, Moltmann seeks to explain Christ's *kenosis* in terms of the Spirit's action. If Jesus' ministry was the function of the Holy Spirit, then it means that "Where the Spirit is not active, Jesus cannot do anything either."[35]

---

see also 52–53 for "impasses of two-nature Christology."

32. Moltmann, *Way of Jesus Christ*, 73.

33. Ibid., 77.

34. Chap. 3 in Moltmann, *Way of Jesus Christ*.

35. Moltmann, *Way of Jesus Christ*, 91. "[W]e have . . . to talk about a *kenosis of the Holy Spirit*, which emptied itself and descended from the eternity of God, taking up its dwelling in this vulnerable and moral human being Jesus" (93).

IN SEARCH OF A NEW PARADIGM IN PNEUMATOLOGY

The title for Moltmann's main pneumatological work, *The Spirit of Life*,[36] succinctly encapsulates its ultimate goal, which is to develop a doctrine of God in support of life, growth, and development. In other words, Moltmann sees the Spirit of God at work everywhere there is promotion of life, growth, inclusivity, and reaching for one's potential; conversely, whatever destroys, eliminates, frustrates, and violates life is not from the Spirit of God. The pneumatology which best facilitates such a life-affirming enterprise is, following the subtitle of the book, a "holistic pneumatology."[37] Moltmann acknowledges the fact that such a paradigm in pneumatology has not yet emerged.[38] What is clear is the inadequacy of traditional approaches to the Spirit. An indication of that mistaken approach of the past, surmises Moltmann, is:

> the established churches' . . . reserve in the doctrine of the Holy Spirit. In reaction against the spirit of the new liberty—freedom of belief, freedom of religion, freedom of conscience and free churches—the only Spirit that was declared holy was the Spirit that is bound to the ecclesiastical institution for mediating grace, and to the preaching of the official "spiritual pastors and teachers." The Spirit which people experience personally in their own decision of faith, in believers' baptism, in the inner experience of faith in which "they feel their hearts strangely warmed" (as John Wesley put it), and in their own charismatic endowment, was declared "unholy" and "enthusiastic." Even today, in ecclesiastical discussions about the Holy Spirit, people like to turn first and foremost to "the criterion for discerning the spirits"—even when there do not seem to be any spirits to hand.[39]

The corresponding reductionistic orientation has been visible in theology, both Protestant and Catholic, where there is "a tendency to view the Holy Spirit solely as *the Spirit of redemption*. Its place is the church, and it gives men and women the assurance of the eternal blessed-

---

36. Moltmann, *The Spirit of Life: A Universal Affirmation*.

37. The English translation of the subtitle *A Universal Affirmation* is not accurate nor very helpful. The German original *Eine ganzhetiliche Pneumatologie* means "holistic pneumatology," and that is the nomenclature also used in the preface (xiii); it could also be translated as "all-encompassing" or "comprehensive." Moltmann also labels his Pneumatology "holistic" elsewhere in the book, see xiii.

38. Moltmann, *The Spirit of Life: A Universal Affirmation*, 1.

39. Ibid., 2.

ness of their souls. This redemptive Spirit is cut off both from bodily life and from the life of nature. It makes people turn away from "this world" and hope for a better world beyond. They then seek and experience in the Spirit of Christ a power that is different from the divine energy of life, which according to the Old Testament ideas interpenetrates all the living." To remedy that "[s]ome theologians have discovered a new love for the charismatic movements; but this can also be an escape, a flight from the politics and ecology of the Spirit in the world of today."[40]

Behind this reductionistic pneumatology is, according to Moltmann, the continuing "Platonization of Christianity," which defines spirituality merely in terms of church life and individual piety. It resists anything bodily and feeds the attitude of distancing from the world. Moltmann finds in the *filioque* clause a reason for this lacuna: "This has meant that the Holy Spirit has come to be understood solely as "the Spirit of Christ," and not at the same time as "the Spirit of the Father." As *the Spirit of Christ* it is *the redemptive Spirit*. But the work of creation too is ascribed to the Father, so *the Spirit of the Father* is also *the Spirit of creation*. If redemption is placed in radical discontinuity to creation, then "the Spirit of Christ" has no longer anything to do with Yahweh's *ruach*."[41]

The net result of limiting the work of the Spirit to the church and its proclamation and sacraments (as is typical of Protestant traditions), was the emptying of the churches while at the same time "the Spirit emigrates to the spontaneous groups and personal experience." That is because "[m]en and women are not being taken seriously as independent people if they are only supposed to be "in the Spirit" when they are recipients of the church's ministerial acts and its proclamation."[42]

Unlike the reductionistic understanding of the term "spirit" in Western theology, the biblical understanding is inclusive and holistic. Moltmann reminds us that

> If we wish to understand the Old Testament word we must forget the word "spirit," which belongs to Western culture. The Greek word *pneuma*, the Latin *spiritus*, and the Germanic *Geist/ghost* were always conceived as antitheses to matter and body. They mean something immaterial. Whether we are talking Greek,

40. Ibid., 8–9.
41. Ibid.
42. Ibid., 9.

Latin, German, or English, by the Spirit of God we then mean something disembodied, supersensory and supernatural. But if we talk in Hebrew about Yahweh's *ruach*, we are saying: God is a tempest, a storm, a force in body and soul, humanity and nature. The Western cleavage between spirit and body, spirituality and sensuousness is so deeply rooted in our languages that we must have recourse to other translations if we want to arrive at a more or less adequate rendering of the word *ruach*.[43]

Above, Moltmann's opposition to the *filioque* clause was registered.[44] He claims that not only does *filioque* help subordinate the Spirit to the Son but it also limits the sphere of operation of the Spirit. Theology has spoken of the Spirit of Christ and of redemption rather than of the Spirit of the Father, the Creator. Consequently, Christ's Spirit and Yahweh's *ruach* have had nothing to do with each other. Thus, the continuity between the work of the Spirit in creation and in the new creation has been severed. In classical terminology, there has been discontinuity between the *Spiritus sanctificans* and the *Spiritus vivificans*, in other words, between the work of the Spirit in sanctifying and making alive.[45]

In his search for a new paradigm in pneumatology, in addition to a fresh look at the Bible and pneumatological tradition, Moltmann makes use of a number of resources from different Christian and ecclesiastical traditions, a hallmark of his theological approach in general, such as the patristic pneumatology of the Orthodox Church or the Pentecostal experience of the young churches or Feminist and other Liberationist theologies, as well as cosmic and "green" pneumatologies. He also takes note of the latest developments in the ecumenical movement, which has come up against questions of pneumatology in many ways, for example, in the encounter of churches with differing experiences and theologies of the Holy Spirit.[46]

43. Ibid., 40.

44. Moltmann also includes a short discussion of the *filioque* at the end of his pneumatology; see ibid., 306–9.

45. Ibid., 8–9.

46. Ibid., 3–5.

IMMANENT TRANSCENDENCE: GOD IN ALL THINGS

If "God's *ruach* is the life force immanent in all the living, in body, sexuality, ecology, and politics,"[47] then it means that the God-world relationship—the key question in current systematic theological reflection—should be reconceived in a new way. The expression that Moltmann uses to describe his panentheistic orientation to pneumatology is "immanent transcendence."

> The possibility of perceiving God in all things and all things in God, is grounded theologically on an understanding of the Spirit of God as the power of creation and the wellspring of life (Job 33:4, 13ff.; Ps 104:29ff.). Every experience of a creation of the Spirit is hence also an experience of the Spirit itself. And every true experience of the self becomes also an experience of the divine spirit of life in the human being. Every lived moment can be lived in the inconceivable closeness of God in the Spirit.[48]

This approach goes against classical theology's overall desire to distinguish transcendence (God) and immanence (creation) in a way Moltmann regards as too radical. Moltmann's harsh criticism of Barth's pneumatology well illustrates his approach. According to Barth, the divine and human spirit have to be kept separate because there is no continuity between the Creator and creation. Furthermore, this separation is accentuated by the fact that not only is the human "spirit" different from the Divine Spirit because of creatureliness but that it is also at variance with God. In other words, there is an antithesis between (divine) revelation and (human) experience. Against this opposition, Moltmann suggests his own alternative: "It is to be found in God's *immanence* in human experience, and in the *transcendence* of human beings in God. Because God's Spirit is present in human beings, the human spirit is self-transcendently aligned towards God. Anyone who stylizes revelation and experience into alternatives, ends up with revelations that cannot be experienced, and experiences without revelation."[49]

A panentheistic theology of the Spirit in the framework of "immanent transcendence" has nothing less than a truly "*holistic doctrine of the Holy Spirit*" as a goal: "It must be holistic in at least two ways. On

47. Ibid., 225–26.
48. Ibid., 35.
49. Ibid., 6–7.

the one hand, it must comprehend human beings in their total being, soul and body, consciousness and the unconscious, person and sociality, society and social institutions. On the other hand, it must also embrace the wholeness of the community of creation, which is shared by human beings, the earth, and all other created beings and things."[50]

Given his principle of immanent transcendence and panentheistic orientation, it comes as a no surprise that Moltmann sees a mutual relationship between the Spirit and the Word. Since "[t]here are no words of God without human experiences of God's Spirit . . . the words of proclamation spoken by the Bible and the church must also be related to the experiences of people today." According to Moltmann, "This is possible if Word and Spirit are seen as existing in a mutual relationship. On the one hand, the Spirit is the subject determining the Word, not just the operation of that Word. The efficacies of the Spirit reach beyond the Word. Nor do the experiences of the Spirit find expression in words alone . . . The Spirit has its non-verbal expressions too."[51] Differently from traditional theology, particularly post-Enlightenment European theology, which often looks at "experience" with suspicion, Moltmann is convinced that a truly holistic pneumatology must not eschew the experiences of men and women but rather incorporate them in its theological reflection. As in many of his monographs, Moltmann begins reflections on the doctrine of the Spirit with his own life experiences[52] and spiritual experiences. "The theology of revelation is church theology, a theology for pastors and priests. The theology of experience is preeminently lay theology. To begin with experience may sound subjective, arbitrary and fortuitous, but I hope to show that it is none of these things. By experience of the Spirit I mean an awareness of God in, with and beneath the experience of life, which gives us assurance of God's fellowship, friendship, and love."[53]

---

50. Ibid., 37.

51. Ibid., 3.

52. For the importance of biography to theology, see Jürgen Moltmann, *Experiences in Theology*, xviii–xix.

53. Moltmann, *The Spirit of Life*, 17.

THE SPIRIT OF LIFE AT WORK IN SALVATION AND THE WORLD

The monograph *Spirit of Life* consists of three parts. In the first part, Moltmann clarifies typical introductory matters of pneumatology such as the possibility of speaking of the Spirit, the Spirit's relation to human experience, the Spirit's role in the Trinity, and so forth. Above all, he lays out his vision for a holistic approach to the Spirit as discussed above. The second part, titled "Life in the Spirit," by far the largest section in the book, looks like a typical *ordo salutis*, an orderly discussion of steps of the reception of salvation by men and women. In fact, this middle part of the book is much more than a typical order of salvation. It is also an extended theological reflection on the implications of conceiving the work of the Spirit in his panentheistic, immanent-transcendence-driven holistic framework at personal, ecclesiastical, socio-political, and environmental levels of life. The discussion of soteriological themes such as justification and sanctification is framed in a way that expands the categories of traditional theology by including communal and creational perspectives. The third part of the book attempts a new way of conceiving the personhood of the Spirit.

Traditionally, the order of salvation has been understood as the "subjective" reception by men and women of the "objective" salvation wrought by Christ. Moltmann's thoroughgoing Spirit-Christology breaks this pattern and makes the work of Christ and the work of the Spirit complementary and mutually conditioning. Whereas in the context of Christology, he "defined the experiences of the Spirit christologically," in the volume on pneumatology, Moltmann seeks to "define the fellowship of Christ pneumatologically." Or to put it this way: "What the Christology presented as 'the discipleship of Jesus' must be seen in our present context as 'life in the Holy Spirit.'" [54] In other words, even in the context of soteriology, Moltmann seeks to overcome the subordination of the Holy Spirit. He is critical of traditional Reformation theology for not paying due attention to the role of the Spirit in salvation. Referring to passages like Titus 3:5–7, which speaks about the "washing of regeneration and renewal in the Holy Spirit, which he poured out upon us richly," Moltmann emphasizes that "'regeneration'" as "renewal" comes about through the Holy Spirit" when the "Spirit is 'poured out.'" Further, by making reference to John

---

54. Ibid., 82.

4:14, the metaphor of the divine "wellspring of life" which begins to flow in a human being, he contends that "through this experience of the Spirit, who comes upon us from the Father through the Son, we become 'justified through grace.'" [55] That said, Moltmann adds an all-important proviso, namely, that he is not going to restrict the experiences of the Spirit merely to experiences of "the Spirit of Christ" but also extending them to the "Spirit of the Father."[56] This is, of course, in keeping with a holistic vision of the work of the Spirit.

Emphasizing that different "stages" of the *ordo salutis* "are not stages in the experience of the Spirit . . . [but rather] . . . different aspects of the one single gift of the Holy Spirit,"[57] Moltmann begins with the conditions of the liberation of life by harshly critiquing the Gnostic juxtaposition of "spirit" to "body" so common in Christian theology. The biblical view of the Spirit as "the life-force of created beings and the living space in which they can grow and develop their potentialities" knows nothing of such dualism.[58] The biblical view points to the principle of "vitality as *love of life*": "This love of life links human beings with all other living things, which are not merely alive but want to live. And yet it challenges human beings in their strange liberty towards life; for life which can be deliberately denied, has to be affirmed before it can be lived. Love for life says 'yes' to life in spite of its sicknesses, handicaps and infirmities and opens the door to a 'life against death.'"[59] Such an inclusive vision of the work of the Spirit facilitates the Spirit's work of liberation, such as in "deliverances from sicknesses and demonic possession, deliverances from social humiliation and insults, deliverances from "godless powers of this world" and, as the Apostle Paul stresses, deliverances from the compulsions of sin and the power of death (Rom 7 and 8)."[60] Consequently, Christians everywhere are called to affirm life: "So the essential thing is to affirm life—the life of other creatures—the life of other people—our own lives. If we do not, there will be no rebirth and no restoration of the life that is threatened. But anyone who really says 'yes' to life says 'no' to war. Anyone who really loves life says 'no' to poverty. So the people

55. Ibid., 146.
56. Ibid., 82.
57. Ibid.
58. Ibid., 84.
59. Ibid., 86.
60. Ibid., 101.

who truly affirm and love life take up the struggle against violence and injustice. They refuse to get used to it."[61]

Liberation theologies in Latin America and elsewhere have captured this vision better than traditional theology.[62] This insight, however, was not totally unknown historically either. Moltmann reminds us of Luther's rediscovery of the "freedom of faith in the liberating gospel" when the Reformer in his treatise "On the Freedom of a Christian" determined that while faith makes people "free lords of all things, and subject to no one," love makes them at the same time "the ministering servants of all things and (freely) subject to everyone." The implication thus is profound: "For justifying faith liberates men and women from the compulsion of evil, from the law of works, and from the violence to death, setting them free for unhindered and unmediated eternal fellowship with God."[63]

If "[d]enied and rejected life is death" and "[a]ccepted and affirmed life is happiness,"[64] then it means that the work of the Spirit of God is not only the "justification of faith" but also the "justification of life," as the title of chapter 6 in *The Spirit of Life* puts it. Moltmann is amazed that Protestant theology has missed the analogy between "God's 'justifying' righteousness and his righteousness that 'creates justice,'"[65] in other words, the integral link between justice and justification. In order for this to happen, the Reformed theologian surmises, the typical Protestant bias of conceiving the universal concept of sin as that kind of collective guilt which makes people blind to "specific, practical guilt" should be corrected; in other words, it is "important for Christians not merely to look at the mythical story, but to see the real history of injustice and violence as sin too to find from God's Spirit the energy to act justly, and the strength for peace."[66] Moltmann firmly believes that "The Protestant doctrine about justification of sinners, and today's theology about the liberation of the oppressed, do not have to be antitheses. They can correct and enrich one another mutually."[67] This can also be seen from the

61. Ibid., xii.

62. Ibid., 109–14.

63. Ibid., 115–16.

64. Ibid., 123.

65. Ibid., 129; see also Moltmann, "Justice for Victims and Perpetrators."

66. Moltmann, *The Spirit of Life*, 126.

67. Ibid., 128.

point of view of Christology: the righteous and merciful God who is himself in Christ (2 Cor 5:19), in and through the passion of Christ "brings into the passion history of this world the eternal fellowship of God, and the divine justice and righteousness that creates life."[68] God's justice is not only for the reversing of injustice in the life of the individuals, it also relates to unjust and sinful structures.[69] One of the tasks of God's Spirit according to the biblical testimonies is to function as the *parakletos* and "judge."[70]

Similarly, sanctification as the work of the Spirit encompasses both "spiritual" and "earthly" life as well as personal and communal dimensions. Sanctification has been traditionally associated with the ministry of the Spirit, as is evident in the ancient creeds. Moltmann's point of departure is the observation that since all life is meant to continue, to grow, sanctification has to do with the furtherance and facilitation of growing life. Sanctification in this more comprehensive perspective encompasses several aspects. It means rediscovering the sanctity of life and the divine mystery of creation, and defending them from life's manipulation, the secularization of nature, and the destruction of the world through human violence. The earth belongs to God and therefore is something to be protected. Out of this attitude grows "reverence for life." This attitude links a religious attitude towards life with a moral respect for it. Sanctification also means the renunciation of violence towards life. Any kind of violence that threatens life and growth opposes the purposes of the Spirit of life. Sanctification of life also includes the search for the "harmonies and accords of life."[71] In sync with this inclusive understanding of salvation, "new birth," a common stage in any *ordo salutis* and a beloved catchword in pietistic and revivalistic spiritualities, means more than just the regeneration through Spirit of an individual. Moltmann reminds us of the cosmic background of the Greek term *palingenesia* which also points to the eschatological renewal of life and world. Thus, the chapter title "The Rebirth to Life."[72]

For such renewed, healed, and empowered life to flourish, the Spirit's role as "The Charismatic Powers of Life" should be rediscovered

68. Ibid., 131.

69. Ibid., 138–42

70. Ibid., 142–43.

71. Ibid., 171–74.

72. Ibid., chap. 7.

in Christian theology.[73] According to Moltmann, "The *whole* of life, and *every* life in faith is charismatic, for the Spirit is 'poured out upon all flesh' to quicken it."[74] When it comes to charismatic gifts, unlike most European theologians, Moltmann spends considerable time discussing gifts such as speaking in tongues and healing of the sick. Again, expanding categories, he also speaks of the "The Charisma of the Handicapped Life."[75] While traditionally the charismata have been divided into two groups: "supernatural" (1 Cor 12:6–8) and "natural" (Rom 12:6–8), both groups have operated within the confines of the church and individual piety. Moltmann insists that the Holy Spirit gives spiritual gifts not only for the church life but also for service in the world, for example, prophetic speech in liberation and ecology movements. "If charismata are not given to us so that we can flee from this world into a world of religious dreams, but if they are intended to witness to the liberating lordship of Christ in this world's conflicts, then the charismatic movement must not become a non-political religion, let alone a de-politicized one."[76]

THE PERSONHOOD AND FELLOWSHIP OF THE SPIRIT

Above it was noted that in his trinitarian doctrine which begins from the threeness and then works towards the unity, Moltmann is keen to affirm the personhood of each member of the Trinity. The third part of *The Spirit of Life* is devoted to new ways of conceiving the personhood of the Holy Spirit. Not surprisingly, the overall context is trinitarian, reflecting Moltmann's "social doctrine of the Trinity."[77] In that outlook, the greatest development in contemporary theology is the replacement of the conception of personhood in terms of substance with a relational and perichoretic understanding that makes better sense for an elusive and dynamic reality of the Spirit.[78] Because of the inadequacy of traditional approaches to defining the personhood of the Spirit,

73. Chapter title in ibid., chap. 9.

74. Ibid., 182.

75. Ibid., 192.

76. Ibid., 186.

77. See Moltmann, *The Trinity and the Kingdom*, 19.

78. Moltmann, *The Spirit of Life*, 269. "Perichoresis" is an ancient way in theology to speak of the "mutual interpenetration" of Father, Son, and Spirit with each other. That is the way Moltmann seeks to affirm unity.

particularly in terms of a generic concept of the "person"[79] or focusing on what Moltmann calls "monotheistic" (in other words, not genuinely trinitarian) approaches, he sets forth a social understanding: "Experience of the Spirit—the Experience of Fellowship."[80] Consequently, Moltmann radically expands the traditional notion of the "communion of the Holy Spirit" to encompass the whole "community of creation" from the most elementary particles to atoms to molecules to cells to living organisms to animals to human beings to communities of humanity. In this "fellowship as process," all human communities are embedded in the ecosystems of the natural communities, and live from the exchange of energy with them.[81] In others words, any kind of community of creation is the fellowship of the Holy Spirit, be it an ecological community or Christian community or a community of man and woman, or, say, a self-help group of AA or the like.[82]

So far so good. This discussion has not yet resolved the problem of defining the personhood of the Holy Spirit even though it has helped open up the Spirit (and the whole of the Trinity) to both human and inanimate communities in God's creation and link them with the energies of the Spirit of Life. Moltmann clearly acknowledges the challenge of such an enterprise. He acknowledges that a "more precise discernment of the personhood of the Holy Spirit is the most difficult problem in pneumatology in particular, and in the doctrine of the Trinity generally."[83] In that enterprise, again in keeping with his exploratory and suggestive theological method—and avoiding "an attempt to arrive at a systematic structure"—he proposes a number of metaphors. These metaphors come under four categories:[84]

1. The personal metaphors: the Spirit as lord, as mother, and as judge

---

79. A dramatic way to describe traditional ways of defining the personhood on the basis of a preconceived idea of personhood in mind (in this case, based on Boethius' well-known formula "an individual substance of rational nature") is such that it "yields a concept reflecting the separated, no-further-divisible, self-sufficient masculine self of our Greek and Roman cultural history." Moltmann, *The Spirit of Life,* 268.

80. A section heading in ibid., 217.

81. Ibid., 225–26.

82. These different forms of fellowship are discussed in chap. 11 of ibid.

83. Ibid., 268.

84. Ibid., 269. Chap. 12 in Moltmann, *The Spirit of Life* is devoted to the detailed exposition of each of these metaphors.

2. The formative metaphors: the Spirit as energy, as space, and as Gestalt

3. The movement metaphors: the Spirit as tempest, as fire, and as love

4. The mystical metaphors: the Spirit as source of light, as water, and as fertility

What is common to the first category of metaphors is that behind each one of them is a notion of "subject" whom/which men and women encounter. These metaphors speak of the experience of liberation since "lord" is connected with freedom in 2 Cor 3:17 and mother and *Paraclete* with experiences of new life, birth, and comfort. These metaphors include both masculine and feminine traits, reflecting inclusivity. The second category of "formative" metaphors speak of forces such as energy, space, and "form," which are not talking about "subjects" but about "forces which impose a profound impress."[85] These "forces" are present in the physical world as well as in, say, love and in Christian life, and these kinds of metaphors of the Spirit can be found all over in the biblical canon. Suffice it to mention only the metaphor of a well (Jer 17:13; John 4:14). Similarly, metaphors denoting movement appear frequently in the Bible in relation to the Spirit. The whole etymological background of the biblical terms *ruach* and *pneuma* comes from "wind," "breath," "tempest," and the like. The last category, named "mystical" by Moltmann, similarly has a biblical backdrop as the Spirit is, for example, compared to water.

The metaphors in themselves, of course, do not yet establish the personhood of the Spirit even when they tell us a lot about the "experiences of the Spirit."[86] Moltmann follows two strategies in trying to define more carefully the personhood of the Spirit, one based on the metaphors of the experiences of the Spirit and one based on inner-trinitarian relationships. Moltmann uses the nomenclature of the "streaming personhood of the divine Spirit" in his attempt, starting from the metaphors that speak of operations of the Spirit and human experiences of the Spirit, to "deduce the contours of his personhood." Deductive in nature, it is, as mentioned, derived from operations rather than from a face-to-face

85. Ibid., 174.

86. It is significant theologically that Moltmann titles the section on metaphors for the Spirit as "Metaphors for the Experiences of the Spirit," in ibid., 269.

encounter. As the Spirit is only known by the Father and Son, human "knowledge" can only be based on operations and efficacies. What the human knowledge reaches is the difference of the acts of the Spirit from those of the Father and Son (otherwise, trinitarian doctrine wouldn't emerge, of course). Now, the question is: What is the revelation of the "unique personhood" of the Spirit in light of the fact that "all God's activity in the world is pneumatic" similarly to "every human experience of God"? In one sense all the metaphors used of the Spirit are also metaphors "for God in his coming to us, and in his presence with us."[87]

In the personal metaphors it is easier to distinguish between subject and the acts of the subject. The lord as subject is transcendent from the act of, say, liberation. Similarly, mother is clearly distinguished from the child she gives birth to. When it comes to metaphors from other categories such as formative and mystical, for example, light—even when of course a distinction can be made between light and the source thereof— it is the connection that is in the forefront. The *Spirit of God*, however, is not an "object" out of which we can move, but rather whatever knowing there is of and about the Spirit, it happens in the Spirit. "The Spirit is in us and round about us, and we are in him."[88] Therefore, we "perceive the personhood of the divine Spirit in the flow between his presence and his counterpart, his energies and his essential nature. It is therefore no wonder that the people affected should talk about the Spirit as power and as person, as energy and as space, as wellspring and as light. This is not cloudiness in human thinking, or 'anonymity' on the divine side; it is wholly appropriate."[89]

Furthermore, Moltmann explains, the Spirit "poured out on all flesh" means nothing else than the self-emptying of the Spirit: men and women perceive and experience God in the force of the Spirit's energies; this is the point of the biblical promise of the Spirit bringing the knowledge of God to men and women.[90]

The other approach to attempting to describe the personhood of the Spirit is based on inner-trinitarian relationships: "It is one thing to work back from the operations of the Holy Spirit to his essential nature; it is quite another to perceive his essential nature from his constitutive

87. Ibid., 285–86.
88. Ibid., 186–87.
89. Ibid., 288.
90. Ibid., 288.

relationships."[91] While one must be cautious about saying too much about the "inner life" of God (immanent Trinity), Christian theology is convinced that "In his trinitarian inter-personhood he [Spirit] is person, in that as person he stands over against the other persons, and as person acts on them." [92] Having scrutinized the traditional models of the Trinity in the Christian West and East, not surprisingly, Moltmann lands on the model he names the "trinitarian doxology." Building on the ancient confession, "Glory be to the Father *and* to the Son *and* to the Holy Spirit, as it was in the beginning is now and ever shall be, word without end," which speaks for the equality rather than subordination of the Spirit and in which the triune God is worshipped for his own sake, Moltmann concludes that only in doxology can we come anywhere near "seeing God." Exactly because in doxology we worship God for what God *is* rather than what God *does*, we transcend in one sense the economic Trinity. "The trinitarian doxology is the only place in Christian practice in which—at least in intention—our gaze passes beyond salvation history to the eternal essence of God himself, so that here we can talk about a doctrine of the Trinity in which the 'economic' themes play no part."[93] Moltmann refers to the important Pauline saying in 2 Cor 3:18: "Now we all, with unveiled face, reflect the glory of the Lord, and shall be transfigured into his likeness from one degree of glory to another; for this comes from the Lord who is the Spirit"[94] This happens in Christian mysticism as the mystic ascends the "ladder of love" towards the Beloved.[95]

AN EVANGELICAL ENGAGEMENT

Evangelicals in general have not offered significant theological dialogues with Moltmann's pneumatology with the exception of one segment of evangelicalism, namely the Pentecostal/Charismatic theologies.[96]

91. Ibid., 289.

92. Ibid., 189–90.

93. Ibid., 301–2.

94. Ibid., 304–5.

95. Ibid., 302.

96. In this discussion, I do not engage the question of the relationship between evangelicalism and Pentecostal/Charismatic Movements. I work with the common assumption that whatever exactly the relationship is, both at the empirical level and in terms of theological convictions, these two spiritual traditions seem to be deeply

On the one hand, Moltmann has made a number of contributions to Pentecostal/Charismatic publications[97] and has given keynote addresses at international events.[98] He has also trained a number of Pentecostal students, many of whom have distinguished themselves as theologians. On the other hand, Pentecostal/Charismatic theologians with a keen interest in pneumatology, have engaged him in a dialogue. The April 1994 issue of *Journal of Pentecostal Theology*, the leading international Pentecostal/Charismatic academic journal, was devoted to "A Global Pentecostal Dialogue with Jürgen Moltmann" with six major review articles plus Moltmann's own response. Using that collection of reviews as the main source of evangelical responses seems to be justified because all of these Pentecostal theologians are also active in evangelical circles, including one who for many years was the chairperson of the Theological Commission of the World Evangelical Fellowship.

Pentecostal theologians have acknowledged with great appreciation Moltmann's pronounced *trinitarian* approach to the doctrine of the Spirit.[99] They also affirm his effort to expand and make more inclusive the work of the Spirit,[100] including the need to connect pneumatology with topics such as sexuality, politics, ecology, and creation.[101] Theologians who themselves live—like Moltmann in the past—in the midst of war and political unrest have applauded the link with

---

intertwined and overlapped.

97. Moltmann, "The Spirit Gives Life: Spirituality and Vitality," 22–37; Moltmann, "A Pentecostal Theology of Life," 3–15. Moltmann also coedited (with Karl-Josef Küschel) the important ecumenical collection of essays on *Pentecostal Movements as an Ecumenical Challenge*.

98. Moltmann was the keynote speaker at the Brighton 91 Conference organized by a large constituency of Pentecostal and Charismatic (including a significant number of Roman Catholic Charismatic) theologians, often considered theologically and ecumenically the most important meeting in that field. Furthermore, in 2004 Moltmann gave a keynote address at a symposium on "Pentecostal Theology of Hope" at the Yoido Full Gospel Church of Pastor Yonggi Cho, the world's largest church, a Pentecostal congregation. In 2007 he was the keynote speaker at the Society for Pentecostal Studies annual meeting at Duke University.

99. Chan, "An Asian Review," 36.

100. Macchia, "North American Response," 25–26.

Kuzmic, "A Croatian War-Time Reading," 17–20; Sepúlveda, "The Perspective of Chilean Pentecostalism," 47–49.

101. Stibbe, "A British Appraisal," 11

suffering.[102] Not surprisingly, Pentecostal reviewers of Moltmann's pneumatology have welcomed his effort to reaffirm and highlight the importance of spiritual experience as a way to constructing a theology of the Spirit.[103] Similarly, Moltmann's ecumenical approach in pneumatology has been acknowledged.[104]

While affirming and appreciating the turn to immanentism and holistic-cosmic orientations in the Spirit's work,[105] there has also been lament about the alleged lack of the transcendence of the Spirit[106] and about the panentheistic orientation.[107] The lack of discussion—or even reference!—to other spirits—What about the Fall? What about evil?[108]—as well as the closely related question of the criteria for the discernment of the spirits, has also been noted by many.[109] Furthermore, questions have also been raised concerning the seemingly uncritical embrace of ecological theology, cosmic Christology, and affirmation of everything bodily.[110] Pentecostals and evangelicals with a keen interest in mission and evangelization have wondered what exactly is Moltmann's view of mission in the world—in light of his enthusiastic discernment of the Spirit of God at work everywhere?[111] Several Pentecostals have critiqued Moltmann's discussion of the charismatic element for its too-generic nature and the tendency to make everything charismatic.[112] Other critical notes by Pentecostals include the selective way Moltmann seems to handle biblical materials.[113] Part of

102. Kuzmic, "A Croatian War-Time Reading," 17–19; see also Macchia, "North American Response," 27–28.

103. Sepúlveda, "The Perspective of Chilean Pentecostalism," 41–43.

104. Lapoorta, "An African Response," 51; Stibbe, "A British Appraisal," 12.

105. Chan, "An Asian Review," 38; Lapoorta, "An African Response," 52–56; Macchia, "North American Response," 29; Sepúlveda, "The Perspective of Chilean Pentecostalism," 43.

106. Macchia, "North American Response," 26–27; Kuzmic, "A Croatian War-Time Reading," 22; Chan, "An Asian Review," 38–39.

107. Kuzmic, "A Croatian War-Time Reading," 20; Stibbe, "A British Appraisal," 12;

108. Stibbe, "A British Appraisal," 13.

109. Chan, "An Asian Review," 39; Stibbe, "A British Appraisal," 15, 16.

110. Stibbe, "A British Appraisal," 13–14.

111. Stibbe, "A British Appraisal," 14; Kuzmic, "A Croatian War-Time Reading," 21, wonders where the need is for conversion in Moltmann's talk about rebirth.

112. Kuzmic, "A Croatian War-Time Reading," 22.

113. Stibbe, "A British Appraisal," 14

this critique is the observation that Moltmann focuses on Paul's Spirit-Christology but is weak and almost neglects Luke's more pronounced pneumatological orientation.[114] Finally, not only evangelical[115] but also other reviewers[116] have noted the lack of clarity in Moltmann's attempt to establish the personhood of the Spirit.

Moltmann's pneumatological vision is a helpful and needed challenge for evangelical theology. In keeping with general Protestant tradition, evangelical doctrine of the Spirit has tended to be limited to themes that have to do with one's personal Christian life and piety, particularly *ordo salutis*, the subjective reception of salvation, some aspects of the life of the church such the as sacraments and ministries, as well as the inspiration of Scripture. What has been lacking is the Spirit's role in creation and the world, including religions and cultures.[117] Furthermore, evangelicals need to be pushed to reconsider the relation of human experience to the divine Spirit; except for Pentecostals, evangelicalism in general has been influenced greatly by Barthian (and to a lesser extent, Fundamentalistic) suspicion. Still, evangelical reflection on the Spirit also has a need to reconsider the relationship between "spirit" and "body" and to work towards a more inclusive view of salvation. Somewhat ironically, the Reformed Moltmann can also inspire evangelicals to embrace more enthusiastically the charismatic dimension of the Christian life, including ecclesiastical life and church ministry. Here Moltmann and Pentecostals seem to be on the same side!

Some of the main challenges—and topics in need of further clarification in the continuing dialogue between Moltmann's doctrine of the Spirit and evangelical doctrines of the Spirit—include the following. Let me just list them here and hope for a long-term, careful mutual learning and comparing of notes:

- How would the turn to panentheism be safeguarded from not making the Spirit of God prisoner to the world? In other words, evangelicals, with many others, are concerned about the mainte-

114. Macchia, "North American Response," 32.

115. Chan, "An Asian Review," 39–40.

116. Müller-Fahrenholz, *The Kingdom and the Power: The Theology of Jürgen Moltmann*, 197–98.

117. A delightful exception is the major pneumatological work by Pinnock, *Flame of Love: A Theology of the Holy Spirit*, which develops a whole systematic theology through the lens of pneumatology and includes topics such as creation and religions.

nance of the freedom of God.

- How would the main Moltmannian criterion for the discernment of spirits, the support for life, be best complemented by other criteria such as the christological one (1 Cor 12:1–3) present in the biblical teaching? A corollary question is this: What is the relation of the Spirit of God to the demonic element(s) and to other spirits?

- Further clarification is needed about the discernment of approaches to pneumatology, enthusiastically embraced by Moltmann, such as cosmic Christology and "Green pneumatology." While evangelicals have a lot to learn about these and similar approaches—which also have deep roots in Classical Christianity, including patristic theologies—they also pose questions about God-world relationship, (some of them) flirting with neo-paganism, and generally reflecting a thin biblical theology.

- evangelicals also want to hear more about the meaning and practice of mission and evangelization in the context of a panentheistic, holistic doctrine of the Spirit. A corollary issue is the question of sin and the Fall.

As mentioned above, Moltmann's way of writing constructive theology is not to repeat things he has developed earlier but rather to deepen, correct, and at times pick up from where he has left off. Therefore, an appropriate way for evangelicals to put Moltmann's pneumatology in perspective is to consider the doctrine of the Spirit in the wider context of his evolving theological vision. That is of course what this essay has attempted to do.

7

Moltmann on Salvation

David Höhne

MOLTMANN ON SALVATION

FOR AN EVANGELICAL TO engage with the writings of Jürgen Moltmann on any topic, especially a topic as close to the heart of evangelicalism as salvation, takes equal amounts of sensitivity, wisdom, and a spirit of adventure. As large and impressive as his oeuvre may be, it is by no means a *Summa Theologica*. Many an interlocutor has bemoaned "conceptual looseness . . . contradictions and . . . speculative tendencies."[1] In his defense, Moltmann's admirers point to the "boldness and fullness of his exploration of the doctrine of God" as more than fair compensation.[2] Thus when entering into theological conversation with Moltmann the critic finds himself at times wandering, at times galloping, and at other times stumbling at forks along Moltmann's "open, inviting path."[3] This path proceeds along several interweaving tracks, "the eschatological horizon of history in the kingdom of God; faithfulness to the earth; new partnerships for the church in the world; and "the narrow wideness of the cross of Christ.""[4] On such a journey Moltmann always seems happy

---

1. Conradie, "The Justification of God? The Story of God's Work According to Jürgen Moltmann Pt. 1," 77.

2. Bauckham, *The Theology of Jürgen Moltmann*, 27.

3. Moltmann, *Experiences in Theology*, xv.

4. Moltmann, *Experiences*, 91.

for his fellow travelers to "have their own theological ideas and to set out along their own paths."[5] Therefore in this essay we shall journey with him while we may, pausing to marvel at the heights of his theological imaginings, empathizing with the depths of his soteriological struggles, yet always reserving the option to depart along a road regrettably less travelled by Moltmann in recent years—that of an exclusive reading of Holy Scripture and *Christian* tradition.

After so many years the number of Moltmann's fellow travelers has expanded to match the breadth of his writings. There seems, therefore, little point in scanning the edges of his theological tapestry in search of another loose thread upon which one might tug. Instead, because his contributions are more latterly imbued with autobiographical reflections,[6] we shall attempt to traverse Moltmann's doctrine of salvation from the inside outwards—that is, as a voyage through his major works from the beginning as he depicts it. There is not room in the present volume for a full theological biography and so, in an attempt to be broadly systematic, the present investigation will chart a course through Moltmann's description of God's saving actions for us and the consequences of these actions for creation. Perhaps other more theologically exacting routes could have been chosen but the present one shall suffice to ensure that what might otherwise be an extensive engagement with a theologian as imaginative and gregarious as Moltmann can be confined to a single chapter in the present volume.

MY GOD, WHERE ARE YOU?

Moltmann's personal journey has always been close to the surface in his writings and never more so since the release of his autobiography, *A Broad Place.*[7] So then, we shall start our expedition through his account of salvation at the beginning—with his personal testimony.

Moltmann's account of "Operation Gomorrah"—the first allied attempt to destroy a large German city in 1943—recalls the first time "I cried out to God . . . and put my life in his hands. I was as if dead, and

---

5. Ibid., xv.

6. See Moltmann, *A Broad Place: An Autobiography.*

7. Ibid. In addition, but to a lesser extent see also Moltmann, *Experiences.*

ever after received life every day as a gift."[8] Significantly, given the place of theodicy in Moltmann's later work, his question was not, "Why does God allow this to happen?" but, "My God, where are you?" In the light of salvation from death—from which the friend standing next to him did not escape—Moltmann reports feeling "the guilt of survival" and searching for "the meaning of continued life."[9] Having been captured and interred, first in Belgium and then in the UK, his sense of guilt and despair deepened with the revelations of Nazi atrocities in Belsen and Buchenwald: "Depression over the wartime destruction and a captivity with no end in sight was compounded by a feeling of profound shame at having to share in shouldering the disgrace of one's own people."[10]

Salvation from this experience came, it seems in two forms: Firstly in friendly encounters with Scottish families amongst whom Moltmann worked as a prisoner of war in various skilled labour settings and, secondly, through the Bible. It appears that it was while reading the words of Psalm 39 that Moltmann felt his "soul called to [by] God," particularly:

> I am dumb and must eat up my suffering within myself.
> My life is as nothing before thee [Luther's version].
> Hear my prayer, O Lord, and give ear to my cry.
> Hold not thou thy peace at my tears,
> For I am a stranger with thee, and a sojourner, as all my fathers were.[11]

The words of lament in the psalm echoed in Moltmann's own experience and when combined with, what must surely be Moltmann's theological *leitmotiv*, "My God, why have you forsaken me?" from the lips of the Markan crucified Christ, the young German POW gained a new hope: "I felt growing within me the conviction: this is someone who understands you completely, who is with you in your cry to God and has felt the same forsakenness you are living in now. I began to understand the assailed, forsaken Christ because I knew that he understood me. [Christ is t]he divine brother in need, the companion on the way, who goes with you through this 'valley of the shadow of death,' the fellow-sufferer who carries you, with your suffering."[12]

---

8. Moltmann, *Broad Place*, 17.

9. Ibid.

10. Ibid., 29.

11. Ibid., 30.

12. Ibid., 30.

With this conviction Moltmann "summoned up the courage to live again." Furthermore he reports being "seized by a great hope for the resurrection into God's 'wide space where there is no more cramping.'"[13] The account finishes with a moving allusion to a medieval picture depicting Christ descending into hell and "opening the gate for someone who points to himself as if he were saying, 'And are you coming to me?'" Such was Moltmann's experience of salvation in that time and that place—an experience that, he reports, has stayed with him after almost sixty years.

It will be seen that many of the themes in Moltmann's theological description of salvation emerge from this testimony. Chiefly, the cross is God's saving act that reveals his genuine compassion for, and identification with, victims of godlessness and godforsakenness on the one hand, and that justifies him in their company on the other. For Moltmann, Christian theology becomes relevant only when it takes the theodicy question as an "absolute presupposition," only "when it accepts this solidarity with present suffering."[14] Human suffering is "the central problem in most religions"[15] and therefore, for Moltmann, a description of salvation must be articulated in terms of the justification of God in the light of such suffering. God's answer to this predicament is the victory of life over death, hope, and freedom in the face of tyranny and despair. Through the resurrection of Christ in the Spirit, a way emerges for those trapped in death and evil, a way out into the broad and open future of God's life, a life characterized by joy and freedom. For Moltmann, Jesus as Messiah is the way into this future and so we move on to consider the path God makes for him, for us, and for himself.

CHRIST, THE DIVINE BROTHER IN NEED

As indicated in Moltmann's testimony, the call of Christ to the forsaken is born out of his identity as "the fellow-sufferer who carries you, with your suffering." In *The Crucified God*, (TCG) Moltmann argued for the triune life of God as the context of God's encounter with evil and suffering. It is in this work that Moltmann makes, perhaps, his signature contribution to a trinitarian description of God's saving actions in Jesus:

13. Ibid., 30.

14. Moltmann, *Hope and Planning*, 35.

15. Moltmann, *The Church in the Power of the Holy Spirit*, 161.

> In the total, inextricable abandonment of Jesus by his God and
> Father, Paul sees the delivering up of the Son by the Father for
> godless and godforsaken man . . . It may therefore be said that the
> Father delivers up his Son on the cross in order to be the Father
> of those who are delivered up . . . if Paul speaks emphatically of
> God's "own Son," the not-sparing and abandoning also involves
> the Father himself. In the forsakenness of the Son the Father also
> forsakes himself. In the surrender of the Son the Father also sur-
> renders himself.[16]

So for the Christian, the God who saves is the Father of Jesus
the Christ, the Father who forsakes his Son for the godless and godforsaken. With Jesus' cry of dereliction (My God, my God, why have you
forsaken me? Mark 15: 34) "all disaster, forsakenness by God, absolute
death, the infinite curse of damnation, and sinking into nothingness is
in God himself."[17] Since anyone who suffers without cause first thinks
God has forsaken him, Moltmann declares that anyone who cries out to
God in this suffering echoes the death-cry of the dying Christ, the Son
of God. Only when Christian theology has recognized what took place
between Jesus and his Father on the cross can it speak of the significance
of this God for those who suffer and protest at the history of the world.[18]

This vision of God born out of the cross of Christ Jesus reveals
three interlaced trajectories for Moltmann's path of salvation. The first
trajectory arcs our conversation into the area of God's impassibility. The
second trajectory draws us into considering the scope of God's saving
actions. The third trajectory, of particular interest in this essay, is the
notion of justice that we might infer from Moltmann's description of
salvation in terms of the resolution of the history of God. We shall inves-
tigate these in sequence bearing in mind that they represent interlocking
flagstones in the same path.

---

16. Moltmann, *The Crucified God*, 243. The reference to Paul here is in conjunction
with a meditation on the words of 2 Cor 5:21 ("He made him sin for us") and Gal 3:13
("He became as curse for us"). See also Moltmann, *The Way of Jesus Christ*, 173.

17. Moltmann, *Crucified God*, 246.

18. Ibid., 225.

THE GOD WHO SUFFERS TO SAVE

Beginning with a central Christian proposition, God is love (1 John 4:8, 16), Moltmann argues that because his love is seen most starkly in the cross, this must imply that God suffers. Over and against classical theism's assertions of God's impassibility Moltmann declares, in *The Trinity and the Kingdom of God*, (TKG) that they "only really say that God is not subjected to suffering in the same way as transient, created beings," and therefore God's impassibility "does not exclude the deduction that in another respect God certainly can and does suffer."[19] Moltmann is strident: "if God were incapable of suffering in every respect, then he would also be incapable of love." At Moltmann's invitation the Spanish mystic, Miguel de Unamuno, has joined our conversation to argue for the *congoja*—pain, sorrow, anguish, and oppression—of God. He asserts, "A God who cannot suffer cannot love either . . . only that which suffers is divine."[20] Unamuno's mystical meditations involve a rather foreboding mix of Hegel, Kierkegaard, Schopenhauer, and the Spanish images of the crucified Christ, with the result that "Christ's death struggle on Golgotha reveals the pain of the whole world and the sorrow of God."[21] The implication then, for Moltmann, can only be that if the cross is to be the demonstration of God's saving love for the world (cf. Rom 5:8–9), then God must suffer in and through the cross in order for it to be a genuine act of saving love. Supporters of Moltmann on impassibility claim that his approach has done much to reinstate the biblical view of God's love over against classical theism. Thus Jansen writes, "In Moltmann, God does not only or primarily love what is like himself—the good in creatures—but what is most unlike himself."[22] Similarly, Wade Willis claims that, "[Moltmann's] doctrine of the Triune God . . . revolutionizes the doctrine of God of the traditional theism in a way in which its inability to respond to suffering is overcome."[23]

Unamuno's fascination with the morbidity and despair of the crucified Christ resonate strongly with Moltmann's earlier attempts to bring together the suffering of the world and the idea of God in a kind of

19. Moltmann, *The Trinity and the Kingdom of God*, 23.

20. Ibid., 38.

21. Ibid., 36.

22. Jansen, "Moltmann's View of God's (Im)Mutibility," 292.

23. Willis, *Theism, Atheism and the Doctrine of the Trinity*, 92.

theologia crucis.[24] In TCG Moltmann claimed that when the classical theist concept of God is applied to Christ's crucifixion "the cross must be evacuated of deity, for by definition God cannot suffer and die."[25] The God of pure causality is not the Christian God for the death of Jesus forces the Christian to "think of God's being in suffering and dying . . . if it is not to surrender itself and lose its identity."[26] In the post-holocaust context of the twentieth century, Moltmann claims, the Christian God must show more than a benign empathy towards the victims of evil. Hence, he argues that God was actively involved in the suffering of his Son: "God not only acted in the crucifixion of Jesus or sorrowfully allowed it to happen, but was himself active with his own being in the dying Jesus and suffered with him."[27] Critics of Moltmann ring the patrapassianism alarm at this juncture but Moltmann evades this accusation by stating the Father suffers the death of his Son: "If God has constituted himself as the Father of Jesus Christ, then he also suffers the death of his Fatherhood in the death of the Son."[28] Even though God suffers at the cross, the Father's suffering is distinct from that of the Son's. These earlier meditations of Moltmann's on the cross event focus on the God who forsakes his Son and, for Moltmann, stand as the ultimate revelation of God's triune nature. The obvious tension within God himself is revisited in Moltmann's later works as the aspect of the portrayal moves from Father to Son. So, in *The Way of Jesus Christ* (WJC) Moltmann explores the death of Christ from a number of angles all of which find a nexus in the Messianic sufferings.[29] Yet we continue to read of Jesus as the child of God dying in abandonment: "God-forsakenness is the final experience of God endured by the crucified Jesus on Golgotha, because to the very end he knew he was God's Son."[30]

---

24. Strictly speaking there is much more to Moltmann's meditation on the cross than originally offered by Luther. In addition there is not a small amount of Hegel and Moltmann also appeals to some of the more radical statements from Bonhoeffer's prison correspondence. Dietrich Bonhoeffer, "An Eberhard Bethge 30.4.44."

25. Moltmann, *Crucified God*, 214.

26. Ibid.

27. Ibid., 190.

28. Ibid., 243.

29. The various angles will be pursued in detail below.

30. Moltmann, *Way of Jesus Christ*, 167.

Moltmann's discussion of divine possibility has been described as a trajectory in the present essay because of the implications that arise when one looks further ahead. Moltmann announces, "To recognize God in the cross of Christ . . . means to recognize the cross, inextricable suffering, death, and hopeless rejection in God."[31] He expands this notion, such that, "the Son's sacrifice of boundless love on Golgotha is from eternity already included in the exchange of the essential, the consubstantial love which constitutes the divine life of the Trinity,"[32] so that "the pain of the cross determines the inner life of the triune God from eternity to eternity."[33] Moltmann's exploration of the doctrine of God has certainly run ahead with great boldness here, even his more sympathetic followers are caused to lag behind. As Bauckham observes, "If this does not make evil necessary, then contingent evil not only affects God in the course of his trinitarian history, but essentially determines his inner life from eternity."[34] Suppose at this early stage we allow Moltmann's rhetoric some latitude;[35] we cannot overlook the fact that, as Wolterstorff suggests, the nature of God's immanent life forms the basis of our understanding of justice in this world and the new creation.[36] As we shall see the restoration of justice will be a central aspect of Moltmann's description of salvation but if this requires us to follow him into resolving divine inner turmoil then the possibility track can only be regarded as entry into a quagmire.

THE SCOPE OF GOD'S SALVIFIC SYMPATHY

The discussion of divine possibility has drawn our path into the depths of God's salvific sympathy. From here we venture out, through the cross of Messiah Jesus, to explore the ever-expanding horizon of the saving God's actions for creation. "The experience of salvation is not really 'my'

31. Moltmann, *Crucified God*, 277.

32. Moltmann, *Trinity & Kingdom*, 168.

33. Ibid., 161.

34. Bauckham, *Moltmann: Messianic Theology in the Making*, 109.

35. We note however Blocher's concern that "the probable interpretation is that Jesus is made the second of the Trinity *as man*, as the man (crucified) with whom God identifies himself, thus defining himself as love, thus differentiating himself as Trinity." See Henri Blocher, "God and the Cross," 132.

36. Wolterstorff, "Is There Justice in the Trinity?"

or 'our' salvation: what is experienced is salvation for everything and everyone."[37] So in WJC Moltmann maintains that Jesus suffered, or at least participated "in the death of all the living, for he was mortal and would have died one day."[38] He is concerned that Jesus' death not be limited to a vicarious action merely for humans. This is pleasing as it does much to preserve not just the humanity of Christ, but also the creatureliness of that humanity. There is a definite sense in which, as the incarnate Word, God has become a creature in his own creation (cf. Col 1:15–17).[39] However, Moltmann's line is uncertain here for in his account it seems difficult to distinguish human mortality from creaturely finitude in order to maintain that Jesus died on the cross, "not only a death for others, but his own natural death as well."[40] In what sense, we might inquire, is death natural? What emerges is that our journey is in Schleiermacher's footsteps, as opposed to the Apostle Paul's.[41] Schleiermacher, and hence Moltmann, "disputes the causal link between sin against God and the physical death of the human being."[42] The Genesis account of the Fall of humankind is dismissed as mythical rather than in any sense prescriptive in order to make way for Jesus' death to include the death of all the transient elements of creation that groan under the weight of mortality. Nevertheless, Moltmann goes on to claim that since the new creation of Rev 21: 4 is a place without death, death is not natural and not a consequence of sin but rather, and enigmatically, "a sign of a tragedy in creation."[43] Christ suffers the sufferings of the present time (Rom 8:18), which inevitably means that God is suffering the plight of the world he made. So the God who saves does so out of compassion for the tragedy of his creation, a tragedy that certainly requires God's actions in Jesus to show it is not necessary.

Moltmann has been amongst the leaders in the twentieth-century reappropriation of trinitarian theology so it is not surprising that his doctrine of God's salvific suffering with creation exhibits explicitly tri-

---

37. Moltmann, *Trinity & Kingdom*, 100.

38. Moltmann, *Way of Jesus Christ*, 169.

39. See Gunton, *Christ and Creation*.

40. Moltmann, *Way of Jesus Christ*, 169.

41. Without the benefits of historical critical readings of Genesis Paul asserts, "The wages of sin is death" (Rom 6:23).

42. Moltmann, *Way of Jesus Christ*, 169.

43. Ibid., 170.

une language. Hence the sufferings of Christ for creation are depicted as a particular form of the Spirit's suffering with creation that Moltmann developed in *God in Creation*. (GiC) Moltmann's panentheistic description[44] of creation has the Spirit of God representing believers and creation alike in their longing for freedom from the bondage of decay with his "sighs too deep for words."[45] The scope of God's suffering with his creation is broadened far beyond the cross as Moltmann writes of the Spirit as "co-imprisoned and co-suffering" with all living things. Thus God the creator, "who has entered into the world through his Spirit, himself holds created being in life (Ps 104: 30), and therefore also suffers with its sufferings."[46]

So, the breadth of Moltmann's descriptive path through the doctrine of salvation rests upon the commensurate extent of God's salvific sympathy with creation. In the power of the Spirit, Jesus died the death of god-forsakenness whenever and wherever it appears in the groans of a world subject to death in godlessness. The notion of the Spirit's benevolent suffering with creation is the contribution of the Jewish kabbalist, Franz Rosenwig. Principally Moltmann is attracted to Rosenwig's work on God's Shekinah: "The Shekinah, the descent of God to human beings and his dwelling among them, is conceived of as a division, which takes place in God himself. God cuts himself off from himself. He gives himself away to his people. He suffers with their sufferings; he goes with them through the misery of the foreign land."[47]

Moltmann applies this to the indwelling of God in creation such that "he [God] gives himself away to the beings he has created, he suffers with their sufferings, he goes with them through the misery of the foreign land. The God who in the Spirit dwells in his creation is present to every one of his creatures and remains bound to them . . . "[48] Importantly

44. Moltmann describes the relationship between God and creation as pan-en-theistic such that: "The one-sided stress on God's transcendence in relation to the world led to deism, as with Newton. The one-sided stress on God's immanence in the world led to pantheism, as with Spinoza. The trinitarian concept of creation integrates the elements of truth in monotheism and pantheism. In the pan-en-theistic view, God, having created the world, also dwells in it, and conversely the world, which he created, exists in him." See Jürgen Moltmann, *God in Creation*, 98.

45. Ibid., 69.

46. Ibid., 69.

47. Ibid., 15.

48. Ibid., 15.

for this excursion, Rosenwig's description ends with God himself in need of redemption: "God himself, by 'selling himself' to Israel . . . and by suffering her fate with her, makes himself in need of redemption."[49] Is Rosenwig leading us along another trail into the quagmire of divine inner turmoil? Perhaps not if we consider Ezekiel's vision of the Lord's glory departing the Temple precincts eastbound to the exiles (Ezek 10). Alternatively, if it is allowed that the Gospel accounts of the trans-figuration of Jesus (cf. Luke 9:28ff.) incorporate Exodus notions of the Shekinah resting on the Tabernacle (Exod 40:34)[50] and this takes place while Jesus is discussing his redemption with Moses and Elijah,[51] then Rosenwig's suggestions are, at least, commensurate with the portrait of God's saving actions already available in Christian Scripture.

THE MESSIAH AS THE SPIRIT EMPOWERED SUFFERER

There is further significance to Rosenwig's contribution to the conversa-tion and this becomes clear when we return to the centre of Moltmann's path, the sufferings of Christ. Critics of Moltmann's trinitarian mediation on the cross seize upon his early focus on relations between Father and Son and denounce him for binitarianism.[52] Even if this was conceded in relation to TCG, Moltmann's later work on the Spirit, *The Spirit of Life*, (TSL) deals with a number of concerns. For here Moltmann writes of the Spirit as the one who "leads Jesus into the mutual history between him-self and God the Father, in which 'through obedience' (Heb 5:8) he will 'learn' his role as the messianic Son."[53] The Spirit who rests upon Jesus is "God's Shekinah . . . the self-restriction and self-humiliation of the eternal Spirit." The Spirit affectively identifies with "Jesus' person and the

49. Moltmann, *Trinity & Kingdom*, 29.

50. Nolland, *Luke 9:21—18:34*, 501.

51. Wright interprets the transfiguration as playing an important part in pre-figur-ing the triumphant return of YHWH to Zion in the work of the Messiah who will return Israel from exile and defeat evil at the same time. N. T. Wright, *Jesus and the Victory of God*, 651. It was in conversation with Moses regarding the redemption of Israel and victory over Pharaoh that YHWH first referred to Israel as "My Son" (Exod 4:22). Jesus has publicly committed himself to a course of action that ends in his death (Luke 9:22); in order for Jesus' Sonship to be preserved he must be redeemed from this fate.

52. See, for example, Jowers, "The Theology of the Cross as the Theology of the Trinty."

53. Moltmann, *The Spirit of Life: A Universal Affirmation*, 61.

history of his life and suffering."[54] The Spirit, according to Moltmann, empowers Jesus and accompanies him. Thus, "it is drawn into his sufferings and becomes his *companion* in suffering." This, according to Moltmann, means the Spirit becomes "the transcendent side of Jesus' immanent way of suffering." The Spirit is united with Jesus "without becoming identical with him," so as to become "the Spirit of the crucified one."[55] Here Moltmann appeals to Heb 9:14, Christ "through the eternal Spirit offered himself without blemish to God." In fact, Calvin is brought into the discussion for his suggestion (in reference to Heb 7:16) that "the power of indestructible life . . . is a way of saying that Christ did not suffer death outwardly or fortuitously, but experienced and affirmed it inwardly . . . through the power of the Spirit." Moltmann takes this to signify that "Christ himself [is] the truly active one [in his death]," and this, "through the operation of the divine Spirit who acts in him."[56] It is through Christ that God's salvific life power absorbs sin, death, and evil in the world and, at the same time, overcomes them.

Moltmann's pneumatological account of Christ's sufferings returns to Gethsemane to complete his trinitarian description of the passion. The Spirit accompanies Jesus in the "experience of God's hiddenness" right through to "experience of God-forsakenness on the cross." Moltmann sees the Spirit's actions as perfecting the relations between Father and Son across the Gospel story: "Whereas in Jesus' baptism God calls Jesus 'my beloved Son,' in Gethsemane Jesus responds by addressing him as 'Abba, dear Father.' Both the call to life and the response in dying are given 'in the Spirit.'"[57] The Spirit enables Jesus to submit to the will of the "hidden, absent, even rejecting Father."[58] Hence Jesus is able to endure God-forsakenness vicariously for a God-forsaken world and as he does, he brings the Spirit into this God-forsaken world.

Moltmann's "christological doctrine of the Spirit"[59] does much to highlight the importance of relations between the Spirit and the Messiah in God's plans for salvation. Yet while the "Jewish" contribution from Rosenwig supports Moltmann's theodicy agenda, it does seem fair to

54. Ibid., 61.
55. Ibid., 62.
56. Ibid., 63.
57. Ibid., 64.
58. Ibid., 65.
59. Ibid., 58.

ask whether the detour was necessary. Moltmann rightly acknowledges the importance of Jesus claiming the Isaiah 61 promise (Luke 4:16ff) as a foundation for Messianic ministry[60] but Moltmann otherwise seems indifferent to the way that the Spirit empowers Jesus with the Scriptures. Jesus' appearance in Nazareth in the Spirit's power follows directly from his triumph in the wilderness over the Satan; a triumph enabled by the Spirit through the Scriptures.[61] In response to the Satan's offer to determine the nature of his sonship (If you are the son . . .), in the Spirit, Jesus chooses the way of discipline (suffering?), he chooses the Father's promised inheritance and he chooses not to pre-empt the Father's promise to save him from death—all "as it is written."[62] In this reading the Spirit makes effective the Father's word of promise to his Messianic Servant to empower Jesus to face death. If this relational dynamic is allowed then the rest of Jesus' story with God in the Spirit gains, we suggest, a greater level of intelligibility. When it comes to the Gethsemane agony, we find Jesus again enabled by the Spirit to submit to God's word in the face of death, here described as "drinking the cup."[63] If it is admitted that the Gospel accounts understand "the cup" in terms of God's wrath against unfaithful Israel (Isa 51) and the nations (Jer 25)[64] then the Gethsemane crisis for Jesus is less a matter of inexplicably facing God's silence, as a matter of submitting to God's spoken word, to the reality that "this [cup] cannot pass unless [Jesus] drink[s] it" (Matt 26:42) so that the Father's will might be done.[65] As obviously terrible as the experience is, the

60. See Moltmann, *Way of Jesus Christ*, 94ff.

61. Kimball describes Jesus' use of Scripture as, "a literal application of the OT (i.e. without midrashic techniques) in a debate pattern similar to certain rabbinic disputations in which questions and answers are drawn from Scripture." Kimball, *Jesus' Exposition of the Old Testament in Luke's Gospel*, 96. Here we are headed towards Vanhoozer's view of Messiah Jesus as, "the pre-eminent performer" in the drama of Scripture. Vanhoozer writes, "The Son 'performs' what God the Father scripted . . . The Son is also the centre of the Spirit's performance in Scripture," See Vanhoozer, *The Drama of Doctrine: A Canonical Linguistic Approach to Christian Theology*, 189.

62. For a fuller justification of this reading see Höhne, *Spirit and Sonship: Colin Gunton's Theology of Particularity and the Holy Spirit*.

63. Following Shepherd we have taken it as given the Spirit continues to work in and for the Messiah even when not named in the text. Shepherd, *The Narrative Function of the Holy Spirit as a Character in Luke-Acts*, 137.

64. Wright, *Jesus*, 572f.

65. Could the interpretation of this event be as simply as the fact that God says "no" to Jesus' prayer?

Spirit is not passively *with* Jesus but actively administering to him the promises of God. In fact we might even go so far as to say that God has not deserted his Son but rather enabled him by the Spirit to achieve the salvation that God wills. Even in the infamous depths of the Golgotha event, when Jesus utters the opening words of Psalm 22 (and Matthew especially proceeds to load his account of the crucifixion with allusions to the poem) might we not also allow the Spirit to minister the promises of vindication to Jesus? "For He has not despised or detested the torment of the afflicted. He did not hide his face from him, but listened when he cried to Him for help" (Psalm 22:24). This would give weight to the testimony of Peter at Pentecost that makes special and explicit appeal to Psalm 16 as a means of interpreting the Messiah's experience in the face of death:

> "For David said about him, 'I saw beforehand my Lord always before me: because he is at my right hand I will not be shaken . . . because you will not abandon my soul in Hades nor will you permit your Holy One to see decay'" (Acts 2:25–28)

When the mission of the Messianic savior is read this way, he is still empowered by the Spirit but to a different end. God's Messiah undergoes the curse of God's wrath in the power of God's Spirit, who enables Jesus to commit himself to God's promise of resurrection vindication for the salvation of sinners from God's curse. Of course, this represents a significantly different understanding of God's saving deeds in Jesus and by the Spirit. Moltmann's circuitous trail that we have travelled through God's salvific suffering for the whole of creation is intentionally divergent from evangelical descriptions that have arisen since the time of the Reformation. This is more readily appreciable once we turn to consider the consequences of God's saving actions for the human being.

THOSE IN NEED OF THE DIVINE BROTHER

Moltmann focuses on Christ's salvific sympathy with the suffering creation in order to lay a road for a "therapeutic Christology."[66] Moltmann's track through the "narrow wideness" of the cross portrays Christ's salvation, as opposed to any other, but "it can talk about the

---

66. Moltmann, *Way of Jesus Christ*, 44.

salvation which Christ brings only as healing,"[67] and this for the whole of creation. Moltmann rightly contends that to talk about salvation one must be critically aware of that from which creation is to be saved—he nominates misery, evil, and suffering. Thus far reference has been made only to godlessness and god-forsakenness as that from which the sympathetic Christ saves. Exactly what these terms mean for Moltmann is not straightforward. As McDougall has observed, "the doctrine of sin remains a lacuna in Moltmann's Messianic Theology."[68] Yet the lack is, ultimately, theological insofar as Moltmann's intentionally passible description of the loving God has him grieving over sin but never angry about it.[69] God's love is injured through "injustice and violence" because, and insofar as, he loves the "unjust and the person who commits violence." So his love must overcome his anger by "reconciling itself" to the pain it has been caused.[70]

If we pursue some kind of explanation for an origin sin in the Creation stories of Genesis Moltmann seems to lag behind: "Admittedly, *in the past* the Christian doctrine of salvation was often applied solely to the eternal situation of human beings in God's sight, in order that eternal salvation might be related to the fundamental existential situation of men and women: their separation from God, their transience, finitude and mortality."[71]

To be fair, Moltmann is rightly reticent to follow a line that focuses "solely [on] the eternal situation of human beings . . ." Protestant doctrines of salvation, especially those governed by the importance of personal assurance could easily be caricatured as "what happens to me when I die and how I feel about it until then." The New Testament portrays a definite cosmic sense in which Christ Jesus is the redeemer, that is, he redeems the *whole* of creation (cf. Eph 1:10).[72]

However, and as we shall see, the "in the past" description of Christian doctrine indicates much of Moltmann's desire to travel in the steps of Modern culture as opposed to Protestant tradition. There are

---

67. Ibid., 44.

68. McDougall, *Pilgrimage of Love: Moltmann on the Trinity and Christian Life*, 147.

69. He may, of course have no warrant to be angry if his eternal inner turmoil is the source of suffering in creation.

70. Moltmann, *Spirit of Life*, 134.

71. Moltmann, *Way of Jesus Christ*, 45. Emphasis added

72. See Gunton, *The Triune Creator*, 1998.

some clear statements about sin in Moltmann's work on creation. Thus, "sin is not something evil about the human being who has been created good; it is an evil and godless power to which human beings have come to be subjected through their own fault."[73] Of course, as we have noted, Moltmann admits that he is following Schleiermacher who "disputes the causal link between sin against God and the physical death of the human being."[74] Hence, Moltmann's focus is less on the nature of sin *per se* and more on how sin affects the *imago Dei* that human beings bear. The sin of the human being "perverts" his or her relationship to God, "but not God's relationship to human beings."[75] If we ask what it means to sin, Moltmann refers to godlessness on the part of the sinner or better: "Sin is the perversion of the human being's relationship to God . . . The relationship to God is turned into idolatry, faith becomes superstition, love of God becomes love of self, fear and hatred."[76]

The notion of a turn to idolatry is borrowed from Luther's Large Catechism. From this Moltmann alludes to Augustine's notion of sin as misdirected desires and finally Kierkegaard's "sickness unto death." Yet, Moltmann prefers to speak of "the energies of sin" that "have to be redeemed."[77] If there is a general sense of god-forsakenness to sin we might look to: "People who forsake the invisible God and worship created things are forsaken by God and 'delivered' or 'given up' to their own greedy desires."[78] That is, "a person closes himself off from the source of life, from God" and hence fails to discover, or fulfill, the purposes to which human beings are, by nature, destined. This occurs "because of hubris, or depression, or "God complex," or a refusal to accept what human existence is about."[79]

Moltmann wants to re-figure the concept of universal sin: "The universal concept of sin is so widespread in Protestantism that it is hard to discover the alternative."[80] However, he finds an alternative view by seemingly pitting the gospel accounts against the Pauline

---

73. Moltmann, *God in Creation*, 232.

74. Moltmann, *Way of Jesus Christ*, 169.

75. Moltmann, *God in Creation*, 233.

76. Ibid.

77. Ibid., 234.

78. Moltmann, *Way of Jesus Christ*, 172.

79. Ibid., 184.

80. Moltmann, *Spirit of Life*, 125.

corpus and focusing on a sociological description of sin in terms of "sinners and tax collectors . . . the outcasts, the poor and the homeless, who cannot keep God's law and are therefore outside the law, without any rights." The Gospel stories are read as filled with power dichotomies where the healthy make the sick, sick; the rich make the poor, poor, etc. Moltmann concedes that there are situations where "people are both victims and perpetrators." "Victims can also be latent perpetrators, and are not necessarily saints just because they are victims." All this rests on the "actual origin story of sin," the Cain and Abel narrative, and the subsequent spread of evil (Gen 4–6). Christian notions of original sin derived from the Garden are dismissed as mythical having no precedence in Judaism. "The weakness about the universal concept of sin underlying the Pauline and Protestant doctrine of justification is that collective guilt of this kind makes people blind to specific, practical guilt."[81] Moltmann's claim is that this leads to resignation about the "fallen-ness" of the world and an indifference to specific sins. Alternatively those who fail to resist evil regimes can take haven in universal duplicity at the expense of those martyred for what was right and who condemn the indifferent in their ways. "The doctrine about sin's universality is really a metaphysical view of sin."[82]

So God suffers the sins, or possibly even the sinfulness, of human beings and he suffers these in himself by the Spirit and through Christ Jesus. Moltmann rightly draws attention to the concrete relational dysfunctions that make up a description of sin—as opposed perhaps to abstract moral codes. It is we ourselves, as sinners, in our contradiction to life, who have to be justified and given back to life again. This is the ultimate goal of God's sympathetic therapy.[83] Moltmann's path from here is clear enough; what is not so clear is how we might follow him. God grieves over sin and somehow deals with his anger (nowhere really explored by Moltmann) in the process of curing the world of it—sin. If this is justice in an ultimate sense, it is extremely difficult to discern how humans, either individually or corporately, could follow such a path so pocked and overgrown by the genuine injustices to which Moltmann wants us to attend. What are we to do with *our* feelings of anger aroused by misery and evil? To answer this we turn to the last part of our jour-

81. Ibid., 126.
82. Ibid., 127.
83. Ibid., 136.

ney together with Moltmann where he explores how God's sympathetic suffering with creation is therapeutic. Here particularly, Moltmann is determined to walk a different path to evangelicals—if they consider themselves to be protestant.

THE HEALING POWER OF DIVINE SYMPATHY

In WJC Moltmann determines to discover the "liberating, redeeming and creative energies" of the Christ's sufferings." What he finds, or the path he builds, is based on four interconnected tracks, each emerging from Pauline testimony. With reference to Rom 4:25, Christ sufferings are "our liberation from the power of sin and the burden of our guilt." His resurrection is "our free life in the righteousness of God."[84] As straightforward as this answer might be in Reformation terms Moltmann gives a twist to the meaning of "justifying faith" that Paul discusses in Rom 4. Thus, with reference to Rom 14:9, Moltmann explains that the meaning of justifying faith is "the redeeming lordship of Christ over the dead and the living."[85] The dead find new community with one another through the dead Christ even as the risen Christ becomes the hope of the living and the dead. The acts of God for Christ, and hence for all who die, are presumably the object of the faith that justifies although Moltmann does not say so specifically.[86] Next, with reference to 1 Cor 15:25–28, the fellowship of Christ with the living and the dead is in anticipation of "the raising of all the dead to eternal life, and to the annihilation of death in the new creation of all things."[87] Justifying faith means community with Christ in the new creation without death. Finally, with reference to Phil 2:9–11, "Even the universal salvation of the new creation is not yet in itself the goal but serves the justification of God—that is, the glorifying of God, the Father of Jesus Christ."[88] The arrival of God in the Sabbath of the new creation marks the end of the theodicy trial of God. "Only then

---

84. Moltmann, *Way of Jesus Christ*, 182.

85. Ibid.

86. Moltmann's description of faith, its substance and its purpose, is always difficult to determine especially given his commitment to universal salvation. See Moltmann, *The Coming of God*, 244ff.

87. Moltmann, *Way of Jesus Christ*, 182.

88. Ibid., 183.

will all creation be able to say: 'True and just, Lord, are all thy judgments' (Rev 16:7)."

Throughout all this Moltmann maintains that Christ's death on the cross can only be an atonement if we see God in it. Yet, "the crucified Christ has nothing to do with a God of retribution, or a divine judge presiding over a criminal court."[89] Furthermore, even though ideas about atonement and reconciliation "go back to the Jewish-Christian community," where Jesus' death is interpreted as expiation and the preaching of the cross contains echoes of Leviticus 16 and Isaiah 53 (cf. 1 Cor 15:3) this could not be compatible with the resurrection. Moltmann admits the possibility of Christ's death portrayed as "expiatory sacrifice [that] takes our sins and God's judgment . . . and saves us from them and their consequences." However, on the basis of the resurrection, he claims that such notions are "bound to disappear once the sin disappears." He asserts that neither the scapegoat nor "Suffering Servant" could return by way of resurrection despite the poet's mention that "He [the Servant] will see [his] seed, he will prolong his days . . . Therefore I will give him the many as a portion, and he will receive the mighty as spoil" (Isa 53:10, 12). Moltmann complains that notions of an expiatory death by Christ for us cut off his death from his resurrection.[90] Yet, one wonders what to make then of the continuation of Messiah Jesus' death scars in his resurrected (cf. John 20:27) and even glorified (cf. Rev 5:6) state? Moltmann deconstructs entirely any notion of God's wrath in order for it to become his compassion. Christ suffers God-forsakenness in a peculiar fashion above and beyond all others but in doing so "human sin is transmuted into the atoning suffering of God."[91]

While salvation of the human being is the immediate goal, the supervening goal is the justification of creation. "Justification is not a unique event, pin-pointed to a certain moment in time. It is a process which begins in the individual heart through faith, and leads to the just new world."[92] The resurrection of the murdered Christ is the beginning of a process whereby, eschatologically, all the dead are vindicated against death itself once it is destroyed: "With God's raising of the Christ murdered on the cross, a universal theodicy trial begins which can only be

89. Moltmann, *Spirit of Life*, 135.

90. Moltmann, *Way of Jesus Christ*, 188.

91. Moltmann, *Spirit of Life*, 136.

92. Moltmann, *Way of Jesus Christ*, 183.

completed eschatologically with the resurrection of all the dead and the annihilation of death's power—which is to say through the new creation of all things."[93]

The exact outcome of this universal theodicy trial is difficult to discern. On the one hand, the dead are vindicated against death and yet, on the other hand, there seems a distinct possibility in which they will be vindicated against God. Certainly God's need to be vindicated in their company lies at the heart of what Moltmann means for God to be ultimately glorified. Moltmann more or less distinguishes his description of salvation's consummation from Hegel's ultimate resolution of absolute Spirit by insisting (via Philippians 2) on distinct outcomes for both Father and Son.[94] However, and many have noticed this, that path seems distinct by a matter of degrees more than anything else. Interestingly, if we are permitted a second glance at Philippians 2, God is said to be glorified when "every knee bows, in heaven and upon the earth, and every tongue confesses that Messiah Jesus is Lord." There appears little if any need for the vindication of unquestionably innocent Jesus on Moltmann's path towards salvation—Moltmann gives the impression that every person bowing the knee and confessing Messiah Jesus as Lord is happy to do so as a matter of course.[95] Absent too is the sense in which the Lordship of Jesus might be vindicated by God's retributive subjugation of the Messiah's enemies "under his feet." (Ps 110:1; cf. Ps 2:9ff).[96]

If we may backtrack partially from the ultimate salvation picture, Moltmann does expect justifying faith to change the individual in the here and now—it is not merely theoretical. "Only justifying faith corresponds to the Christ crucified 'for us,' for it is only through justifying faith that the liberating power of Christ's resurrection is experienced."[97] Moltmann goes back to his Reformation roots to discuss the dialectic between Paul and the law and observes, "If the crucified Christ was counted among the sinners and 'made sin,' then the risen Christ liberates from the power of sin." The Spirit mediates life through the gospel of the risen Christ anticipating in believer's victory over death through libera-

---

93. Ibid.

94. Moltmann, *Coming of God*, 330.

95. The notion of reconciliation could easily be seen as a peace that results from total subjugation—willing or otherwise. See O'Brien, *Commentary on Philippians*.

96. See Moltmann, *Coming of God*, 240ff.

97. Moltmann, *Way of Jesus Christ*, 184.

tion from the power of sin. "God is just because he makes the unjust just and creates justice for those who suffer under injustice."[98]

Moltmann portrays the Spirit as the one who brings the justification of life. The Spirit of God brings life to a world that has become unjust by restoring righteousness to both the victims and perpetrators of injustice. From John 16:7f. the Spirit of truth convicts the world of sin and so begins the process of setting all things right. The Spirit of Christ accuses the guilty and defends the accused; He is the merciful judge all in one. Here again Moltmann criticizes Reformation descriptions of justification. He acknowledges continuity between the Reformers and Paul in descriptions of sin (cf. Rom 2–3) noting "the saving and justifying gospel is therefore directed with equal universality to all sinners, and calls them all to faith, 'for they are justified by grace as a gift through the redemption which is in Christ Jesus'"[99] (Rom 3:30). Moltmann finishes this off with a kind of doctrine of providence whereby the Spirit acts as judge to unsettle the wicked and give them no peace, to destabilize corrupt structures of violence. In the positive sense the Spirit makes Christ's atoning power present amongst the perpetrators but it is not clear to what end. The Spirit is the divine life of love that ensures that humanity is perpetuated despite its worst efforts. The Spirit makes it possible for people to be kind to each other where ever it might happen. The Spirit is the one who is responsible for anything right and just that actually does happen in the world.[100]

CONCLUSION

Here at the end we have gained something of the breadth of Moltmann's "open inviting path." Moltmann's description of salvation takes us from cruciform pains in the eternal and consubstantial love of Father, Son, and Spirit out through the "narrow wideness of the cross" towards the open horizon of the Spirit's salvific sympathy with all of creation. There are certainly sections of the journey where one feels angels, if not evangelicals, might fear to tread. As Webster reminds us, "God communicates

---

98. Ibid., 184.

99. Moltmann, *Spirit of Life*, 124.

100. Ibid., 143.

himself not out of lack but out of fullness:"[101] there is nothing in divine life that needs resolving. Moltmann's commitment to theodicy takes him on a particular route towards a doctrine of the God who is passible enough to grieve sin but not such that he might be angered over it. Nevertheless, his theological wrestling with the significance of the cross for God plays an important role in ensuring that our dogmatic assertions concerning God's aseity, however eloquent, remain assertions.

For Moltmann we have seen that the scope of God's saving actions is directly proportional to God's need for absolute justification. This may accord with the prophet's words, "I take no pleasure in the death of the wicked" (Ezek 33:11), and thus the promise of a new creation without death (Rev 21:6). However, Moltmann's insistence that salvation is from tragedy leaves behind "early Jewish Christian" portrayals of Messiah Jesus as Lord. Thus, instead of the Son empowered by the Spirit to entrust himself to the Father's promise in order to exhaust divine wrath towards sin, we have the desperate victim of inexplicable circumstance acting as the channel through which "all things are made new." Instead of the Father justifying the righteousness of the Son by raising him in the power of the Spirit, and vindicating him over and against the enemies of salvation, we have the therapeutic grief of the Spirit ensuring that life is indomitable. Finally, it is in this hope (God will make everything better) that we are to journey into the wide-open future of God's glory—a path obviously rougher for many.

101. Webster, "God's Perfect Life," 149.

8

Moltmann's Ecclesiology in Evangelical Perspective

Timothy Bradshaw

ECCLESIOLOGICAL ROOTS: BARTH AND BARMEN

MOLTMANN EXPLAINS HIS ECCLESIOLOGICAL and theological orientation in 1952:

> The Protestant state churches, which had kept silent or rejoiced in the Hitler period, did not appeal to me. I was impressed only by the Confessing Church, with the Barmen Theological Declaration of 1934 and its clear Yes and No. However, it could not establish itself in the post-war period. When after 1945 Adenauer and Bishop Dibelius restored the old 1933 conditions, though these had not hindered Hitler and the German Christians, I joined the groups which succeeded the Confessing Church, the "Brotherhoods" and the "Society for Protestant Theology." And these were critical of both politics and the churches.[1]

Moltmann was powerfully attracted initially to Barth's ecclesiology, ultimately moving to go beyond its christocentric theology despite its record as having proved a hard rock in the face of the Nazification of the church during the 1930s. In particular Moltmann found the

---

1. Moltmann, *How I Have Changed*, 14.

famous *Barmen Declaration*,[2] written by Barth in 1934 for the Protestant churches in Germany, to have been a powerful expression of the Christian gospel in facing up to the infiltration of all cultural ideologies into the churches. *Barmen* issued the crystal clear message that there is "one Word of God," who is Jesus Christ, and that to seek to add to that one Word, to coordinate other ideals and programs to that of Christ, is to contaminate the church. To place the swastika next to the cross, and *Mein Kampf* next to the Bible, as was done by the "German Christians," was to bring idolatry into the holy of holies. The German Christians desired to participate fully in this new nationalistic way of life, a way of action and being as a people, a *Volk* with its own particular vocation and civilization, its own *Volkstum*. For Barth this was to allow false idolatries, cultural and experiential feelings of German identity and aspiration, to condition Christian theology. It had led to a ghastly coordination of the anti-Christ with Christ, a displacement of the truth of Jesus Christ, a new lordship in the church.

Perhaps the most famous Catholic theologian to allow himself to be swept up in the cultural euphoria of the Nazi revolution was Karl Adam, who saw Hitler in messianic tones as the liberator of the German genius who revealed the unity of German blood and identity, who epitomized "our German self, the *homo Germanus*," a "man of the south, the Catholic south."[3] How this God-given moment in creation and culture could be related to Catholic Christianity, for Adam, was through the Thomistic scheme of grace presupposing nature: "The dependence of Catholic Christianity upon a living national *Volkstum* is a direct consequence of that principle with which the Catholic Church and its theology describes the relationship of grace to nature . . ."[4] Here indeed was a vital "point of contact," the spirit becomes effective "on the blood, in the blood, through the blood," as grace completes nature, coordinating Catholic dogma with Nazi racial doctrine.

Barth's voice proved to be one of the truly great theological models of Christian theology and theology forged in the deepest possible crisis of culture and politics on the world stage. And yet, as Scholder says, this piercingly one-sided approach had its problems and in particular, "Its crucial weakness lay in the fact that the church's concentration on

2. Found in, e.g., Cochrane, *The Church's Confession Under Hitler*, 237–42.

3. Scholder, *The Churches and the Third Reich*, 427.

4. Ibid.

theological existence blocked direct insight into the significance of the Jewish question."[5] This perceived narrowness of approach shifted Moltmann from his early deep adherence to Barth and Barmen to a theology and ecclesiology that wanted a wider angle on theological existence for today, an angle that would not be able to transcend theologically such dire issues as mass persecution of human beings and their genocidal murder. It would, of course, be grossly unfair to Barth to imply that he in any way turned away from such horrific political criminality, and indeed his christocentric theology played out against it, as against South African Apartheid.[6] Moltmann tells us that after 1945 only the Barmen church impetus had given any encouragement for a new start to churches that had so signally failed the test of the 1930s and had revealed their flaws by being swept up in cultural enthusiasm to the point of distorting their theology and ecclesiology. Moltmann was impressed with Barmen and its clear "yes and no."

It is interesting also to note that Moltmann, prior to writing his *Theology of Hope*, found Barth's *Church Dogmatics* akin to a "beautiful dream: too beautiful to be true on this earth, from the annihilation of which in the war we had just escaped. Only the doctrine of predestination with its theology of the cross (in *Church Dogmatics* II.2) touched my heart."[7] In terms of the doctrine of the church, Barth relates this at the deepest level to the doctrine of election set out in *Church Dogmatics* II.2. Reconciliation, for Barth, is the event of God's gracious election fulfilled objectively in Jesus Christ and subjectively in people by the Holy Spirit. Christology, after the resurrection of Jesus from the dead, entails the church, since the resurrection of Jesus Christ from the dead means that God has decided that Christ would not be Christ without his own people, that Christology is inclusive.[8] The church is very closely bound to its Lord: "Where this community lives by the Holy Spirit, Jesus Christ Himself lives on earth, in the world and in history."[9] The interval between the resurrection and the parousia of Christ is to give humanity space to come to confess the saving truth of God's act in Christ for us. The church is vitally important in this self-declaration of the truth of

---

5. Ibid., 439.

6. See Horn, "From Barmen to Belhar and Kairos," 105–20, esp. 113.

7. Moltmann, *History and the Triune God*, 1991, 126.

8. Barth, *Church Dogmatics*, 4/1 354.

9. Ibid., 353.

Jesus Christ in the world. Moltmann retains this note of the church's role in witness in the world, but loosens his theology and ecclesiology from Barth's anchor in the electing will of God realized in the community which God has determined should always be with Christ in the Spirit, indeed should be a form of Christ in history.

> At that time we were very Barthian and wanted to get away from the misalliances of "throne and altar," "faith and the bourgeoisie," "religion and capitalism," characteristic of culture Protestantism, and move in the direction of "Christ alone" and radical discipleship in the service of peace . . . [W]e sought the centre of scripture and became exclusively christocentric, *solus Christus*. However, we got into difficulties with this narrow understanding of Barth and this "Barmen orthodoxy" when we wanted to give positive answers to the political possibilities and cultural challenges of the post-war period. Every "centre" has a surrounding area, otherwise it is not a centre.[10]

We might say that Moltmann wished to give theological, rather than just practical, significance to this "surrounding area," the area of the world and history. Moltmann felt constrained by Barth's very tight, albeit crystal clear, christological focus. He felt the need to expand from this so as to embrace political and cultural questions thrown up in history as a *matter of theology*, since such phenomena were not disconnected from God, the God of history.

EXODUS CHURCH

Moltmann's *Theology of Hope* sets out his new pathway in theology and church, stimulated by the "principle of hope," a principle engaging him through the Jewish Marxist thinker Ernst Bloch. For Bloch "the principle of hope" is the driving force of human initiative and from that he looks for the arrival of the undreamt of "new thing" from the future. The future is decisive rather than the past, the present being the seedbed of the tendencies and latent urges which open out on the future and which we must seize upon and develop. The nerve of the concept of history is "the new," says Bloch and Moltmann agrees.[11] History must be capable of real

10. Moltmann, *How I Have Changed*, 14–15.
11. Moltmann, *Theology of Hope*, 263.

meaning and genuine growth in time, and this requires the possibility of the new and a denial of determinism from the past. Historical momentum involves the possibility and hope of salvation and also therefore the possibility of danger in the unexpected future. And history itself must be theologically significant as coming from God and for the purposes of God. This is the main point of Moltmann's move from Barth, the need to grant history real theological significance, the mission of God in this ongoing movement. The only sign of the omnipotent divinity of God we have is "the fireglow" of the raising of Christ from the dead. "That God is God accordingly cannot be the eternal source and background of the proclamation of Christ, but must be the promised, but as yet unattained, future goal of Christian proclamation. Barth's very expressions, in their originally Platonic terms, of the 'eternal Spirit' and the eternally self-identical 'substance' of the Bible show a tendency towards uneschatological, and then also unhistorical, thinking, which is still to be met even in the later terms of the word of God and his self-revelation."[12]

We are on the way to the fullness of revelation, it is not yet here, its completeness lies ahead. "This universal and immediate presence of God," says Moltmann, "is not the source from which faith comes, but the end to which it is on the way. It is not the ground on which faith stands, but it is the object at which it aims."[13]

Moltmann is stressing the fact of our existence in history and its importance. Epistemologically he is not really concerned to establish facts nor develop meanings. He looks to Scripture and its narratives and finds their eschatological impetus, their flesh and blood events, to be of real importance issuing from the hand of God from the future. The resurrection of Jesus is the key event in this trajectory of life and faith. The church's statements are based on what happened to Jesus, his death and resurrection, and these events are about one figure, bridging into the historical Jesus and his life. This fact of the resurrection is the revelation of the kingdom of God in history, the lordship of God in the death and resurrection of Jesus, a transformation of the idea of the kingdom and one experienced by the Christian church. This goes beyond ethics and personal self-understanding, it is a new creation and a call to trust in the promise of God who is drawing us on into the future fulfillment of the kingdom. We are called "to suffer under the

12. Ibid., 281.
13. Ibid., 282.

forsakenness and unredeemedness of all things and their subjection to vanity."[14] This kingdom entails the "future of Jesus Christ," meaning not the awaited return of someone who is absent so much as his imminent arrival, his presence which must be awaited and which leaves us in the dialectic of suffering and hope, the experience of being in history and wrestling with it, a very gritty and realist view of the Christian path. In contrast to Barth, "The revelation of Christ cannot then merely consist in what has already happened in hidden ways being unveiled for us to see, but it must be expected in events which fulfill the promise that is given with the Christ event. This Christ event cannot then itself be understood as fulfilling all promises, so that after this there remains only the sequel of its being unveiled for all to see."[15] Moltmann here brings the Christian view of revelation and kingdom into history in a fully realist way and breaks with Barth. "What then does the future of Christ bring? Not a mere repetition of history, and not only an unveiling of it, but something which has not yet so far happened through Christ . . . the fulfillment of the promised righteousness of God in all things."[16] The Christian disciple is to live in this dialectic of dying and rising, the baptismal pattern, suffering and rejoicing, secure in the hope that is set before us. This is the dialectical shape of the messianic hope and the essence of what the church is.

The final chapter of the *Theology of Hope* is entitled "Exodus Church" and sets out "the question of the concrete form assumed by a live eschatological hope in modern society."[17] Moltmann understands the body of Christian disciples, *Christenheit*,[18] as the pilgrim people of God, and he defines the social shape of this body in modern society. This means Christians in their daily walks of life, not merely as organized by church structures. This "weekday" role of Christians in their worldly callings in society was a Reformation imperative that Moltmann feels has been lost and is crucial to recovering the eschatological understanding of Christian existence and the radical summons of hope and resisting accommodation to the norms of this world. The Christians

14. Ibid., 223.

15. Ibid., 228.

16. Ibid., 228–29.

17. Ibid., 304.

18. Ibid., 304 "*Christenheit*" is the original German term, meaning the totality of Christians, in the translated edition here rendered "Christianity," the belief system.

in the world are a "world-transforming, future-seeking missionary practice,"[19] a movement seeking to change the world rather than interpret and understand it, as said Marx, but, unlike Marx, with a hope in God to lead this movement onwards. We might say that this looks like the *"Christus Victor"* view of the early church with its eschatological expectation for a new age entirely brought about by the God of Jesus Christ who had won the victory over the oppressive powers of darkness, the second Adam who reversed the disobedience of the first Adam. But Moltmann is opening the process of the victory up and saying that the body of Christians in the world not only participate in this victory as already won but *enact it* as they press forward in history to the future, in faith. This is the "historifying of the world in the Christian mission," its transformation through the effort of the faithful in and through the God of hope. This transforming mission, which it seems for Moltmann *is* the church at its deepest level, requires a confidence and hope in the world. This is a kind of critical realism about history, "seeking for what is possible in this world in order to grasp it and realize in the direction of the promised future of the righteousness, the life and the kingdom of God."[20] The church is the Christian way of being directed towards the messianic righteousness in hope, always open to the coming of God, always seeking obediently to act as a counter-cultural movement against compromising with the worldly way.

Moltmann prefaces his ecclesiology of "exodus church" with a penetrating review of the place of Christianity in modern society, using Hegel as his guide.[21] Postindustrial Western society has freed itself from the domination of religion, and as a result Christianity found itself responding to this change in various ways. Firstly it took a turn into subjectivity and privatization of faith, *"cultus privatus"* replacing the *"cultus publicus,"*[22] since society as a whole was becoming secular and faith an individual personal kind of experience. Rationalization has disenchanted the world, but humanity in faith can reflect on its own spirituality and sense of transcendence; God is no longer the God of history, but of our private faith-existence, according to Moltmann's critical appraisal.

19. Ibid., 288.

20. Ibid., 289.

21. For a probing evangelical appraisal of the use of the narrative of the exodus by political theology, see O'Donovan, *The Desire of the Nations*, 22.

22. Moltmann, *Theology of Hope*, 310.

Christianity tends to retreat from issues of objective social justice and political engagement. We live a torn existence, in the bleak rationalized, managed society of secularism alongside an inward subjectivity. This leads to Christianity ceasing to act as a thorn in the flesh of society towards its less than humane ways of conducting itself.

Also religion becomes a cult of co-humanity in our secular modern era; Christianity offers a place for community among people in their bleak alienation of life in our harsh economically driven world. Christian congregations can offer warmth and neighborliness of an "authentic" kind, not available elsewhere, a kind of Noah's Ark in a cold lonely world.[23] The church in this role is a place of refuge, rather than engaging with the surrounding world. And thirdly Moltmann sees religion as the "cult of the institution," and here he means that Christianity still has a role in many societies as the cultural "glue" remaining for many people, a tradition with which they identify, without which they would have no cultural orientation at all. This is the residual "folk religion" or cultural Christianity, still present in the form of established churches in England, Germany, and Scandinavian nations. This is Christianity with a role of "an institutionalized non-committal outlook," one existing within the secular milieu of society in general, and not an agency to challenge or engage society with the message of the gospel.

It must be said that this last point of Moltmann's describing a background social role foisted on the church has been neutralized by the very fast advent of "multiculturalism" in Europe, as a large Islamic minority presence has asserted itself and led to secularists and church leaders to push any "established" representative Christian presence firmly out of the public forum.[24] It remains true, however, that the "non committal" attitude of national or "folk" churches persists, but now for the added reason that any other attitude might "offend" other religions. The "beneficial unquestioningness" of established Christianity remains, perhaps because such an attitude is considered safer than to allow real inter-religious debate. States do not want ideological differences to be highlighted and established churches may in fact be gaining the role of "ministries of religion," agencies for ensuring that all religions are kept happy and quiet as they cater for their own communities.

---

23. Ibid., 320.
24. See, e.g., Bradshaw, *Chaos or Control?*, 4–46.

Moltmann follows up his acute sociological description of the place of churches in society with "Christianity within the horizons of the expectation of the kingdom of God" and "the calling of Christians in society," the two final sections of "Exodus Church." Essentially he sees Christians, the church, engaging with society and culture in a counter cultural "eschatological" fashion: whenever that dynamic ceases, it is no longer Christian, no longer church, but is accommodating itself to the ways of the world. The church might even be said to be defined as a *via negativa*, a continual thorn in the flesh of the prevailing mores. The church should not be a privatized, subjective state giving meaning for the individual, nor a Noah's Ark community of shelter from the flood waters of cold secularism, nor a cultural chaplaincy to society in general, offering rituals for births, marriages, and deaths. *Christenheit*, the body of believers, is like the yeast in the dough, to leaven the lump and make the bread rise, or the salt in the stew to give it taste, although in a way that involves change and challenge rather than comfortable synthesis, according the Moltmann. Moltmann's *Christenheit* is taken to oppose and challenge the culture of industrial society, the bourgeois lifestyle of complacent selfishness, and "venture on an exodus" to break away from the "Babylonian captivity" of the roles being placed on the church as just set out. Christians are not to be conformed to this age but to "break through social stagnation" by preaching hope: "Hope alone keeps life—including public, social life—flowing and free."[25] "Change" seems to be a key imperative for the church, and stagnation, settling down, is to be challenged at every turn by the "exodus church."

We should also note that the changes and challenges to the *Christenheit* in history are, as Moltmann agrees with Hegel, the fruit of the movement of the Spirit "acting precisely in this torn and divided state of objectification and subjectivity. It is not the romanticist's self-preservation from this tornness and his way of shutting himself off from it, but only self-emptying surrender to it that proves the power of the spirit."[26] The new thing can be achieved as the Spirit moves from the future, and the church, or *Christenheit*, dies to live, bows to the suffering and bewilderment produced by the secularizing culture, so as to find itself and its mission. *Christenheit* "has its essence and goal not in itself and not in its own existence, but lives from something and exists for

25. Moltmann, *Theology of Hope*, 324.
26. Ibid., 310.

something which reaches far beyond itself."[27] It is open to the future, God's future mediating the eschaton into history as a process whose goal can be attained by following the promise given by God in Christ. Baptism and the Lord's Supper are future oriented practices of the church, sealing people for "the future of the kingdom of God" and waiting expectantly seeking communion with the coming Lord: the kingdom of God is *at* hand, rather than being *on* hand or at our disposal. Likewise, the word of God in the church points us forwards and is never grasped, transcending itself. The hope of the church is oriented by the horizon of expectation, which gives hope shape and meaning.

This orientating horizon is described by Moltmann in terms resonant of Hegel: "Only when a meaningful horizon of expectation can be given articulate expression does man acquire the possibility and the freedom to expend himself, to objectify himself and expose himself to the pain of the negative, without bewailing the accompanying risk and surrender of his free subjectivity."[28] With this horizon of expectation to catch us, this life of self-giving is the gaining of life. To lose our life is to gain it, to surrender our freedom to this promised end means true freedom overcoming the pain of the negative. And this horizon is given to us by Christ's mission to the world, "it has its nature as the body of the crucified and risen Christ only where in specific acts of service it is obedient to its mission to the world."[29] The church becomes the church when it dies to live, bows its head in service to the world. Here we perceive Moltmann's ongoing debt to Barth whose ecclesiology is marked by an actualism of faith according to which the church truly becomes the church as it lives in faith to its Lord. Here, for Moltmann, the church is truly the church *as it serves* the world in utter self abnegation and obedience, in trust of the oncoming future. This is life in the Spirit. The church is this mission, this Christ-shaped and Christ-inspired way of being in the world and to the world. The church discovers itself in and as it engages in this costly service and suffering. The church is "to take up mankind—or to put it concretely, the Church takes up the society with which it lives—into its own horizon of expectation of the eschatological fulfillment of justice, life, humanity and sociability"[30] and lives its life

27. Ibid., 325.
28. Ibid., 327.
29. Ibid.
30. Ibid., 328.

for this. This is the "apostolate" of the church in which it "finds its own essence—namely that which makes it the Church of God."[31] The church is for the world and for the kingdom of God.

The calling of Christians in society is accordingly one of struggle against the complacency of the status quo in Western societies certainly, questioning unjust structures and changing history towards justice and peace. The church is to unsettle and be a catalyst for change. The horizon of the kingdom of God calls us to be for what is good and liberating for all, to suffer in that calling, to discover the cross of the present. This is "creative discipleship," refusing to be conformed to the wisdom of this age but to change it, and this matters for our being in the world, in our professions and social roles, not simply in church life. This discipleship involves a consciousness raising: "It must consist in the theoretical and practical recognition of the structure of historic process and develop- ment" and of future potentialities. Moltmann's closing pages of *Theology of Hope* offer a highly sophisticated analysis of the Western psychosocial condition of people in modern society, a condition of estrangement, of individualism and frustration. Marx's prescription has not cured this, nor has inward reflection and ironic detachment resulting in an unsocial human experience. The Christian horizon brings hope, finding oneself in and with others, the call to spend ourselves for the kingdom and to reshape our social and political institutions. This is not a matter of a socialist revolution in the strength of humanity, of self redemption, but of openness to God and hope that the resurrection of Jesus must "bring about a new understanding of the world . . . To disclose to it the horizon of the future of the crucified Christ is the task of the Christian Church."[32]

Moltmann's first great book brings us a doctrine of the church clearly in line with the theology of liberation. The church is an agency in society that knows the truth of history and its goal and has the min- istry of opening up sinful structures that entrap and estrange people, in line with the kingdom of God taught, initiated and anticipated by Jesus. The great emphasis is on the church as action, as mission, its essence is in this activity of transformatory provocation to change. Individual sin is not in focus, but that does not mean it is not a concern of Moltmann's ecclesiology. In terms of classical evangelical theology and practice, Moltmann can be taken as making an emphasis rather

31. Ibid.
32. Ibid., 338.

than rejecting the other, more individual, one. As is the case with the best liberation theology, the Old Testament strikes important notes, as the "exodus" theme used by Moltmann indicates. There is a prophetic, and in terms of the kingdom, apocalyptic, imperative sounding through his ecclesiology, the word of the Lord denouncing wrong in the name of divine justice, harmony and peace.

We might characterize this "exodus church" as striving for sanctification and in a corporate mode: the church is awakened to the historical process and is called to implement the Christ-shaped kingdom. Engaging the ossified static structures of society that cement the preferential option for the wealthy, Moltmann teaches the church to become what she really should be in sanctifying social patterns, in social reform. As this happens, we infer, individual lives will be sanctified and opened to the Spirit. This happens as we suffer, endure the "pain of the negative," "die to live," a way of being resonant with Hegel's reading of Christianity. Moltmann does stress the historical and social process of the church's mission as it engages the structures, or we could say the powers and principalities as interpreted by many theologians of liberation. Moltmann is urging Christians to gain an awareness of the process of history and to be inspired to "light a candle" rather than curse the darkness. He is not urging a Marxist bloody revolution of violent seizure of power and it would unfair to see Moltmann as offering Marxism in Christian dress.[33]

In terms of the premillennialist discussion so lively among evangelicals in the USA, Moltmann's ecclesiology teaches the reverse of the church ruling the world in any sense or at any juncture in time. Rather, as we will now see, the Christian way is the rejection of power, the way of the "crucified God."

THE CHURCH OF THE ECONOMIC TRINITY

Moltmann's successive volumes enrich this ecclesiology with a radical trinitarian theology which never retracts his earlier vision but shows its grounding in the divine economy of Father, Son, and Spirit. This development was signaled radically in Moltmann's *The Crucified God*, which sought to think through the logic of divine sympathy with the

---

33. For an interesting diagrammatic demonstration of Marx's view of history in comparison with Jewish eschatology, see Russell, *History of Western Philosophy*, 383.

godforsaken, suffering, miserable human beings, a sympathy enacted and revealed at Calvary. With Barth before him Moltmann insisted that God was in Christ suffering for the human race and that this revealed the very character of God and the fact of the Trinity. Jesus Christ is the divine Son who suffers death for us, his Father suffering the abandonment of his Son and indeed hands over or delivers up the Son to annihilation,[34] while the Son simultaneously gives up his life freely and lovingly for the godforsaken, plumbing the depths of their despair and suffering. In this act the Son and the Father are at one. This event "contains community between Jesus and his Father in separation, and separation in community."[35] Here is the very core of Moltmann's theology.

This historical event is also an event in God's own trinitarian life, which itself is of an historical nature, and is disclosed by Jesus' death and resurrection. "Christian faith," says Moltmann, rather than using the word "church," "does not believe in a new 'idea' of God. In the fellowship of the crucified Christ it finds itself in a new 'situation of God' and participates in that with all its existence."[36] This has happened and its significance is that the faithful find themselves in the trinitarian history of God and theologize about God accordingly. This theology recognizes what has happened and what is true, and it accords with the whole Jewish experience of God. Christ communicates the Fatherhood of God and the power of the Spirit for Christians, in parallel to the Hebrew experience of the divine *Shekinah* presence of the transcendent God in all the suffering of the people. The death of the Son opens the covenant to all, unconditionally. "But in that God himself creates the conditions for communion with God through his self-humiliation in the death of the crucified Christ and through his exaltation of man in the resurrection of Christ, this community becomes a gracious, presuppositionless and universal community of God with all men in their common misery."[37] Here is another statement of ecclesiology, describing the church as the group who know they are loved by God in their unhappy consciousness from the pure grace of God suffering with them. Sinful miserable humanity can know it is accepted freely, since Christ has occupied the place of the criminally godforsaken: "Man is taken up, without limitations and

34. Moltmann, *The Crucified God*, 241.

35. Ibid., 243–44.

36. Ibid., 274.

37. Ibid., 275.

conditions, into the life and suffering, the death and resurrection of God." And this life of communion with Christ is in the trinitarian life of God. The emphasis is on a church suffering with Christ, rather than being forgiven and justified in Christ.

Moltmann here is viewing the church as transcending religion and institution, rather disciples are "taken up" into this divine life story. As Barth teaches "The Holy Spirit as the "abolition [*Aufhebung*] of religion" in the Hegelian sense of a taking up and exaltation of it, indeed for Moltmann a universalizing of participation in God. This is no smooth pantheism, however, blurring the finite into the infinite since: "a trinitarian theology of the cross perceives God in the negative element and therefore the negative element in God, and in this dialectical way is panentheistic."[38] God has absorbed the pain of what opposes God in the death of the particular man Jesus at Calvary, and so made communion, at-one-ment, a reality in which we participate. God has journeyed into the very heart of annihilating darkness and begins to become "all in all." We can recognize suffering and hopeless rejection in God, taken up, reconciled, detoxified. Even Auschwitz is taken into God, God was on the gallows there and the faith of Jesus the Jew was expressed, we might say, as the *Shema* was prayed during the brutalization and murder of the worshippers. Moltmann points to the final resurrection of the dead for the healing of such victims, for the "abolition of all rule and authority," for the annihilation of death, then the Son will hand the kingdom over to the Father, then there will be eternal joy. "This will be the sign of the completion of the trinitarian history of God and the end of world history, the overcoming of the history of man's sorrow and the fulfillment of his history of hope."[39] The church is the herald of this good news of hope for the healing of the nations.

Here we have a remarkable christological, staurological, and trinitarian view of *Christenheit* in the life of the economic Trinity taking up our history and promising a future of joy overcoming sorrow. This note of future joy is welcome as a development of the ecclesiology of the "exodus church" with its stress on struggle and suffering to transform the world. Evangelical theology, of course, wishes to press the expiatory core of the death of Jesus, the Son of God, bearing our sin as well as sharing our pain. Moltmann's ecclesiology seems to stress sanctification

38. Ibid., 277.
39. Ibid., 278.

by suffering with Christ. But Moltmann's reading does offer a view of the church as humanity renewed by the suffering of Christ, called to walk the way of the cross in the power of the Spirit, and to herald this good news to all the nations in a non-judgmental way. We are very much "in Christ" as the members of the church, on the basis of free grace. And we are given a gritty summons to costly discipleship about the real problems of life and God's presence with us in these. Evangelicalism, if not formal evangelical theology, has been prone to lapse into a curious lack of realism, into a pretended cheerfulness as if to admit problems were to betray a lack of holiness—an odd habit for Christians who stress justification by grace rather than by personal capacity to cope perfectly with difficulty and tragedy, to need to seem serene at all times.

We should note Moltmann's economic Trinity is linked to his doxological Trinity of the completion of history, rather than an eternal Trinity of a Platonic structure as he sees it. Whereas Calvin and Barth see the church rooted in the eternal electing will of God to be for us in Christ and his saving work, Moltmann eschatologizes this and roots salvation in the future hope of the coming messianic kingdom, the trinitarian fulfillment of history. The church trusts in the Father who gave up his Son for us and takes us up in him into fellowship in the Spirit. This is a given reality of grace, a whole new way of life and the church knows it and must herald it to all nations. This good news is rooted in the divine love which has endured the pain of human suffering, and we can add, this pain absorbed by God includes human shunning of the divine love, as shown in the prophetic symbolism of Hosea and his painful buying back of his unfaithful wife from slavery. The church is a dynamic prophetic and messianic movement, announcing the truth of the suffering God and enacting it physically in and to the world.

SHAPE OF THE CHURCH

Moltmann's work following his radical treatise *The Crucified God* draws out the implications of that trinitarian reconciliation of humanity, recognized and followed by the church. But, in contrast to the teaching of Barth, Jesus' work is not yet completed, the reality of ongoing history is linked essentially to the completion of history by the Son. Only then will the ambiguity of history in all its terror and misery, which make it hard for people to have faith, be removed and God the Father glorified. *The Church in the Power of the Spirit* tells us that "God experiences history in order to effect history. He goes out of himself in order to gather into himself. He is vulnerable, takes suffering and death on himself in order to heal, to liberate and to confer new life. The history of God's suffering in the passion of the Son and the sighings of the Spirit serves the history of God's joy in the Spirit and his completed felicity at the end."[40] Moltmann deeply respects the christocentrism of the *Barmen Declaration* of 1934, but wishes to expand it so as to say that the church is present wherever the manifestation of the Spirit takes place. This happens wherever enmities are overcome, where what is torn apart is healed and mended, divisions reconciled. Unity is the will of the Father and this process must be continued in history so as to fulfill the work of the Son as negation and destructiveness is endured and overcome. The church must engage in this, and recognize itself where it happens. This today must include the work of those who repair and protect the created order from the depredations of human greed and exploitation, the green guardians of God's world. "The whole being of the Church is marked by participation in the history of God's dealings with the world."[41] The boundaries of the church, for Moltmann, seem to be much more flexible and porous than its institutional forms allow.

The church's shape is loose knit, is fellowship in the Spirit echoing the messianic way of Jesus' wisdom and praxis. There is almost a Franciscan quality to Moltmann's ecclesiology as he draws the cosmos into its scope, the well being of the ecological order, brother sun and sister moon. Fellowship with the poor is a major note of the church as it disturbs the complacencies of the bourgeois western societies. The history of Jesus, his lifestyle, is vitally important to Moltmann in his shaping of how the church should be. Just as Barth spoke of the "Way of the Son into the Far Country," so Moltmann speaks of *The Way of Jesus Christ*, adding the subtitle, "Christology in Messianic Dimensions." Ecclesiologically Moltmann looks to the Synoptic Gospels for the way of being human lived out by Jesus, as did Francis of Assisi, and challenges the churches to live accordingly. This can be a helpful message for evangelicalism, which has tended to be accused of preferring Paul to the Gospels in shaping church life and praxis.

40. Moltmann, *The Church in the Power of the Spirit*, 64.

41. Ibid., 65.

But Moltmann cannot be said to pit the Jesus of the Gospels against the Jesus of Paul or other New Testament witnesses. His eschatology is very Pauline, as is his teaching on the Spirit indwelling human beings. The kingdom of the Son is marked by suffering servanthood, that of the Spirit by the creative energies of the new creation, from the eschaton but arriving in advance, pointing us towards the completion of the creation and towards our deification.[42] There is almost an eschatological anthropology being stated here, not simply a doctrine of the Spirit in the church: "If through the Spirit men and women in their physical nature become God's temple (1 Cor 6:13bff.), then they are anticipating the glory in which the whole world will become the temple of the triune God (Rev 21:3)." The church is the church most fully as it embraces the cause of the poor and godforsaken, as it acts in the way of Jesus, and this is to be indwelt by the Spirit bring the energies of the kingdom, the great eschatological completion of creation. Again the boundaries of the church seem to be defined by the triune God, certainly in the view of God and the final kingdom.

Moltmann's developing theology expanded its horizons and this is hardly surprising given that eschatology was always such an imperative. The fulfillment of all things must embrace all the created order, apart from its abusive evil and rejection of God its creator. This will include the cosmos itself, groaning until its ultimate liberation (Rom 8:18–26). In discussing social forms of the church at levels from the very local to the global, and in the context of global military, ecological, and social dangers, Moltmann underlines the fellowship of the Holy Spirit:

> which crosses frontiers and denominational borders, and a new orientation towards the kingdom of God and the new creation of things. Hitherto the kingdom of God has generally been viewed as orientated towards the church. The important thing today is to orientate the church towards the kingdom of God. Only then can the churches take the step which today is the most important step of all: to see the themselves not merely as a church of human beings but as a church of the cosmos, and to perceive that the social and ecological crises in the world are crises in their own life too.[43]

Needless to say, there is no contradiction between a biblically orientated evangelical theology and a deep concern for the cosmos and social

---

42. Moltmann, *The Trinity and the Kingdom of God*, 213.
43. Moltmann, *The Spirit of Life*, 247–48.

well being, and Moltmann's wide horizons, expanded beyond humanity, are rooted in the openness of the cosmos to the future of God.

Christologically this works out in terms of "the greater Christ," and Moltmann's concern about impending ecological catastrophe makes him speak of "Christ chaos" in the light of the reduction of much of our planet to a rubbish heap.[44] Indeed this situation is now so serious as to warrant speaking of the conversion of Christian faith itself, challenging its anthropocentrism towards a cosmocentric faith. Christ is the head of the reconciled cosmos: "the body of Christ is the crucified and raised body of Jesus—the body of Christ is the church—the body of Christ is the whole cosmos."[45] Moltmann is not, we need to note, collapsing Christ into a cosmic mysticism here, as if to define Christ in terms of natural rhythms of nature, rather "Cosmic Christology talks about a reconciled, Christ pervaded, cosmos and in this way differs from every other cosmic mysticism, old and new, whether Indian or post-modern."[46] This is surely an agreeable insight for evangelical theology. For Moltmann the ontological foundation for cosmic Christology is the death of Christ, inseparable from his resurrection and future consummation. It is this great eschatological creative act that offers personal redemption and this must include the redemption of nature. And moreover the cosmos is not only "nature" but includes the wealth of cultures in the world, "the heathen": Christianity was not just one more competing religion but instead: "it acted as the peacemaker and unifying community of the Creator and Reconciler of all things . . . The purpose was integration into the reconciliation and peace which was the eschatological horizon of the cosmos."[47]

While evangelical theology might query this emphasis, it would generally welcome the view that Christianity is not simply one more religion in the world, rather it is the self-disclosure and saving act of God the creator, who cares about the cosmos, its animals, materials, structures, and peoples. The church is therefore a guardian or trustee for humanity, in obedience to Christ "who made peace by the blood of his cross" at the heart of the cosmos, and in whom all things hold together (Col 1:15–20). Moltmann's left of centre political commitments

44. Moltmann, *The Way of Jesus Christ*, 275.

45. Ibid., 275.

46. Ibid., 278.

47. Ibid., 284.

fall under this aspect of his theology, he thinks that social wrongs and injustices are to be repaired by engaging and improving social structures for the poor and dispossessed. How this is done is a matter of political and economic debate no doubt, but that it is a Christian imperative is not, as the Lausanne Covenant proclaims, for example.[48]

CHURCH STRUCTURE

Finally let us see how Moltmann deals with church order. He deploys his trinitarian theology, with its social perichoretic shape, to fashion a thunderous attack on all absolute political and ecclesiastical power and authority. He connects monotheism to the phenomenon of absolute power structures and he champions social trinitarianism as its antidote.[49] The allegedly distant and controlling God is displaced by the loving Father, self-giving Son, and empathetic Spirit of the Christian gospel. Mono-episcopacy echoed the disaster of Constantinianism and ultimately turned the church into a line management organization, claiming power for itself and demonizing those outside it.[50] Friendship is the key model for church relationships, replacing the master-slave model of the Roman Imperial rule, and this leads Moltmann to conceive church order in terms of a local congregational perichoretic model of free interchange and appreciation. Many "free" evangelical ecclesiologies will welcome this wholeheartedly, especially Moltmann's stress on the priority of the local congregation and real friendship over against the regional and national structures of established churches, and mono-episcopal church order. Interestingly he is criticized by liberal and postmodern theologians for sacralizing human structures such as the family as vital for congregational life,[51] taken by critics to be a concession to bourgeois culture and ideology.

Moltmann's deconstruction of oppressive absolute lordship is found throughout his works, for example he calls for an end to patriarchy and

48. See Chester, "Lausanne Covenant," 537–39.

49. Otto, "Moltmann and the Anti-Monotheism Movement," 293–308.

50. Moltmann, *Theology and the Kingdom of God*, 140.

51. Sedgwick, "Anglican Theology," 178–93, 191. See, e.g., Moltmann's claim in *The Spirit of Life*, 246: "The genesis of the local congregation is the proclamation of the gospel and the celebration of the sacraments, but it is fed most of all by the tradition of Christian families."

an adoption of matrifocal culture in the church. He equates the absolutist God with the rise of the cruel impersonal machine model of life, the self-giving God of the Trinity deconstructs that to render a model of church and society of interactive love and friendship. He is criticized for a naiveté in his view of authority and power, for example by Stephen Sykes, and for sacralizing a socialistic political system that can be equally oppressive as a right of centre one.[52] It may be true that if a church does not uphold any structure for its use of power that can open the way for the most powerful personality to take control. "Office bearers" in the church—preachers or celebrants, for example—act in Christ's name, says Moltmann, and is keen to locate them as arising from the congregation and yet not as merely democratically representative, rather bringing the word of Christ to them.[53] Moltmann here is teaching standard congregationalist evangelical theology of the ministry,[54] rejecting clerical monotheism and hierarchy.

The traditional "marks of the church" are that it is one, holy, catholic, and apostolic: Moltmann's interpretation of these make a fitting way to conclude. The unity of the church is primarily that of Christ who gathers the church, rather than an institutional unity. The holiness of the church lies in Christ's holiness, and in Christian responsive holiness in poverty, self-giving, and joyful empathetic suffering. Apostolicity is eschatological, rather than a claim to a historic succession: instead the church lines up with the arrival of the Spirit from the future as it marches towards the eschaton in hope and joy. Catholicity is universality, openness to all, again a prefiguring of the eschatological completion of all things, conditioning prayer to this promised unity of the nations.[55] Moltmann's reinterpretation of these traditional marks is fresh and insightful.

CONCLUSION—SOME EVANGELICAL CRITICISM

This radical eschatological reorientation of ecclesiology is refreshing, it challenges any temptation of a beleaguered Western church to turn inwards on itself, to draw up the defenses against secularism and other

52. Sykes, *Power and Christian Theology*, 79.
53. Moltmann, *The Church in the Power of the Spirit*, 304.
54. See, e.g., Forsyth, *The Church and the Sacraments*, 1917.
55. Moltmann, *The Church in the Power of the Spirit*, 1977, 338–39.

faiths, and maintain itself during the siege. Moltmann offers an outward looking vision, catching the messianic note of ultimate optimism and telling us to ride this wave in hope and joy, while pointing us to the cost of discipleship in christological realism. This is no "cheap grace." Engaging with this theologian of hope and suffering can only be healthy for evangelical theology.

And yet evangelical theology will wish to register some questions about Moltmann's ecclesiology. This is a "servant model" of the church, combined with a "herald model," to use Dulles' classifications, and evangelicals find these actions of the church very necessary indeed.[56] We might suggest the term "suffering servant" model. But does Moltmann have a sufficient account of what the church is, the very identity of the church in the eyes of God; that is, the being of the church as well as its action? Here is the key question evangelicals may wish to put. In the New Testament the church is the bride of Christ, the body of Christ, beloved in a deep way paralleling that of husband and wife. The church's being is rooted in divine grace by her election and by the justifying grace of the cross and resurrection, in which the divine verdict of the Father was given, once and for all, *tetelestai*. This is the foundation of God's church. *Simul justus et peccator*, the Christian person is in Christ of the grace of Christ, and nothing can separate us from the love of God in Christ Jesus because of his "finished work." Yes this work calls us on into the future of creation, into the kingdom, into battle with social and political forces that oppose the way of Jesus Christ. But our salvation and being in Christ by the Spirit is sealed now, as well as in the future. Baptism, sacramental sealing of our new life in Christ is for Moltmann our sealing for the future of the kingdom that is being brought by the risen Christ, and the Lord's Supper is waiting for the coming Christ.[57] Evangelical ecclesiology wishes surely to add that Baptism is into the finished death of the Lord, once for all, to lead to a sharing of the risen life of Christ (Rom 6:4). This is a present reality, now, which is not to deny Moltmann's own emphasis resonating with Paul's affirmation that "we shall certainly be united with him in a resurrection like his" (Rom 6:5). The Christian knows that "our old self was crucified with him so that the sinful body might be destroyed and we might no longer be enslaved to sin" (Rom 6:6). The church has already the identity of being in Christ on

56. Dulles, *Models of the Church*.

57. Moltmann, *Theology of Hope*, 326.

the ground of his sacrifice for us, to free us from sin: our suffering is an outworking of this new given identity, existing now. Likewise conversion to Christ is a work of the Spirit now, rooted in God's eternity of love,[58] which surely does also entail a "conversion to the future"[59] and seeks the kingdom together with the Matthean community of the beatitudes, but is a given reality now, in the now of divine grace rooted in the divine electing will of the Trinity of love. In short, this focus of finality seems to be historicized by Moltmann, in utterly worthy fashion, into a future fulfillment, so much so that the present seems occluded.

The dialectic of suffering and hope is not, in fact, the primary dialectic of the gospel, which is sin and grace. "This universal and immediate presence of God," says Moltmann, "is not the source from which faith comes, but the end to which it is on the way. It is not the ground on which faith stands, but it is the object at which it aims."[60] As *Ephesians* tells us, the grace of the triune God is the ground of our faith, the ground of the church now, then and in the future. The New Testament envisages the concrete identifiable church as the object of Christ's special love, his "bride," the body of which he is the head, such are the intimate analogies of the apostolic ecclesiology. The church exists now on the basis of an accomplished justifying work of God in Christ, crucified and risen, and rooted in the electing will of God. This great emphasis must be guarded securely, however much we wish also to stress the future hope.

Such evangelical hesitations about Moltmann's ecclesiology connect with his Christology. The resurrection of the crucified Jew, Jesus, reveals him "as the Lord on the way to his coming lordship, and to that extent in differentiation from what he will be;"[61] the emphasis is on the unfinishedness of the identity of Jesus, this is on the way, towards the future. But the church knows that this resurrection is the final verdict of the Father on Jesus' identity as the Son, to whom disciples give their lives, trusting in his finished work of salvation, whatever the future may hold. In fact the future holds "wars and rumors of wars," famines and disasters, but the end is not yet.[62] The task of the church is to have faith, to love our neighbors and our enemies, in the forgiving grace of the cru-

58. See, e.g., Fee, *Paul, the Spirit and the People of God*, ch 8.

59. Moltmann, *The Church in the Power of the Spirit*, 80.

60. Moltmann, *Theology of Hope*, 282.

61. Ibid., 87.

62. Mark 13:7 compare Rev 6.

cified risen Christ. This may involve suffering, but love is the apostolic act rather than suffering in itself, albeit linked to hope, as a precursor to the coming kingdom in which God will be all in all. The church is the church, "ransomed healed restored forgiven," complete in its identity in Christ, living out its life of love in the world, utterly dependent on the grace of God and the gifts of the Spirit. The identity of Jesus is indeed now known and given to the church, it does not await completion. "God has sent the Spirit of His Son into our hearts, so we cry Abba, Father" (Gal 4:6), the Son is of the very heart of God, the church is his body chosen and precious to him, sure in its baptismal identity, and praising the Father in the Spirit here and now. All that Moltmann says about the church facing the future is necessary, but may not be sufficiently grounded: his eschatological economic trinitarianism produces a dynamic theology of the church in action, but is there a sufficient ontology of the church in Christ?

To end at the beginning: does the immense stress on the future of history and "the as yet unfulfilled future identity of this one agent in history,"[63] leave Moltmann in danger of being open to seduction by the latest powerful movement of modern culture? Barth's focus on Jesus Christ as the one Word of God has the great merit of protecting against that danger. For example the modern secular ecological movement might entail some presuppositions hostile to the gospel, which the church should assess with caution. Evangelicals wish to confess Jesus as the Christ, whose *finished* work grounds the church and gives it assurance of salvation, as it faces the challenges of sin in history, a history which does not have the potential to save and heal itself.

63. Moltmann, *Theology of Hope*, 194.

9

Reclaiming the Future

The Challenge of Moltmann's Eschatology

Daniel Castelo

OF THE MANY THEOLOGICAL topics with which Jürgen Moltmann is associated, the one that continues to be prominent is hope specifically and eschatology more generally. In a manifesto-esque statement in *Theology of Hope* that has been quoted time and time again, Moltmann remarks, "From first to last, and not merely in the epilogue, Christianity is eschatology, is hope, forward looking and forward moving, and therefore also revolutionizing and transforming the present. The eschatological is not one element *of* Christianity, but it is the medium of Christian faith as such, the key in which everything in it is set, the glow that suffuses everything here in the dawn of an expected new day."[1] Although TH was not Moltmann's first work, it was the text that announced Moltmann on the theological scene. Almost instantly, the text received praise and became a modern theological classic with the German Reformed scholar and sometime pastor experiencing the kind of success and fame that only few (and usually those being older) theologians do in their lifetimes. By his own confession, Moltmann was surprised of the immediate and warm reception of his work; in his mind, he was simply elaborating a theme that he found "in the air," one that

---

1. Moltmann, *Theology of Hope*, 16; hereafter referenced as TH.

other theologians and philosophers had been considering for a while.[2] And yet Moltmann's voice and the thematic he employed so early in his career have resounded for some time now. What is it about Moltmann's eschatological vision that made him such an important theological voice? And now, given the passing of a few decades, what features of his project continue to be relevant and which others suffer because of their contextual particularity?

BACKGROUND

Although Moltmann rose to prominence in the 1960s, his generation suffered the ignominy and humiliation of the events and circumstances surrounding World War II. Moltmann himself was a POW in the war (1945–48), and he found faith at this time because of the efforts of English-speaking chaplains. This context had a powerful influence not only upon his own life generally but his theological interests as well; Moltmann has remarked that in his despair as a POW, he found "that comfort in the Christ who in his passion became [his] brother in need, and through his resurrection from the dead awakened [him] too to a living hope."[3] In relation to this period of his life, he has also stated, "And in this collapse [I] found a new hope in the Christian faith, which brought me not only spiritual but also (I think) physical survival, because it rescued me from despair and from giving up. I returned to Germany a Christian and with the new 'individual approach' to study theology, in order to understand that power of hope to which I owed my life."[4] Given this context, one cannot overestimate the importance surrounding how Moltmann came to faith for his theological vision. For Moltmann, Christianity is first and foremost a hopeful faith in the midst of despair, tragedy, and loss.

---

2. Meeks mentions Wolfhart Pannenberg, Walter Kreck, Wolf-Dieter Marsch, Gerhard Sauter, and Johann Baptist Metz as other contributors to this emerging eschatological framing of theology (one that did not necessarily constitute a "school" per se); see Meeks, *Origins of the Theology of Hope*, 1; for broader considerations of this movement and its internal variations, see Capps, *Time Invades the Cathedral*.

3. Moltmann, *Experiences in Theology*, 4.

4. Moltmann, *History and the Triune God*, 166; see also his account in Moltmann, *A Broad Place*, 30.

Upon returning to Germany from the displacements of the war, Moltmann began to study at Göttingen, and several teachers and influences helped shape his views toward hope around that time. Gerhard von Rad helped him see the importance of promise in the Old Testament; Ernst Käsemann emphasized the role of apocalyptic and Christ's parousia in New Testament studies; Hans Joachim Iwand emphasized both the coming kingdom as well as the notion of *promissio* within Reformation christological construals; Otto Weber, Moltmann's supervisor, eventually put him in contact with the Dutch theologian Arnold van Ruler, who also impressed upon him the importance of the kingdom of God motif; Ernst Wolf inspired his reflection on social ethics; and there were others. When Moltmann moved to Wuppertal in the late 1950s, he continued to think along these lines, and many of these strands converged with his reading of Ernst Bloch's *The Principle of Hope* while he was on vacation in the Swiss mountains in 1960. Moltmann admitted later that he did not notice the beauty of his surroundings because of the questions that surged to his mind as he was reading this text; some of these questions included, "Why has Christian theology neglected this theme of hope, which is so distinctively its own? What is left of the earliest Christian spirit of hope in present-day Christianity?"[5] These concerns are vital, for whereas Christian reflection had repeatedly emphasized faith and love in a number of distinctive traditions and movements, the third of the theological virtues had rarely been considered.[6] With a century like the twentieth, the timing of hope's rise to prominence was more than apropos.

The effect of Bloch on Moltmann's early work cannot be over-estimated, for Bloch proved to be a significant impetus for the way Moltmann pieced the different strands of his training together. An "esoteric Marxist" and atheist, Bloch, who would later become Moltmann's colleague at Tübingen, took the unlikely approach to consider Judaism's promissory and messianic themes in the Old Testament as grounds for a Marxist utopian vision in the present. According to Bloch, both biblical religion and Marxism anticipate a different future with the assumption

---

5. Moltmann, *History and the Triune God*, 169.

6. Moltmann at times does speak in terms of the theological virtues and his recovery of the third of that sequence; however, he is careful to delineate that whereas the category of "theological virtues" may sound other-worldly, his concerns in emphasizing the theme of hope involve a forward-looking perspective that affects life here and now.

that things can change in light of an apprehended and projected horizon; in short, biblical religion historically introduced the eschatological conscience, one that in turn was picked up by Marxism. Therefore, ideas like praxis, process, and others that are open and experimental in nature are heavily emphasized in *The Principle of Hope*. Two features of Bloch's project that have proven especially influential upon Moltmann's eschatological reflections have been Bloch's anthropology of hope and his ontology of "not yet being."[7]

As to the first point, Bloch believed that being human meant hoping, that humans function first and foremost as entities who are constantly on the move and striving toward a future; they are essentially "creatures of hope." With this kind of assumption about human existence, Bloch could bring together Jewish religious history and Marxist utopian striving together under one heading, namely as social and political expressions of what is at the core of humanity. When Moltmann picks these themes up in terms of the religiosity of human beings, his arguments resonate with Bloch's project: "[Man] is a world-open creature who himself can and must everywhere build his own environment in his cultures. And yet there is an element and an environment without which he cannot live as man, and that is hope. It is the breath of life."[8]

This anthropological move bears some similarities to the second element, the ontology of "not yet being." For Bloch, reality is not so much a static or closed system in that the possibilities for the future are inherent already in what is; rather, reality is open to the truly new, or the *novum*, in that the interactions between emerging potentialities lead to dialectical processes that in turn produce new outcomes and further unforeseen possibilities. Reality, then, is open, experimental, and a process. One can see how in the cases of the anthropological and the ontological realms Bloch is advocating for the conceptual possibility of a utopian vision. This feature of "not yet being" plays a role in both how Moltmann elaborates God's being and the nature of the kingdom of God.

Although Bloch is not an extensively referenced figure in TH,[9] Moltmann was self-consciously trying to reconfigure what he perceived

---

7. Both are mentioned in Moltmann, *The Experiment Hope*, 20.

8. Moltmann, *The Experiment Hope*, 21.

9. Some editions of TH have an appendix that has Moltmann engage Bloch in a sustained fashion; it can be found in Moltmann, *Religion, Revolution, and the Future*, 148–76. If one does not have an edition of TH that has this appendix, however, there

to be the promising suggestions of Bloch within a Christian, specifically eschatological, framework. Bauckham even goes so far as to make the analogy that Moltmann used Bloch in a similar fashion (in terms of an appropriation of a view of reality, concepts, categories, and the like) to how Aquinas used Aristotle and Augustine the Neo-Platonism of his day.[10] If such an analogy holds, then it is no wonder that Bauckham can remark that Moltmann thought that Bloch represented "the most appropriate philosophy for articulating an eschatologically oriented Christian theology."[11] Naturally, some within the theological community thought that Moltmann was "baptizing" Bloch and simply engaging in theological faddishness.[12] From Moltmann's own perspective, he simply wanted to "undertake a parallel action in Christianity on the basis of its own presuppositions."[13] The language of "parallel" is quite intentional and frequently used by Moltmann in speaking on this matter: He was self-consciously not trying to imitate or extend Bloch's agenda but attempting to do something different that could subsequently yield convergences and resemblances, a gesture consonant with Moltmann's conviction that theology ought to be dialogical. Despite such explicit distancing, Moltmann has consistently had to dispel the tendency by observers to conflate his project in TH with Bloch's.

METHODOLOGY

Moltmann has insisted that he has never been interested in establishing his method ahead of time: "Up to now these questions about method have not greatly interested me, because I first wanted to get to know the real content of theology. For me, what was important was the revision of theological issues in the light of their biblical origins, and their renewal or reworking in the challenge of the present."[14] He continues: "My

are echoes of Bloch in the text itself: Bauckham goes to the trouble of documenting several of these, and they are sundry; see Bauckham, *Moltmann: Messianic Theology in the Making*, 10.

10. Bauckham, *Moltmann: Messianic Theology in the Making*, 9.

11. Ibid., 9.

12. The language of "baptizing" was explicitly used by Barth in correspondence directed to Moltmann; see Moltmann , *A Broad Place*, 109–11.

13. Moltmann, ed., *How I Have Changed*, 15.

14. Moltmann , *Experiences in Theology*, xiv.

theological methods therefore grew up as I came to have a perception of the objects of theological thought. *The road emerged only as I walked it.* And my attempts to walk it are of course determined by my personal biography, and by the political context and historical *kairos* in which I live."[15] On the one hand, this kind of methodological openness can be positively construed in that it avoids preemptive closures that are a result of being consistent with one's methodology; however, Moltmann is right to point out that "figuring it out along the way" means that his theology is determined significantly by the vicissitudes and particularities of his own context, and although there is a degree of such determination in all theologizing, this *location* especially comes through in Moltmann's eschatological proposals.

Moltmann believed that theology, for it to be fully alive and relevant, must attend to and be shaped, both methodologically and thematically, by the experiences, passions, fears, and aspirations of those engaged in the theological task at a given time and place: "For me, theology comes into being wherever men and women come to the knowledge of God and, in the praxis of their lives, their happiness and their suffering, perceive God's presence with all their senses."[16] Barth had the newspaper in one hand and the Bible in another, and the result was the *Church Dogmatics*; Moltmann saw what was around him alongside the biblical depiction of God and God's works and produced TH. In looking back at TH and *The Crucified God*, Moltmann says, "I did not attempt to write these books as theological textbooks, informative on all sides, balanced in judgment and reassuring in wisdom. In them I wanted to say something in a particular cultural, theological and political situation, and took sides. They were written from the time for the time, and are thus to be understood as contextual theology, set within the conflict of contemporary life."[17] Because of this orientation, Moltmann demonstrates a species of occasionalism in his theological reflection. For instance, Bloch plays an important role in Moltmann's early career, but in time he distanced himself from Bloch while admitting a greater indebtedness to the work of Franz Rosenzweig. This occasionalism complicates the task of evaluating Moltmann, but certain general features do come to the fore for considering his eschatology.

15. Ibid., xv.
16. Ibid., xvi.
17. Moltmann , *History and the Triune God*, 173–74.

GENERAL FEATURES

In reflecting on his career and theological contributions, Moltmann elevates the following three themes as central to any Christian theology of hope: 1) "the concept of the divine promise," 2) "the concept of the raising of the crucified Christ as God's promise for the world," and 3) "an understanding of human history as the mission of the kingdom of God."[18]

1) If eschatology is about hope, then it is telling how Moltmann defines the latter: "Hope is nothing else than the expectation of those things which faith has believed to have been truly promised by God."[19] In this light, Moltmann believes that the history and witness of God's people are essentially promissory or messianic. Unlike some other religions, both Judaism and Christianity believe that God comes to humanity and relates to them and makes promises for a reality that is yet to come: "According to the Israelite view . . . the past is a promise of the future."[20] Relying on his reading of Scripture and following the work of Walther Zimmerli, Moltmann can say that a promise is "a declaration which announces the coming of a reality that does not yet exist . . . If it is the case of a divine promise, then that indicates that the expected future does not have to develop within the framework of the possibilities inherent in the present, but arises from that which is possible to the God of the promise."[21] A grounding moment for this understanding is found in Gen 12:1–3, the call of Abram and all the promises therein. These promises of blessing come from the one who revealed himself to Moses through the Tetragrammaton, a name that Moltmann takes to mean in part, "I will be there for you." This promissory history rests on the constancy of God's character to fulfill these speech-acts: God can and will fulfill God's promises because God is God.

In that God relates to humanity in a promissory way, God does not simply promise within history those things that will be in the future but God comes to us from the future into history and both makes and fulfills promissory/messianic expectation within it. If God is beyond the time continuum of chronicity, then the promises God

---

18. Moltmann , *A Broad Place*, 101.

19. Moltmann, *Theology of Hope*, 19.

20. Ibid., 18.

21. Ibid., 103.

makes within time are in a sense already realized in God's future. In this manner, God comes to us from God's future and both inculcates a sensibility of openness and introduces possibilities that are totally new from what could be anticipated or assumed given how things have been. For Moltmann, two prominent examples of these "new developments" would be Jesus' resurrection from the dead and the inbreaking of God's kingdom in the proclamation of the gospel. There is a sense then that a dialectic of history and futurity are at play in Moltmann's eschatological vision, largely stemming from both the historicity of Israel's identity as well as how that identity is repeatedly directed to a future that God promises to enact; in other words, it is a dialectical reality for those who are a "people on the way."

In this first point, one sees important convergences and divergences with Bloch's program. Moltmann appropriated the idea from Bloch that Judaism is future-directed through its promissory and messianic framing. In important ways, the story of God's people is one that depicts them "on the way." However, Bloch, in being an atheist, found that this expectation was misdirected in that he agreed with Ludwig Feuerbach that religion was simply a human projection; where Bloch differed from Feuerbach was that the latter believed this projection had to be absorbed and reconfigured in human experience whereas Bloch believed that the projection into the future was a real gesture outward, one that is at the heart of religion and that requires a utopian vision.[22]

It is precisely at this point in which Moltmann would interject and say that this longed for future is really not that hopeful if it cannot hope in something truly transcendent, i.e., something that does not simply operate in terms of "not yet being" but one that can even extend to "no longer being."[23] In other words, Bloch's vision cannot account for any hopefulness beyond death, for a *novum ex nihilo*; in contradistinction to Bloch, Moltmann's account of biblical hope, one resting primarily on the resurrection of Jesus, can suggest the work of transformation and

22. Bauckham, *Moltmann: Messianic Theology in the Making*, 16. A quote from Moltmann may help here: "For Bloch . . . the future of the risen Christ and the future of God is—methodically following Feuerbach's formula of reduction—'nothing else but' the future of hidden man and of the hidden world. What separates him from Feuerbach is the change from mysticism to Millenarianism, from mystical ecstasy withdrawing from the world to revolutionary subversion of the world, from Meister Eckhart to Thomas Münzer" (Moltmann, *Religion, Revolution, and the Future*, 152).

23. Bauckham, *Moltmann: Messianic Theology in the Making*, 18.

redemption from the *nihil* that reality tends to: "If God creates what is new out of nothing, then the poor, abandoned, and the dying are closer to him than are the efficient and militant heroes of the revolution who help mankind."[24]

2) As noted by the above quotes from his imprisonment during the war, Moltmann believes Christ to be central to his project; he is not interested in "the future" *per se* but in Christ's future since the events surrounding Christ, especially his resurrection, open up new possibilities for existence. This moment is a fulfillment of the messianic expectation one can see throughout the Old Testament, and it is the basis for Christian hope in God's continued promises of the universal renewal of all things. Christian eschatology's focus on the resurrected Jesus and his future distinguishes itself from all utopian visions.[25]

This eschatological orientation could easily revert to a false trust in optimistic progress, one that has historically overtaken a number of regions throughout the world in different forms. Moltmann was able to differentiate his project from this faith in modern progress by highlighting Christ's role throughout, first in terms of his resurrection and subsequently in line with the crucifixion, as one sees in TH and *The Crucified God*, respectively. Moltmann's dialectical strategy was bequeathed to him by his esteemed teacher Hans Joachim Iwand, who in turn drew from the master of dialectic himself, Hegel. Moltmann analogously was able to connect Hegel's dialectically historical process of reconciliation to Christ's resurrection and crucifixion, the former moment indicating a hopeful future in which all of creation will be reconciled while the latter showing God's solidarity with those who appear godforsaken today. Thus, the "already-not yet" tension often associated with eschatological reflection is dialectically posed and christologically grounded in Moltmann's eschatology.

Once again, one sees a significant difference here with the work of Bloch. For Moltmann, the raising of the crucified Jesus precisely opens up possibilities for hope to those who are marginalized and who are suffering and dying in a way that Bloch's vision cannot. The limits of Bloch's project manifest themselves within the "immanent transcendent" that he sets up for himself because of his atheism. For Moltmann, this vi-

---

24. Moltmann, *Religion, Revolution, and the Future*, 18.
25. Moltmann, *Theology of Hope*, 17.

sion stops short of being truly hopeful because it cannot account for that which derails hope most significantly, namely death.

3) In light of the last point, Christ's resurrection is indicative of how the kingdom is "already" manifest in terms of the ongoing possibilities that Christians can participate in and promote; as Moltmann remarks, "The kingdom of God has identified itself with Jesus in the resurrection of the crucified one. In his words and deeds Jesus has anticipated the kingdom of God and has opened the coming of the kingdom."[26] Rather than bound to the past, Christian existence can look to the future, specifically God's future, one that has on its horizon the fulfillment of God's promises and the transformation of the created order.

For this reason, the Christian life can be awakened and impassioned by what God is doing in the world so that believers can stand in the contradictory tension between what is promised and what is present reality; put another way, "biblical eschatology leads to criticism of the status quo and to movements for change."[27] Christian hope is essentially subversive because it throws to light the limits of "how things are" in realation to "how they can be" and even, in Christian terms, "how they will be."

The role of the Christian is to join in that work and to hope in God that things will be different. To quote Moltmann again: "If it is correct to say that the Bible is essentially a witness to the promissory history of God, then the role of Christian theology is to bring these remembrances of the future to bear on the hopes and anxieties of the present."[28] In this light, works like Bloch's can help Christians reclaim features of their testimony for the greater good of the world. Christians can be inspired by different movements to look deeper into their own tradition and to seek allies for promoting political and social aims that can lead to much needed change. It is here where Moltmann finds theology's critically dialogical orientation important, for he wishes to move from the particularity of the death and resurrection of Jesus to the universality that has always been inherent to the Christian gospel; the latter would imply that the Christian faith has to engage in a deep and sustained way with the wider world.

26. Herzog, ed., *The Future of Hope*, 23.

27. Bauckham, *Moltmann: Messianic Theology in the Making*, 15.

28. Moltmann, *The Experiment Hope*, 8.

Many of the above impulses that Moltmann developed in TH and elsewhere were further extended in his "contribution" to theology titled *The Coming of God*. Rather than casting the whole of theology under a single motif (as he did with the trilogy of works beginning with TH), Moltmann's subsequent "contributions" to theology are more particular and focused in their scope. In the case of *The Coming of God*, several prominent themes within eschatology are considered; these include eternal life, the kingdom of God, the new creation, and glory. Moltmann intentionally follows the logic of TH and extends it, as when he remarks, "Here, in dispute with consistently futurist eschatology and the absolute eschatology of eternity, I propose to follow the line taken in *The Theology of Hope*, and put forward *Advent* as eschatological category, and the category of *Novum* as its historical reverse side."[29] In trying to avoid the extremes associated with past eschatological proposals (e.g., depictions of a timeless eternity or the future of time), Moltmann uses dialectic once more to link history and the future by God's breaking in from the future into historical existence.[30] The Blochian notion of God having the future as God's very essence plays a role here as in TH.[31] In addition to a more robust account of his understanding of Bloch's phrasing of God's ontology, Moltmann also offers his support for millenarianism. He does not hold to a historical millenarianism (one which points to its present actualization or fulfillment through political, economic, or other social means), but he does endorse an eschatological millenarianism, one that ties God's coming from the future, messianic expectation, and present-day praxis together. He remarks: "Christian eschatology—eschatology, that is, which is messianic, healing, and saving—is millenarian eschatology."[32] Impressively, this text focuses on God's coming, God's filling the new earth and the new heavens, and God's glory; in other

---

29. Moltmann, *The Coming of God*, 6.

30. "If transcendental future is the source of time, then it does not abolish time as does timeless-simultaneous eternity, nor does it lose itself in the maelstrom of the general transience of all temporal being. It rather throws open the time of history, qualifying historical time as time determined by the future" (Moltmann, *The Coming of God*, 26).

31. Moltmann, *The Coming of God*, 23.

32. Ibid., 202. For some important elaborative and critical engagements with Moltmann's millenarianism particularly and some features of his eschatological vision more generally after the publication of *The Coming of God*. See Bauckham, ed., *God Will Be All in All*.

words, a prominent role to God's participation and God's fullness is on display at various points in the work, making it a fitting, culminating moment in Moltmann's eschatological proposals.

ONGOING RELEVANCE

Although not alone in this achievement, Moltmann is significantly responsible for helping make eschatology a serious topic of theological study today. Classes, books, conferences, and other activities and mediums often use the theme of eschatology as a guiding motif, and part of eschatology's rise as a topic worthy of consideration on its own terms has to be traced to the person and work of Moltmann. In order to grasp more concretely the way Moltmann's eschatological vision has contributed to a number of streams within Christian theology, one could move to study particular movements or groups. Two will be surveyed in what follows.

A species of political theology is a consequence of Moltmann's dialectical depiction of Christ's resurrection and crucifixion.[33] If Christ has been raised from the dead, then there is a sense in which the kingdom of God has broken into the world, and yet that inbreaking is only partial in that Christ's crucifixion is indicative of a world that still stands in need of redemption. For those who stand within this tension now, they are charged with the task to do all that they can to put the world to rights; they are to participate in the possibilities made available because of Christ's resurrection so that the kingdom of God can become clearer and more actual in the present as it will be in the future. An extensive quote is important here:

> If the real predicament underlying the theistic world view was the theodicy question (*Si Deus, unde malum?*), the Christian initiative for the overcoming of this predicament today, using the possibilities of the modern world, must enter the battle for God's righteousness on earth politically in the battle against human misery. Therefore, cosmological theology must now be

---

33. Over time, Moltmann has moved more in the direction of emphasizing the crucifixion and less so the resurrection in this regard; telling is his opening remarks to his work *God for a Secular Society*: "Remembrance of the crucified Christ makes [theology] critical towards political religions and idolatries" (1). One wonders as to the rationale for the shift, which has been considerable over time.

replaced by *political theology*. In political theology the future of God is mediated in the world changing powers of man, so that today this future makes these powers and possibilities of man legitimate in their use and they anticipate it at the front of the present misery.[34]

Furthermore, Moltmann's political theology is quite German in that it is "best, although not exclusively, interpreted against the backdrop of German philosophy and German politics."[35] He aligns himself with the work of another German theologian, Johann Baptist Metz, a figure who also works in terms of the eschatological. This German quality to his political theology has made it challenging at times to translate it to other contexts, although efforts have been made to create such links.[36]

Another expression of the influence of Moltmann's eschatology has been modern-day Pentecostalism. In its classical North American forms, Pentecostalism has considered itself an eschatological movement, especially through the "latter rain" motif, one in which the two seasons of rainfall in Palestine function typologically for the outpouring of the Spirit at Pentecost and in "the last days."[37] Given the prominence of signs and wonders in the early days of Pentecostalism, early adherents believed that these indicated that Christ's return would be soon. In time, however, the movement came to adopt a dispensational fundamentalist eschatology that was in significant tension with some of its earlier impulses, especially ones related to the role and function of the charismata in current worship practices, the prophetic and reconciling work of the Spirit in identifying and healing gender and racial divides in present-day Christian fellowship, and an overall sense of mission for evangelizing and reaching the lost.[38]

As a way of countering this fundamentalist morphing, some Pentecostal scholars began to look for alternatives, and Moltmann's eschatological proposals proved helpful. Features of Moltmann's vision that were employed by Pentecostals included the primacy of the work of

---

34. Herzog, *The Future of Hope*, 46–47.

35. Adams, "Jürgen Moltmann," 227.

36. One example is Chopp, *The Praxis of Suffering*.

37. For a treatment of this theme in light of Moltmann's eschatological vision, see Althouse, *Spirit of the Last Days*.

38. A classic article that analyzes this tension is Sheppard, "Pentecostalism and the Hermeneutics of Dispensationalism."

Christ; the present, transformative work of the Spirit; and the pending sense of ecclesial mission. All of these themes can be framed for both Moltmann and Pentecostals in terms of eschatology; therefore, many Pentecostals have gone on to accept prominent features of Moltmann's project, including the way the kingdom is an inbreaking reality from the future, a reworked sense of apocalyptic, and so forth.[39] Although important differences continue to exist between the camps, their interchanges have proven fruitful for both: Moltmann was one of the first reputable theologians to take seriously Pentecostal claims and identity, partly because of his recognition of the importance this strand of Christianity has globally for empowering the masses, and in turn Pentecostals have found in Moltmann a dialogue partner more congenial to their eschatological, trinitarian, and ecclesiological commitments.

PRESSING CONCERNS

Moltmann has been a controversial figure in theology in part because of his eclectic use of sources and figures for elaborating his theological vision. Because of his daring to be dialogical, Moltmann has often included the thought and themes of voices that some would not be inclined to find theologically generative. On the one hand, such an approach appears fresh and alive; from another vantage point, his work has at times appeared too occasional or at least insufficiently explicit in his engagement with past figures, arguments, and works within the vast tradition of Christian theological reflection. Given the theme of this chapter, it would be appropriate to return to the most significant non-Christian influence for Moltmann's eschatology.

As mentioned above, Ernst Bloch influenced Moltmann in a myriad of ways, including his ontology. Along these lines, Moltmann at times makes remarks that many Christians would find quixotic if not alarming. One of the most prominent of these would be the statement that God's primary mode of being is the future, a claim that can be traced to Bloch's *The Principle of Hope*. Moltmann himself can say: "The place where God's existence and communion are believed and hoped for is the place 'in front of us' and 'ahead of us.' This is not a spatial, but a temporal

---

39. One work that shows this influence in a number of ways is Land, *Pentecostal Spirituality*.

definition of place. God is not 'beyond us' or 'in us,' but ahead of us in the horizons of the future opened to us in his promises. Thus the 'future' must be considered as mode of God's being."[40] Within the same essay he also remarks, "God is not the ground of this world and not the ground of existence, but the God of the coming kingdom."[41] On Blochian terms, these claims make perfect sense: For Bloch, God is a symbol of the future (the *Deus spes*), and his existence therefore is of little consequence. Because of Moltmann's wish to use Blochian ontological categories, however, a number of subsequent tensions arise.

Within TH, one cannot find a fully developed ontology; although sharing similarities with Bloch and Hegel, Moltmann's ontological musings are not entirely consistent or sufficiently developed; in this light, the proposals of TH offer a basis or foundation for ontology, but not much more. This conceptual ambiguity is why Moltmann is sometimes associated with process theism or even open theism, yet the affiliation is not entirely true: Within Moltmann one sees moves and gestures that could lead to the aforementioned options, but clearly Moltmann does not say enough to make the association undeniably accurate. A sampling of quotes demonstrates the complexity of the matter: "Anyone who speaks of God in Christian terms must tell of the history of Jesus as a history between the Son and the Father. In that case, 'God' is not another nature or a heavenly person or moral authority, but in fact an 'event'"[42] and "The Trinity is no self-contained group in heaven, but an eschatological process open for men on earth, which stems from the cross of Christ."[43] These prior remarks seem to lead to one direction, but elsewhere one can find Moltmann saying, "*Adventus* designates *that which is coming*. If we apply this to theology we are not able to speak of a 'becoming God' but only of a 'coming God.' This is the difference between eschatology and process philosophy."[44] At other points, Moltmann is willing to speak of God's superabundance and plenitude.[45]

40. Herzog, *The Future of Hope*, 10; something similar is expressed in Moltmann, *Theology of Hope*, 16.

41. Herzog , *The Future of Hope*, 10.

42. Moltmann , *The Crucified God*, 247.

43. Ibid., 249.

44. Moltmann , *The Experiment Hope*, 53.

45. See Moltmann , *Experiences in Theology*, 105.

Given the long history of theological reflection regarding ontological matters and questions, it is surprising the extent to which Moltmann fails to engage this tradition and the manner in which Blochian ontological categories are adopted according to their conceptual logic.[46] The framing of eschatology along Blochian lines also creates missed opportunities, including a dialogue between Moltmann and past Christian voices on the actuality-possibility interface. For some venerable Christian schools of thought, God is depicted as *actus purus*, suggesting that God is the only one who is fully actualized as compared to other beings who are mixes of actuality and potentiality. In this model, actuality, and not potentiality, is valued most. On Moltmann's account, the accent seems to fall on the opposite side of the continuum in which possibility is prioritized more; in comparing Bloch and William James, Moltmann draws the following conclusion: "But common to both is the fact that they value the category of possibility higher than the category of reality . . . If we understand reality as the realization of possibility, then this necessitates an ontology of that which is not yet but is possible or stands in possibility."[47]

A second matter that could be pressed for further critical inquiry regarding Moltmann's eschatology is its implied activism. As noted above, Moltmann believes his eschatological vision calls for Christians to join with others in anticipating the open possibilities implied by God's future. Although the claim that humans are inherently "hopeful creatures" may be contested in its own right, the more serious difficulty of Moltmann's dialogical and subsequently collaborative efforts with others outside the church is the degree to which one can know when something truly is a sign of God's inbreaking kingdom or when it is something else. One example from Moltmann's corpus demonstrates the point; in the essay "God in Revolution," one that originally was presented as a lecture at the World Student Christian Federation Conference of 1968, Moltmann elaborates a number of theses as a way of starting a discussion rather than offering a closed-off, answer-laden presentation. "Thesis One"

46. Although it may be too much to say that Moltmann "baptized" Bloch, one can see why somebody like Barth would make the claim: Although Moltmann does not assume some of the conclusions Bloch does, a deep, conceptual resonance is shared so that the language of "parallel" is strained; these conceptual "lines on a plane" actually do cross at more than one point.

47. Moltmann , *The Experiment Hope*, 25. One caricature of "Greek metaphysics" occurs on page 50.

states, "We live in a revolutionary situation. In the future, we shall experience history more and more as revolution. We can be responsible for the future of man only in a revolutionary way."[48] Moltmann continues to elaborate that for him revolution means the transformation in the foundations of a system when people cultivate a critical consciousness in which they can compare what is actual with what is possible.[49] One wonders the degree to which these sentiments are culturally conditioned so that when the assumption fades that one lives in a "revolutionary situation," the question remains as to how this might play in reconfiguring or altering a given construal of eschatological hope. Such a concern is pointedly expressed in "Thesis 3": "The eschatological (and messianic) tradition of hope can give rise to a new birth of Christian faith in the revolutionary present." On the one hand, "taking sides" with the oppressed and the "damned of the earth" sounds legitimate enough, but Moltmann continues in the chapter to advocate the potential necessity of violence. Although Moltmann shows constraint on this score, the matter is remarkably underdeveloped in spite of inviting such a radical possibility. Moltmann raises the all-important question here: "How are we to bring about the kingdom of nonviolent brotherhood with the help of violent actions?"[50] From a vantage point of several decades later, one worries that both an understanding of the kingdom and of the use of violent force to bring about this kingdom runs the risk of conflating the category of eschatological hope with a certain ideological and contextually laden construal of human progress. Put another way, "taking sides" is a very complicated affair, and one wonders to what degree and in what manner Moltmann's proposals can be applied if it is understood they should be in a given situation.

CONCLUSION

Moltmann will long be remembered as a theologian of hope. His eschatological vision of the theological enterprise has been influential, generative, and controversial. Evangelicals may find some of his eschatological views unsavory or peculiar, but they nevertheless have shaped

48. Moltmann , *Religion, Revolution, and the Future*, 130.

49. Ibid., 131.

50. Ibid., 144.

the current theological climate to the point that eschatology is no longer a locus simply about "the end times." It remains to be seen to what degree Christian eschatology will continue to be significantly shaped along Moltmannian terms since at present the influence is still detectable after these many decades.

10

An Evangelical Assessment of Jürgen Moltmann's Ethics

Paul Parker

THE HEART OF EVANGELICAL faith is a personal relationship with Jesus Christ as one's Lord and Savior. Without this there can be no evangelical ethics or theology. Whatever else may be said, personal faith in Jesus Christ goes to the very core of evangelicalism—and to the heart of Jürgen Moltmann.

As most persons read Professor Moltmann's books they gradually become aware of his background as a German youth who was conscripted into his county's military in the waning months of World War II, nearly killed on more than one occasion, and eventually captured by Allied forces. During his imprisonment he fell deeply into despair before experiencing rebirth and new life through Jesus Christ.

Moltmann is correct not to dwell on his war experiences in his theological works. He knows that they were not daring adventures but involuntary experiences of death. But those who wish to understand his thought must pay close attention to what he rightly has not until his recent autobiography. From his first writings to his most current, the perceptive reader will come to understand the formative power and continuing influence of his war experiences on his theology and ethics—and more importantly, the crucial role of his imprisonment and liberation. We should draw from his frank acknowledgement that the stupidity and terror of war as well as his imprisonment and liberation have "put their stamp on my life."[1]

In 1929 when Moltmann was still a toddler his parents built their house in a small, politically liberal, socialist-inspired community of like-minded persons who longed for a simplified life close to nature and one another. He describes their settlement as warm, robust, pragmatic, "joyous, and intentionally void of religious belief and practice."[2] This voluntary community was his first experience of a diverse and mutually affirming "community" which eventually becomes important to his understanding of human nature, the church, and God.

Drafted into the air force in February 1943, Moltmann's first assignment was to staff an anti-aircraft battery that was built on stilts above the waters of the huge Outer Alster Lake on the edge of the city of Hamburg. Moltmann saw no combat until July 24, 1943, when the Allies executed "Operation Gomorrah" with nine consecutive nights of relentlessly bombing Hamburg. Near the end of the campaign his battery was hit, decapitating his fellow soldier, wounding him, and tossing him like trash into the lake. Moltmann remembers that "during that night I cried out to God for the first time in my life and put my life in his hands . . . My question was . . . 'My God, where are you?' And then there was the other question, the answer to which I am still looking for today: Why am I alive and not dead, too, like my friend at my side? During that night I became a seeker after God."[3] For the first time in Moltmann's life, at the age of seventeen, the question of God became personal.

In July 1944 he was called-up to a heavy weapons company of an infantry battalion on the Western Front. From September onward his unit retreated under constant attack by the advancing Allies. Over the next several months, the soldiers of his unit were either killed, captured, or separated to the extent that in early February he found himself wandering alone between enemy positions without purpose or provisions. On February 15, 1945, an Allied patrol discovered him and he surrendered. He was nineteen years old.

Already despairing of life, Moltmann was now totally dispirited and confined in a Belgium prisoner of war camp (not due to Belgium abuse

---

1. Moltmann, *A Broad Place*, 19.
2. Ibid., 5.
3. Ibid., 17.

but to the characteristically dehumanizing nature of prisons and to the brutality and false hopes perpetuated by the hard core Nazi prisoners.)

Gradually, over the next several years, three experiences led him to new life and hope. First, in August 1945 he was transferred to a Scottish prisoner of war camp. While imprisoned and performing forced labor, he and his fellow prisoners experienced genuine, nonjudgmental hospitality from local Scottish workers and their families. Through their nonjudgmental kindness—to him, the undeserving enemy—he began to find within himself a sense of worth, but also profound shame. He had begun to learn what Germany had actually done to the millions of Jews and millions of other "undesirables" in its death camps—and he began to see himself "through the eyes of the Nazi victims." Moltmann confesses that he was overcome with such a sense of shame "the weight of which has never left me to this day."[4]

The second event was his experience of the salvific power of the Bible. Moltmann had received a free Bible from an army chaplain who was distributing them throughout the POW camp. As he read in the evenings after work he found that the Psalmist showed him how to pray for healing (Ps 39) and that Jesus' cry of dereliction (Mark 15:34) introduced him to the God who understood him and accepted him in all of his emptiness. Moltmann writes:

> I was slowly but surely seized by a great hope for the resurrection into God's "wide space where there is no more cramping" . . . I have never decided for Christ once and for all . . . I have decided again and again . . . Right down to the present day, after almost 60 years, I am certain that then in 1945, and there, in the Scottish prisoner of war camp, in the dark pit of my soul, Jesus sought me and found me . . . *Whenever I read the Bible . . . I am always assured of its divine truth.*[5]

In the spring of 1946 Moltmann was transferred again, this time to an "educational camp" set up in Cuckney, England, for the youngest German POWs for the completion of their high school education. In that POW camp in the winter of 1947, completely outside his family's tradition and expectations, Moltmann affirmed God's claim on his life to become a pastor and began his theological education. He recalls that

---

4. Ibid., 20–28. See also Moltmann, "Wrestling with God: A Personal Meditation."

5. Ibid., 30f. Italics not in original.

he "received what he had not deserved, and lived from a spiritual abundance he had not expected."

The third event that shapes Moltmann's ethics and theology while in the prison camp was an international Student Christian Movement conference held in the summer of 1947. Moltmann and a few other young POWs were surprised to receive invitations, and they attended, but with weighty misgivings. They were, after all, the enemy. What Moltmann found, however, was undeserved and unanticipated acceptance—real "liberation" although he was still very much in prison. Finally, in April 1948 after more than five years in batteries, bunkers, foxholes, and POW camps, Moltmann was discharged—but he had already been liberated by Christ almost three years earlier.

These were the experiences that freed Moltmann from shame, despair, and death to a new birth, which has shaped his life, ethics, and theology. Through enemies who had loved him like a brother, he experienced the love of God. And through the biblical text he experienced liberation by the grace of God through Jesus Christ and a call to ministry.

Although Moltmann's life story of the Good News of Jesus Christ is unique to him, it is familiar to us: it is "our story" and the story of the experience of billions of others throughout the centuries and around the world. It is the story of a new community, biblical revelation, a personal experience of salvation, and a commitment to pass to others the gospel of Jesus Christ, which he has so undeservedly received. Whenever Moltmann does theological and ethical reflection, these experiences are foundational:

> *When I saw the mud huts* in the slums of Mathare Valley outside Nairobi *I remembered the hovels in which we prisoners* sought protection from the snow and rain behind the barbed wire . . . It all came back to me. I must have looked like that: contorted, shabby, with hunger pangs in my stomach, despair in my heart, and a curse against God and humanity on my lips. *I recognized myself in them.*[6]

He goes on: "*Today I see before me the millions of the imprisoned*, the exiled, the deported, and the silenced everywhere in the world where people are pushed into this darkness."[7] And he continues with explicit commitment to do Christian theology from the perspective of a POW.

6. Moltmann, *The Passion for Life*, 97. Italics not in original.

7. Moltmann, *The Power of the Powerless*, 30. Italics not in original.

Who am I? And as whom do I reflect on the theme of "hope in the struggle of the people"? . . . I cannot help speaking as a professor of theology and as an academician. I cannot help speaking as a pastor. But *I will try also to speak as a prisoner . . .* and to use my experiences as a pastor and my responsibilities as a professor *to serve that community out of which I come and which has had a much deeper influence on me than anything that came later.*[8]

When Moltmann does Christian ethics, he is intentionally thinking from the perspective of "a prisoner"—but his experience is significantly different from the typical prisoner. Moltmann does ethics not as a POW, but as a "liberated" POW—and not just as one who was eventually repatriated with his country and family, but most importantly, as one who was set free by God in Jesus Christ while still a prisoner of war.

Moltmann eventually comes to understand that while his POW experience was life-altering and crucial for his understanding of God and the world, it was sufficiently different from those who are still trapped in oppression to cause him to rethink his scholarly agenda. In late 1977 at a Latin American conference he "suddenly discovered":

I don't belong anywhere, since I'm not oppressed, not black, and not a woman. I can support these liberation movements and learn from them, but my existence is not in them . . . I've been involved in the peace movement and ecological movement [but professorial responsibilities] do not leave one much time. Feminist theology has influenced me more strongly than I realized . . . So, what should I do?[9]

Out of this new self-awareness, he turned to writing his greatest systematic theological contributions: *The Trinity and the Kingdom of God* (1980), *God in Creation* (1985), *The Way of Jesus Christ* (1989), *The Spirit of Life: A Universal Affirmation* (1991), and *The Coming of God* (1995).

It is important to read Moltmann's works with the understanding that his hope in the God of the future arises from his experience of God liberating him while still in the POW camp and then from the POW camp. Moltmann does not begin with a political agenda that he then theologically rationalizes. He begins with his experience of salvation, of liberation, of Jesus Christ coming to him and finding him through

---

8. Moltmann, *The Passion for Life*, 97. Italics not in original.

9. Moltmann, *How I Have Changed*, 19f.

Scripture and through living Christians, all by the grace of God. For Moltmann, theological statements must be "verified by one's experiences or by empathy with others' experiences."[10] His ethics and his theology will be difficult to understand, and even more difficult to accept, for those who think Christianity is primarily about getting the doctrines right, and for those who have never known themselves to have been "dead" and then reborn through Jesus Christ. Moltmann's experience of liberation—by Jesus Christ mediated through Scripture and the church by the grace of God—is the source of his ethics, theology, and pastoral ministry.

EVANGELICAL ETHICS FOLLOW THE WAY OF JESUS CHRIST

Moltmann observes with dismay that there are practically no mainstream Christian ethicists who include in their methodology an explicit and thorough Christological foundation. Across the spectrum of ethical discourse, virtually "no specifically *Christian* ethic can be detected." And this approach is intentional. Christians in the West have addressed the moral issues of their day from inside the institutions of cultural privilege, political power, and prestigious universities. An explicitly christological foundation would not fit well with contemporary discussions of politics, economics, technology, and social mores.[11]

However, Moltmann worries with good reason that if there is no unique contribution of Jesus Christ to Christian ethics, can there be any unique contribution of Jesus Christ to understanding God? And if there is no uniquely Christological contribution to Christian ethics or to Christian theology, in what sense could Jesus be the Christ? Can Jesus be the Messiah in any relevant way?

Moltmann maintains that if Jesus Christ is to be taken seriously as the Messiah, he must be essential not only for Christian theology but also for Christian ethics. If Christian ethics is to be Christian, it must "involve a practical discipleship that follows the messianic path Jesus' own life took; and that means an ethic which has to be made identifiably Christian." Although each Christian's moral decisions will inevitably reflect one's identity, time, and place (e.g., male or female; Asian or North

10. Ibid., 20.

11. Moltmann, *The Way of Jesus Christ*, 116–19.

American; twelfth century or the twenty-first), Jesus as the Messiah must be central. For Moltmann, who was rescued by Jesus Christ, this is not just a scholarly debate. "Christian ethics is really about nothing less than the messiahship of Jesus . . . What is at stake is the acknowledgement of Christ."[12]

The whole of Christianity turns on the specifically messianic nature of its ethics. To know Christ is to follow Christ. Christian discipleship, following Jesus, is Christian ethics. How can one be a Christian yet not even try to follow Christ?[13] If Christian ethics are truly Christian, then the way of Jesus must still today be ethically normative.[14]

Moltmann develops this emphasis by drawing on a number of different sources from his own heritage such as the Barmen Theological Declaration (1934), medieval German Anabaptists like Hans Denk, and contemporary American Mennonites like John Howard Yoder. For these theologians, faith and ethics are inseparable. Just as Jesus is inseparable from Christian faith, Jesus is inseparable from Christian ethics.

"Christology and christopraxis become one . . . Christ is perceived and known not only with mind and heart, but through the experience and practice of the whole of life." What is central for evangelical faith is true for Moltmann: one cannot know Christ if one does not follow him. Quoting the sixteenth-century Denk, Moltmann affirms that "'No one is able verily to know Christ except he follow Him in life.' . . . Christian ethics cannot be anything except ethical Christology."[15] It is epistemologically and politically consistent and crucial to understand that truth is determined through praxis, that is, through the experience of taking action that follows Jesus and critical reflection upon that experience which spills forth in a new socially relevant actions.[16]

When individuals and communities of faith follow the way of Jesus, they should expect to suffer for it. The cross of Christ is often still the result of taking the way of Christ in an unredeemed world. It is "impossible," says Moltmann, to reconcile the example of Jesus, and

---

12. Ibid. 118.

13. See Moltmann's new book on ethics for his renewed emphasis on Christian discipleship and the messianic way of Jesus. Moltmann, *Ethik der Hoffnung*, 14, 38, 44, 45, 70–74, et passim.

14. Rasmusson, *The Church as Polis*, 72, 117.

15. Moltmann, *The Way of Jesus Christ*, 119.

16. Rasmusson, *The Church as Polis*, 48f.

his ethical and theological teachings with the present world situation. Nuclear weapons, political domination, retributive punishment, pollution, environmental degradation, and poverty in the midst of wealth, just to name a few examples from Moltmann, are unacceptable to those who follow the way of Jesus Christ. Knowledge that the way of Jesus Christ and the way of the world are incompatible is not difficult to grasp, except by those who have accepted the way of world as normative and either ignored or rationalized the way of Jesus. The church must therefore become "the great alternative to the world's present system. The church is to be a 'contrast-society,' and through its existence it calls into question the systems of violence and injustice."[17]

EVANGELICAL ETHICS ARE THE ETHICS OF AN ALTERNATIVE COMMUNITY

Christianity is a doomed ideology—abstract and weak—without the church. The church is the future of Christianity or else Christianity has no future, and "the future of the church is the kingdom of God."[18] Although this has always been the case from the first century until today, there has been a new empowerment of the church that began during the Enlightenment and continues with increasing vitality into the twenty-first century. Moltmann observes that in the twentieth century the church has become more clearly "an independent and resisting community, a community with a universal mission, and an all-embracing hope for the kingdom of God as the future of the world."[19]

From the early fourth century (when the church comingled the authority of Jesus Christ with the authority of the Roman Empire) until the Age of the Enlightenment, Christianity had become "a matter of the state." The state determined the religion, adjudicated theological disputes, established church polity, directed daily religious practice, and administered ecclesiastic discipline. Since the Enlightenment in the West, however, religious authority has been progressively wrestled from the hands of the state. And since World War II, the entire world has experienced growing religious freedom, although not fully, but even so far

17. Moltmann, *The Way of Jesus Christ*, 122.
18. Moltmann, *Sun of Righteousness*, 7.
19. Moltmann, *Sun of Righteousness*, 17–19.

as its enshrinement in the UN Charter for Human Rights. As Moltmann quips, "the one who was crucified by state power cannot easily become the God of a state religion." The "separation of church and state" has given to churches and to individual Christians the freedom to determine their own religious identity, beliefs, and practice—but it has also had two unanticipated consequences: in the West, generally, and to a lesser but still significant degree world-wide, religion has become individualized and privatized. For many, Christianity is now *mis*understood as an individual's private concern.[20]

Moltmann rejects both of these modern "truths." Just as the coming messianic kingdom of God rejects state religion, it also rejects privatized and individualized Christianity. The church must remind both "the rulers and the ruled" that the coming kingdom of God is not only spiritual, but also social, economic, and very much political. The church belongs to no particular state, culture, economic system, or political movement, and cannot be individualized or privatized because it is "the vanguard" of the universally inclusive kingdom of God. "Christian faith as discipleship of the crucified Christ" cannot be controlled by the government or individualized and privatized by "a market society."[21]

Since it was the world powers that executed Jesus, the church that follows the way of Jesus Christ will necessarily be a contrasting alternative to the way of the world. Moltmann makes clear in *The Crucified God* (1972) that God's resurrection of Jesus Christ, whom the state crucified, means that "churches which take his name must dissolve their alliances with the powerful and seek solidarity with the humiliated who exist in the shadow of the cross . . . The cross of Christ is the foundation and critique of Christian theology."[22] If the ethics of the church were identical with the ethics of the world, then the kingdom would have already come "on earth as it is in heaven." Since the kingdom has not fully come, however, the ethics of the church must be a contrasting alternative to the ethics of the world. Whatever else evangelical ethics are, they must be a clear and distinguishable alternative to the ethics of the state, culture, and prevailing ideologies. And today just as in Jesus' day, a contrasting

---

20. Moltmann, *How I Have Changed*, 108f.

21. Ibid., 109. This is one of several areas where Moltmann draws on the wisdom of the still influential 1934 Barmen Theological Declaration of the Confessing Church.

22. Ibid., 18.

alternative ethic will be regarded as a threat to the privileged, the power-ful, and those in authority.

Just as the Law and the Prophets declared, Moltmann asserts that the church's alternative ethics must be an ethics of peace—real, personal, inner, social, political, and economic—which is "indispensably linked with the Messiah . . . If this peace does not come—in a tangible, social sense—then the Messiah has not come."[23] Moltmann does not shrink from the biblical expectation that when the Messiah comes, he will bring world peace. "Without the practical witness to peace of the community of his people, Jesus cannot be the Messiah."[24]

The church is to be an example of the peace of the messianic kingdom—a real alternative contrast-society. Christ is the head of the church and the church is the body of Christ, a community of brothers and sisters, equals who have entered a covenantal community with God and each other where "all are priests and kings equally." All are priests with no division between laity and clergy. All sisters and brothers are free and equal members of the community; each one is uniquely gifted for the up-lifting of the entire congregation—even the world—under the authority of Christ.[25] Church polity could be represented by the par-ticipatory models of democracy, Latin American base communities, or some other inclusive, egalitarian, and liberating arrangement. St. Paul wrote to the church in Corinth about the nature of the church in the same manner and in a way that is strongly prescient of the trinitarian na-ture of God: "There are many gifts but the same spirit" (1 Cor 12:4). The church is characterized by the same "unity in diversity and diversity in unity" that characterizes God.[26] For Moltmann, the entire church must become a church of messianic peace—real socio-political peace.

EVANGELICAL ETHICS ARE MESSIANIC ETHICS

Biblical scholars agree that Jesus' central proclamation was that "the time is fulfilled, and the kingdom of God has come near; repent and

23. Moltmann, *The Way of Jesus Christ*, 118.

24. Ibid., 135.

25. For an important discussion of Just Peace and the church as an alternative com-munity see chapter 4 of Moltmann's *Ethik der Hoffnung*.

26. Moltmann, *Sun of Righteousness*, 20ff.

believe the good news." But Moltmann laments that many scholars have very little to say about the kingdom. The kingdom of God is often left undefined or vaguely described as if its meaning were either unknowable or broadly known, accepted, and followed, neither of which is the actual situation. Moltmann takes the New Testament seriously as a reliable source of information about the life and teachings of Jesus, and therefore finds Jesus' kingdom message to be theologically and ethically clear and commanding.

To explain Jesus' understanding of "the kingdom of God," Moltmann draws on texts throughout the Gospels, but most succinctly from Jesus' first recorded sermon in Luke 4:18ff and from Matthew's account of Jesus' Sermon on the Mount. According to Luke, when Jesus preached in the synagogue in Nazareth, he opened the scroll to the messianic text of Isaiah 61:1f in which the prophet reaches back to the Books of Moses on the jubilee year, the year of *liberation* (Lev 25). Jesus drew on the Law and the Prophets for his understanding of God's messianic kingdom that will be fulfilled with the same commitments as the year of liberation—but with two world-shattering extensions.[27]

The jubilee year was the year following the seventh of seven sabbatical years, i.e., every fiftieth year, when the requirements of the sabbatical year (debts forgiven, slaves freed, and fields laid fallow) were combined with the requirement of the jubilee year (land returned to the families of its original owners for an approximate egalitarianism.) In the first radical change, when Isaiah reached back in time to pull Moses' year of liberation into the messianic age, he expanded the institution of the jubilee from every fiftieth year to every day of every year. In the messianic age, the underlying commitments of the jubilee's liberating program become perennial, not the four literal criteria, but the jubilee's commitment to liberating egalitarianism. In the messianic kingdom, freedom characterized by equality becomes permanent. For the second radical change, Jesus followed the prophets' universalization of the messianic kingdom by opening its doors to Gentiles: the now perpetual commitments to freedom and equality are for everyone. This was as challenging, offensive, and even revolutionary in Jesus' day as it is today. When Jesus proclaimed that the Messiah's perpetual egalitarian liberation was not just for Jews but for everyone, "all in the synagogue were filled with rage. They got up, drove him out of the town, and led him to the brow of the

27. Moltmann, *The Way of Jesus Christ*, 119f.

hill on which their town was built, so that they might hurl him off the cliff. But he passed through the midst of them and went on his way" (Luke 4:28ff). The way of Jesus is dangerous.

By the mid 1990s Moltmann has become clearer than ever that Jesus' announcement of the messianic kingdom of God was the perpetual and universal institutionalization of an egalitarian community (economic and socio-political) that rejects all forms of domination including environmental degradation. Moltmann understands Jesus' messianic kingdom as "a programme for a complete social . . . and ecological reform . . . Those who recognize him as the Christ of God should follow him" in the messianic kingdom of social, political and economic egalitarianism that refuses to devalue friend or foe or even the environment. For Moltmann, "to act according to any other justice . . . would be denying the messiahship of Jesus." The identity and existence of the church hang in the balance with messianic ethics. Only those who follow the way of the Messiah can know the Messiah.[28]

In the Sermon on the Mount Jesus teaches his disciples in the first century and the twenty-first century the same messianic interpretation of the Torah and the Prophet. But from then until now many have dismissed Jesus' Sermon on the Mount as impossible, idealistic, impractical, unreasonable, and even irresponsible folly. Some have claimed that the free market, nuclear deterrence, and the war against terror are the only realistic options in a corrupt and sinful world. Indeed, the ethics of the community of the Messiah stand in contradistinction to the ethics of the state, prevailing culture, mainstream ideologies, and international politics. The messianic community rightly understands itself as a "contrast society"—recognizable and identifiable as an alternative to the exclusive and dominant communities. Because the community of Christ is open to all persons at all times, it is impossible for it to withdraw into social isolation or ideological sectarianism. Of course there will always be Christian communes and subgroups (there are many different ways to be faithful), but they will be for the universalization of the perpetual free and equal messianic kingdom, not flight to an impossible purity. Christian discipleship and Christian community go together. "And in this unity 'the law of Christ' is not an undue burden. It is a matter of

---

28. Ibid., 120–22.

course—'the light burden' (Matt 11:28–30) for all the weary and heavy-laden who in it find rest."[29]

Are messianic ethics really possible? Can the Sermon on the Mount actually be lived? Is the universal, egalitarian, liberating messianic reign of God to come *in human history* "on earth as it is in heaven"? Characteristically for Moltmann, Christian ethics must be relevant and effective. He asks: "Is Jesus' messianic interpretation of the laws of the year of liberation . . . realistic and practicable?" And he answers: "In light of the approaching kingdom of God . . . it is the only reasonable thing . . . The apocalyptic dimension of the approaching kingdom, and the end of the present world system, are constitutive for messianic interpretation of the laws of the year of liberation."[30] Moltmann answers the honest concerns of suffering human beings not with political calculations, economic theory, psychology analyses, or denominational programs, but "theologically: anyone who considers the Sermon on the Mount to be in principle impossible of fulfillment, mocks God . . . God gives no commandments that cannot be fulfilled."[31]

FOR EVANGELICAL ETHICS, EVERYTHING HAS CHANGED

Moltmann's premise is clear: since Jesus is the Christ and in him the messianic kingdom of God has come near, everything has changed (2 Cor 5:17). Evangelical ethics supplants the world's way with the way of the Messiah. The way of the world is no longer acceptable.[32] Jesus is Lord—not the state, economic structures, political powers, or cultural norms. The messianic kingdom of God subverts all other authorities.

When the children of Israel languished under the harsh rule of the Egyptian empire, the ancient Israelites cried out to the God of their fathers for liberation. Moltmann reminds his modern readers that ancient Israel recognized YHWH as *their* God because the LORD liberated them from slavery. Liberation from slavery was the divine act by which biblical Israel recognized YHWH as their God. YHWH was not known as their God because he supported ancient Egypt's empire, religion,

29. Ibid., 125f.

30. Ibid., 121.

31. Ibid., 127.

32. See Moltmann, *Ethik der Hoffnung*.

slavery, or economy. YHWH proved himself to be the Israelites' God by subverting Egyptian political, social, cultural, and religious authority to set them free. Therefore, says YHWH, Israel is to have "no other gods before me." The messianic proclamation of Jesus Christ is that the divine act of liberation will be fully realized worldwide—"his righteousness and justice will guarantee eternal peace on earth."[33]

Moltmann quotes approvingly the great Danish theologian, Søren Kierkegaard: "*God's almighty power is his goodness. Goodness means giving oneself totally, but in such a way that in almighty fashion one withdraws oneself, making the one who receives independent. All finite power creates dependency. Almighty power alone is capable of creating independence.*"[34] God does not possess all power, omnipotently willing and doing all nature and history. God's almighty power is not utterly overwhelming power that obliterates human freedom and responsibility. God's almighty power is universal goodness expressed by creating others to exist with him eternally in freedom. Ergo, Moltmann affirms what appears to contradict Kierkegaard, but does not: "*God's almightiness consists of his liberty.*"[35] God's almighty power consists of his freedom to limit his power in order to create free human beings.

"True Christianity is a movement of hope in this world . . . for sick souls and bodies . . . and a movement of liberation for life."[36] Liberation from every form of bondage is what the institution of the jubilee was to have accomplished; liberation is the message of the prophets; liberation is the hope of the kingdom; and liberation is the mark of divine action that Moltmann himself has experienced. Why is God so committed to liberation, even to something as mundane as liberation from poverty? Moltmann asks rhetorically, "Why does YHWH love the little, unimportant people"—the slave, the poor, the sick, the widow, the orphan, the sojourner, and even a prisoner of war who deserves death for the crimes of his country? And he answers: When God liberates the powerless, God creates their value and dignity. God's love creates all being and value *ex nihilo*. God creates and sustains human

---

33. Moltmann, *Sun of Righteousness*, 90.

34. Ibid., 109. Italics not in original.

35. Ibid., 110. Italics not in original.

36. Ibid., 115.

worth where those in power deny it.[37] For those who know Jesus as the Christ, everything has changed.

As one who has himself been liberated, Moltmann believes that the work of God for world-wide, messianic liberation must be pursued through "the preferential option for the poor"—those who are socially marginalized, politically expendable, economically disadvantaged, and any who are tossed aside like trash.[38] No empire anywhere on earth at any time in history has ever preferred the weak, the poor, the outcast, and the foreigner—yet this is exactly the way of Jesus' messianic kingdom of God. Because the kingdom has come, everything has changed, the old has passed away and the new has come. There can be no question for Moltmann but that God's liberation of all persons must focus on those with the greatest needs—a clear and distinguishable ethic to every other worldview.

Moltmann asserts that one of the major reasons that Christians have very little genuine hope for the coming of Christ is that Western Christianity has become "a civil religion." He points out that from the time of Constantine, generally, "renunciation of hope for the parousia was the price paid for Christianity's integration into the Roman Empire." Whereas first century congregations prayed, "*Maranatha,* come Lord Jesus, come soon (1 Cor 16:22), Constantinian imperial churches prayed, *pro mora finis*—that the end might be delayed—hoping thereby to recommend itself as a religion that supported the state and preserved the world."[39]

As it was in the fourth century Constantinian compromise, it is still in twenty-first century cultural Christianity: those who prosper (or hope to prosper) in their socio-political situation and those who work within "the empire" to preserve the prevailing system of "justice" are unlikely to hope for the messianic kingdom where everything has changed. Why hope for change when one benefits from the status quo? Why would the rich, the elite, the powerful, and the well educated look forward with joy to the economic and socio-political equality of the coming kingdom? It is unlikely that anyone will hope for the kingdom to come on earth as it is in heaven unless they have experienced genuine conversion or are among the suffering and powerless. For "the poor," however, and for

37. Ibid., 123f.
38. Ibid., 145.
39. Moltmann, *The Way of Jesus Christ*, 313.

those who have experienced "true conversion," hope for the messianic kingdom is crucial. Jesus Christ's gospel of the coming kingdom of God is their salvation literally, spiritually, materially, now, and forever. In this sense, the coming and universal, perennial, egalitarian, and liberating messianic kingdom of Christ is only for the poor.[40]

Nonviolent resistance to evil and peace are the way of Jesus Christ: For Moltmann, the messianic expectation of world peace is essential to legitimate the claim that Jesus is the Christ. "The center of the Sermon on the Mount is liberation from violence; enmity is to be surmounted by the creation of peace."[41] "The reality of God" that sustains the entire universe—both the good and the evil—has broken the circle of violence that begets violence to end violence by violence.[42]

The Messiah "brings to creation the peace that surmounts not only acts of violence, but also the violence used to restrict acts of violence . . . Wickedness is not merely the first act of violence but the vicious circle of violence and counter-violence." If Jesus is the Messiah, he is the Lord with "sovereign power over violence and counter-violence." Precisely because, and only because, Jesus is the Messiah "non-resistance to evil [i.e., benevolent, nonviolent resistance to evil] shows up the absurdity of evil."[43] Benevolent, nonviolent resistance to evil robs evil of its legitimation: first, by demonstrating the resistor's *freedom* from the ostensibly inevitability of violence; and second, by showing the resistor's *good will* even to the point of vicariously suffering for the enemy when retribution against the enemy is the accepted norm. It is the integration of "means" and "ends" into one whole. Benevolent, nonviolent resistance to evil is Paul's interpretation of Jesus' preaching, "Repay no one evil for evil . . . Do not be overcome by evil but overcome evil with good." (Rom 12:17–21)

Moltmann does not believe that commitment to nonviolent resistance to evil is the repudiation of relevance nor capitulation to evil. To overcome evil with good "does not mean a de-politicization, nor does it mean the renunciation of power," but is the redemption of power. Since power is neither renounced nor exploited but redeemed, it can be used

---

40. Ibid., 313f.

41. Ibid., 127.

42. Moltmann, *On Human Dignity*, 125ff; Moltmann, *The Power of the Powerless*, 51ff.

43. Moltmann, *The Way of Jesus Christ*, 128–30.

in every relationship and all institutions. "Nonviolent conquest of violence is not merely possible on the personal level. It is possible politically too," interpersonally as well as internationally. The kingdom of God has come; everything has changed.[44]

"Nonviolent action is action that liberates the enemy from violence. It is what Jesus calls loving one's enemy" and it supplants the world's way of using violence to conquer the enemy. Rather than responding in the manner that one has experienced from the other, nonviolent resistance to evil takes "responsibility for one's enemy" to free them from the compulsion to respond with violence. Jesus proclaims that God loves the just and the unjust without discrimination (God sends the sun to rise on the good and the evil, Matt 5:45) and the community of his disciples is to love both friend and enemy in the same indiscriminate manner thus liberating the world from the compulsion to violence.[45]

This kind of love for the enemy cannot be scripted, nor prescribed in a law or regulation, nor can it be "a recompensing love, returning what one has received." Legislation, retribution, and historic cultural norms cannot be love. Enemy love is surprising. It is "creative love. Anyone who repays evil with good is creating something new" beyond all rights, demands, and expectations.[46] Enemy love is not "subjection," nor "endorsement," nor "surrender" to evil, but is the "intelligent conquest of hostility." To love the enemy the way God loves the good and the evil alike, "deprives the enemy of his hostility . . . Ultimately, therefore, it is the only reasonable thing if we are to ensure lasting peace on earth." If Jesus is the Messiah who introduces the kingdom of God to the world, nonviolence is "the logic of life," the only path for human success or even survival. "In our own age, in which we cannot afford any major nuclear war, *service for peace that renounces violence, and love of one's enemies, prove to be the only reasonable and wise behavior . . . Peace is a plausible objective.*"[47]

---

44. Ibid., 130.

45. Ibid.

46. For a groundbreaking study of the surprising nature of kingdom ethics, see Stassen, *Just Peacemaking: The New Paradigm for Ethics of Peace and War,* and especially his earlier work on which it is based *Just Peacemaking: Transforming Initiatives for Justice and Peace.*

47. Moltmann, *The Way of Jesus Christ,* 131–32. Italics not in original.

Of course, the cost can be high and few Christian have been willing to pay it. Jesus' execution was real and for those who follow the way of Christ, "martyrdom" is a real possibility. Moltmann reminds his readers that Gandhi, Martin Luther King, Oscar Romero, the six Jesuit professors (and their cook and her daughter in El Salvador on November 16, 1989), and countless others over the centuries have followed Jesus in life, to the death. Peace is the only hope of humanity, but nonviolent peacemakers will suffer for it.

Nevertheless, lethal self-defense and armed defense of the innocent may be historically necessary: Moltmann's early essays explain that although "the concept of nonviolence belongs to the eschatological remembrance of faith in Jesus . . . it is not the idealistic principle of nonviolence that is consonant with the gospel, but the responsible action of love . . . [namely,] the sacrifice of personal innocence to the point of incurring guilt."[48] Military action may be the historical form of Christian love when such force is necessary to liberate individuals or entire nations from tyranny. Moltmann explains: "Brotherhood-in-arms among the oppressed is neighborly love in situations of crisis. For in a political context the commandment about neighborly love means resisting tyranny, liberating the oppressed, and promoting the equal rights of everyone."[49] Even capital punishment can be a form of Christian love in the real world of human societies: "The divine protection of human life that is imperiled by other human beings can, in history, take the form of the death penalty, as a kind of emergency measure of self-defense."[50]

According to Moltmann "the problem of violence and nonviolence is an illusory problem. There is only the problem of the justified and unjustified use of force and the question of whether the means are appropriate to ends."[51] He further explains (although not far enough) that "violence is the unjust use of force"—and unjust is defined by the exercise of power that is not "subject to law."[52] Although Moltmann rejects just war theory for its lack of dependence on the gospel of Jesus Christ,

48. Moltmann, *The Experiment Hope*, 136–37, 143.

49. Moltmann, *The Power of the Powerless*, 109.

50. Ibid., 9.

51. Moltmann, *Religion, Revolution and the Future*, 143; Moltmann, *The Way of Jesus Christ*, 130.

52. Moltmann, *The Way of Jesus Christ*, 130.

he discusses many of the same concerns as just war theorists (although less thoroughly) when considering the Christian use of lethal force.

Corresponding to the principles of *jus ad bellum* and *jus in bello*, Moltmann argues that Christians have the duty to resist and the right to use violence when they have: just cause (viz., "tyranny: continuous violation of the law, violation of the constitution, and violation of human rights which is itself legalized by laws and constitutions"); the right authority (e.g., military action must be sanctioned by the persons suffering under oppression, the United Nations, national law, or a constitution drafted by the population it governs); right intentions (e.g., to end oppression, restore human rights, or establish a just order); probable success (e.g., Moltmann uses terms like liberate, effective, and transformation); the last resort (i.e., no other action is as likely to succeed); and the right means (i.e., whatever actions have a reasonable chance to alleviate tyranny and establish justice.) In the real world of power and powerlessness, "counter-violence is often the only remedy."[53]

Forgiveness and the reality of the kingdom of God is the only human hope: How is one to make sense of Moltmann's dialectical argument? "Killing remains killing and cannot be justified . . . or approved . . . Guilt remains guilt." Violent resistance to tyranny is "caught up in the vicious circle of force and retaliation."[54] And yet militaristic resistance to tyranny may be a legitimate form of Christian love. Part of his answer is to say that violence may at times be necessary, but it is still sinful and therefore requires forgiveness.[55] But to argue that something is both required by God and sinful raises even more questions about human freedom, responsibility, sin, and accountability which Moltmann does not adequately address. Does God indeed require "brotherhood in arms" with one brother against another brother? Such a self-contradiction also violates Moltmann's understanding "the logic of life" which is voluntary, self-sacrificial, nonviolent, resistance to evil.[56] Is it really possible to rec-

---

53. Moltmann, *The Experiment Hope*, 137–43; Moltmann, *The Power of the Powerless*, 9, 35, 107; Moltmann, *Religion, Revolution and the Future*, 143f. For a discussion that stitches together Moltmann's thinking and just war theory see Parker, "God and the Moral Life," 171–80.

54. Moltmann, *The Power of the Powerless*, 35.

55. Moltmann, *The Experiment Hope*, 142ff.

56. Moltmann, *The Way of Jesus Christ*, 133ff.

oncile Moltmann's allowances for war and capital punishment with non-violent resistance to evil as the "the only reasonable and wise behavior"?

Another way that Moltmann might be seen to bring his conflictive positions into balance is with the view that the kingdom of God has not yet arrived in full. Yes, it is certain, and "it already determines the present of the people who walk in the way of the Lord," but the reign of God is not yet fully present. The jubilee-inspired and prophetically envisioned messianic kingdom of God is still coming. And when God's messianic order is fully established on earth, the final victory will be God's alone.[57] But it is unsatisfying to remove the socio-political reality of the messianic kingdom of God from contemporary world affairs. Wars and injustices of every kind confront Christians daily—individually, within communities of faith, and nationally. Decisions and actions are required—and the kingdom of God is set aside as "not yet"? What about Moltmann's evocation of the examples of Jesus, Romero, and Martin Luther King? Since the kingdom has come, hasn't everything changed?

Moltmann does not find it necessary to resolve the conflict between Jesus' call for peace and its historical limitations. What Moltmann does find necessary is to commit to the prophetic vision of the messianic kingdom of universal, perennial, egalitarian liberation. It is the way of Jesus Christ. It is necessary to struggle *against* tyranny and environmental destruction and *for* human rights and environmental health. Although Moltmann is not committed to absolute pacifism, he is strongly inclined to nonviolent resistance to evil in order to achieve real, historic, social, political, economic, environmental, cosmic, eternal liberation through Jesus Christ. Moltmann declares that "any means of liberation may be appropriate" so long as it achieves God's liberation; but it is only in the particular historical situation (and Jesus' messianic kingdom is part of every historical situation) that a person is able know what means are "appropriate."[58]

Whatever the means of liberation, "the Sermon on the Mount is valid" and must be the way of the church or else Christianity will become nothing more than civil religion in support of the state, cultural norms,

---

57. Moltmann, *On Human Dignity*, 125–27; Moltmann, *The Power of the Powerless*, 32–35, 51–54; Moltmann, *Religion, Revolution and the Future*, 68; Moltmann, *The Way of Jesus Christ*, 134.

58. Moltmann, *On Human Dignity*, 7, 14f, 19f, 25f, 33f; Moltmann, *Religion, Revolution and the Future*, 143–45; Parker, "God and the Moral Life," 175–80.

and the economic status quo. For Moltmann the Sermon on the Mount is "the litmus test" of the church's identity. The church's commitment to follow Jesus' messianic preaching must undermine all forms of violence and domination—personal, institutional, national, and international. If the Messiah has come, peace will prevail.

Bibliography

Adams, Nicholas. "Jürgen Moltmann." In *The Blackwell Companion to Political Theology*, edited by Peter Scott and William Cavanaugh, 227–40. Malden, UK: Blackwell, 2004.

Alexander, Denis R. and Ronald L. Numbers, eds. *Biology and Ideology from Descartes to Dawkins*. Chicago: University of Chicago Press, 2010.

Althouse, Peter. *Spirit of the Last Days*, JPTS 25. London: T. & T. Clark, 2003.

Alvez, Rubén. *A Theology of Human Hope*. St. Meinrad, IN: Abbey, 1975.

Antognazza, Maria Rosa. *Leibniz: An Intellectual Biography*. Cambridge: Cambridge University Press, 2009.

Assmann, Hugo. *Theology for a Nomad Church*. Translated by P. Burns. Maryknoll, NY: Orbis, 1976.

Atkinson, D., and D. Field, eds. *Lausanne Covenant*. Leicester, UK: InterVarsity, 1995.

Bauckham, Richard J. "Evolution and Creation: (9) in Moltmann's Doctrine of Creation." *Epworth Review* 15 (1988) 74–81.

———, ed. *God Will Be All in All: The Eschatology of Jürgen Moltmann*. Minneapolis: Fortress, 2001.

———. *Moltmann: Messianic Theology in the Making*. Basingstoke, UK: Marhsall, Morgan and Scott, 1987.

———. *The Theology of Jürgen Moltmann*. Edinburgh: T. & T. Clark, 1995.

———. "Time and Eternity." In *God Will Be All in All: The Eschatology of Jürgen Moltmann*, edited by Richard Bauckham, 156–226. Edinburgh: T. & T. Clark, 1999.

Barth, Karl. *Church Dogmatics*. Translated by G. T. Thomson et al. and edited by G. W. Bromiley and T. F. Torrance. 4 volumes in 13 parts. Edinburgh: T. & T. Clark, 1936–75.

Blocher, Henri. "God and the Cross." In *Engaging the Doctrine of God*, edited by Bruce L. McCormack, 125–41. Grand Rapids: Baker, 2008.

Bonhoeffer, Dietrich. "An Eberhard Bethge 30.4.44" In *Widerstand Und Ergebung*, edited by Christian Gremmels, 401–8. Munich: Kaiser, 1998.

———. *Letters and Papers from Prison*. London: SCM, 1967.

Borges, Jorge Luis. *The Total Library: Non-Fiction 1922–1986*. Translated by Suzanne Braun Levine. London: Penguin, 1999.

Bradshaw, Timothy. *Chaos or Control? The Crisis of Authority in Church and State*. Milton Keynes, UK: Paternoster, 2010.

Brueggemann, Walter. *Theology of the Old Testament: Testimony, Dispute, Advocacy*. Minneapolis: Fortress, 1997.

Brunner, Emil. *Natur und gnade: zum gespräch mit Karl Barth*. Tübingen: Mohr (Siebeck), 1934.

Buxton, Graham. *The Trinity, Creation and Pastoral Ministry: Imaging the Perichoretic God*. Milton Keynes, UK: Paternoster, 2005.

Cameron, Nigel M. de S., ed. *Issues in Faith and History*. Edinburgh: Rutherford House, 1989.

Capps, Walter H. *Time Invades the Cathedral*. Philadelphia: Fortress, 1972.

Carroll R., M. Daniel. "God and His People in the Nations' History: A Contextualized Reading of Amos 1–2." *Tyndale Bulletin* 47.1 (1996) 39–70.

————. "Living between the Lines: A Reading of Amos 9:11–15 in Postwar Guatemala." *Religion & Theology* 6.1 (1999) 50–64.

————. "The Prophetic Text and the Literature of Dissent in Latin America: Amos, García Márquez, and Cabrera Infante Dismantle Militarism." *Biblical Interpretation* 4.1 (1996) 76–100.

Chan, Simon K. H. "An Asian Review: Review of Jürgen Moltmann's, *The Spirit of Life: A Universal Affirmation*." *Journal of Pentecostal Theology* 4 (1994) 36.

Chester, Tim. *Mission and the Coming of God: Eschatology, the Trinity and Mission in the Theology of Jürgen Moltmann and Contemporary Evangelicalism*. Paternoster Theological Monographs. Milton Keynes, UK: Paternoster, 2006.

Chopp, Rebecca S. *The Praxis of Suffering*. Maryknoll, NY: Orbis, 1989.

Church of England Mission and Public Affairs Council. *Sharing God's Planet: A Christian Vision for a Sustainable Future*. London: Church House, 2005.

Cochrane, Arthur. *The Church's Confession under Hitler*. Philadelphia: Westminster, 1962.

Conradie, Ernst M. "The Justification of God? The Story of God's Work According to Jürgen Moltmann Pt.1." *Scriptura* 97 (2008) 77.

Conyers, A. J. *God, Hope, and History: Jürgen Moltmann and the Christian Concept of History*. Macon, GA: Mercer, 1988.

Cosden, Darrell. *A Theology of Work: Work and the New Creation*. Paternoster Theological Monographs. Carlisle, UK: Paternoster, 2004.

Crocker, Robert, ed. *Religion, Reason, and Nature in Early Modern Europe*. Boston: Kluwer, 2001.

Crisp, Oliver D. "Karl Barth on Creation." In *Karl Barth and Evangelical Theology: Convergences and Divergences*, edited by Sungwook Chung, 77–95. Milton Keynes, UK: Paternoster, 2006.

Deane-Drummond, Celia. "A Critique of Jürgen Moltmann's Green Theology." *New Blackfriars* 165 (1992) 554–65.

Duce, Philip, and Daniel Strange, eds. *Getting Your Bearings: Engaging with Contemporary Theologians*. Leicester, UK: Apollos, 2003.

Dulles, Avery. *Models of the Church*. Expanded edition. New York: Image, 1987.

Erickson, Millard. *Christian Theology*. Grand Rapids: Baker, 1998.

Evans, C. Stephen, ed. *Exploring Kenotic Christology: The Self-Emptying of God*. Oxford: Oxford University Press, 2006.

Fee, Gordon. *Paul, the Spirit and the People of God*. London: Hodder & Stoughton, 1997.

Finlan, Stephen, and Vladimir Kharlamov, eds. *Theosis: Deification in Christian Theology*. Eugene, OR: Pickwick, 2006.

Forsyth, P. T. *The Church and the Sacraments*. London: Independent, 1917.

————. *The Person and Place of Jesus Christ*. London: Hodder & Stoughton, 1909.

Franke, John. *The Character of Theology*. Grand Rapids: Baker, 2005.

García Márquez, Gabriel. *One Hundred Years of Solitude.* Translated by G. Rabassa. New York: Harper & Row, 1970.

Gibson, David. "The Day of God's Mercy: Romans 9–11 in Barth's Doctrine of Election." In *Engaging with Barth: Contemporary Evangelical Critiques,* edited by David Gibson and Daniel Strange, 136–67. Nottingham, UK: Apollos, 2008.

Gilkey, Langdon. "God." In *Christian Theology: An Introduction to its Traditions and Tasks,* edited by P. C. Hodgson, and R. H. King. Philadelphia: Fortress, 1985.

———. *Nature, Reality, and the Sacred: The Nexus of Science and Religion.* Minneapolis, UK: Fortress, 1993.

Grenz, S. J., and Olson, R. E. *20th Century Theology: God and the World in a Transitional Age.* Downers Grove, IL: InterVarsity, 1992.

Gunton, Colin E. *Christ and Creation.* The Didsbury Lectures. 1992. Reprint. Eugene, OR: Wipf and Stock, 2005.

———. *The One, the Three and the Many: God, Creation and the Culture of Modernity.* Cambridge: Cambridge University Press, 1993.

———. *The Triune Creator.* Edinburgh Studies in Constructive Theology. Grand Rapids: Eerdmans, 1998.

Gutiérrez, Gustavo. *A Theology of Liberation.* Translated by Sister C. Inda and J. Eagleson. Maryknoll, NY: Orbis, 1973.

Hall, Douglas John. *Thinking the Faith: Christian Theology in a North American Context.* Minneapolis, UK: Fortress, 1991.

Hart, John W. *Karl Barth vs. Emil Brunner: The Formation and Dissolution of a Theological Alliance, 1916–1936.* New York: Lang, 2001.

Harvie, Timothy. *Jürgen Moltmann's Ethics of Hope: Eschatological Possibilities for Moral Action.* Aldershot, UK: Ashgate, 2009.

Herzog, Frederick, ed. *The Future of Hope.* New York: Herder and Herder, 1970.

Heschel, Abraham Joshua. *The Prophets.* 2 vols. San Francisco: Harper and Row, 1962.

Höhne, David A. *Spirit and Sonship: Colin Gunton's Theology of Particularity and the Holy Spirit.* Farnham, UK: Ashgate, 2010.

Horn, Nico. "From Barmen to Belhar and Kairos." In *On Reading Karl Barth in South Africa,* edited by Charles Villa-Vicencio, 105–19. Grand Rapids: Eerdmans, 1988.

Hudson, W. D. *The Marxist Philosophy of Ernst Bloch.* London: Macmillan, 1982.

Jansen, Harry. "Moltmann's View of God's (Im)Mutibility." *Neue Zeitschrift Fur Systemaische Theologie und Religionsphilosophie* 36.3 (1994) 284–301.

Jenkins, Philip. *The New Faces of Christianity: Believing the Bible in the Global South.* New York: Oxford University Press, 2008.

Jónsson, Gunnlaugur A. *The Image of God: Genesis 1:26–28 in a Century of Old Testament Research.* Coniectanea Biblica, Old Testament Series, 26. Stockholm: Almquist and Wiksell, 1988.

Jowers, Dennis W. "The Theology of the Cross as the Theology of the Trinity: A Critique of Moltmann's Staurocentric Trinitarianism." *Tyndale Bulletin* 52.2 (2001) 245–66.

Keller, Catherine. "Last Laugh: A Counter-Apocalyptic Meditation on Moltmann's *The Coming of God.*" *Theology Today* 54 (1997) 381–91.

Kimball, Charles A. *Jesus' Exposition of the Old Testament in Luke's Gospel.* JSNTS 94. Edited by Stanley E. Porter. Sheffield, UK: Sheffield Academic, 1994.

Klein, Eliahu. *Kabbalah of Creation: The Mysticism of Isaac Luria, Founder of Modern Kabbalah.* Berkeley, CA: North Atlantic, 2005.

Kuzmic, Peter. "A Croatian War-Time Reading: Review of Jürgen Moltmann's, *The Spirit of Life: A Universal Affirmation.*" *Journal of Pentecostal Theology* 4 (1994) 17–20.

LaCugna, Catherine M. *God for Us: The Trinity and Christian Life.* San Francisco: Harper Collins, 1991.

Lapoorta, Japie J. "An African Response: Review of Jürgen Moltmann's, *The Spirit of Life: A Universal Affirmation.*" *Journal of Pentecostal Theology* 4 (1994) 51–58.

Lewis, Alan E., "Unmasking Idolatries: Vocation in the *Ecclesia Crucis.*" In *Incarnational Ministry: The Presence of Christ in Church, Society and Family,* edited by Christian D. Kettler, and Todd H. Speidell, 110–28. Colorado Springs: Helmers and Howard, 1990.

Lewis, Gordon, and Bruce Demarest. *Integrative Theology.* Grand Rapids: Zondervan, 1996.

Licona, Michael R. *The Resurrection of Jesus: A New Historiographical Approach.* Downers Grove, IL: InterVarsity, 2010.

Macchia, Frank D. "North American Response: Review of Jürgen Moltmann's, *The Spirit of Life: A Universal Affirmation.*" *Journal of Pentecostal Theology* 4 (1994) 25–26.

Mackintosh, H. R. *The Doctrine of the Person of Jesus Christ.* Edinburgh: T. & T. Clark, 1913.

McDougall, Joy Ann. *Pilgrimage of Love: Moltmann on the Trinity and Christian Life.* Oxford: Oxford University Press, 2005.

McCormack, Bruce, ed. *Engaging the Doctrine of God: Contemporary Protestant Perspectives.* Grand Rapids: Baker Academic, 2008.

McCormack, Bruce L. *Orthodox and modern: studies in the theology of Karl Barth.* Grand Rapids: Baker Academic, 2008.

McGrath, Alister. *Christian Theology: An Introduction,* Oxford: Blackwell, 1997.

McPherson, Jim. "Life, the Universe and Everything: Jürgen Moltmann's 'God in Creation.'" *St Mark's Review* 128 (1986) 34–46.

Meeks, M. Douglas. *Origins of the Theology of Hope.* Philadelphia: Fortress, 1974.

Míguez Bonino, José. *Doing Theology in a Revolutionary Situation.* Philadelphia: Fortress, 1975.

———. "Reading Jürgen Moltmann from Latin America." *Asbury Theological Journal* 55.1 (2000) 105–14.

Molnar, Paul D. *Divine Freedom and the Doctrine of the Immanent Trinity: In Dialogue with Karl Barth and Contemporary Theology.* New York: Continuum, 2005.

———. "The Function of the Trinity in Moltmann's Ecological Doctrine of Creation." *Theological Studies* 51 (1990) 673–97.

Moltmann, Jürgen. *A Broad Place: An Autobiography.* Translated by Margaret Kohl. Minneapolis: Fortress, 2008.

———. "A Christian Declaration on Human Rights." *Reformed World* 34 (1976) 58–72.

———. *The Church in the Power of the Spirit: A Contribution to Messianic Ecclesiology.* Translated by Margaret Kohl. London: SCM, 1977.

———. *The Coming of God: Christian Eschatology.* Translated by Margaret Kohl. London: SCM, 1996.

———. *Creating a Just Future: The Politics of Peace and the Ethics of Creation in a Threatened World.* Translated by John Bowden. London: SCM, 1989.

———. *The Crucified God: The Cross of Christ as the Foundation and Criticism of Christian Theology.* Translated by Margaret Kohl. London: SCM, 1974.

———. "The Destruction and Healing of the Earth." In *God and Globalization, Vol. 2: The Spirit and the Modern Authorities*, edited by M. L. Stackhouse, and D. S. Browning, 166–90. Harrisburg, PA: Trinity, 2001.

———. "The Ecological Crisis: Peace with Nature?" *Scottish Journal of Religious Studies* 9 (1988) 5–18.

———. *Ethik der Hoffnung*. Gütersloh: Gütersloher Verlagshaus, 2010.

———. *Experiences in Theology: Ways and Forms of Christian Theology*. Translated by Margaret Kohl. Minneapolis: Fortress, 2000.

———. *Experiences of God*. Translated by Margaret Kohl. Minneapolis; Fortress, 2007.

———. *The Experiment Hope*. Translated by M. Douglas Meeks. Philadelphia: Fortress, 1975.

———. "'From the Closed World to the Infinite Universe': The Case of Giordano Bruno." 1998. In *Science and Wisdom*, 158–71. Minneapolis: Fortress, 2003.

———. *The Future of Creation*. Translated by Margaret Kohl. London: SCM, 1979.

———. "God and Space." In *Science and Wisdom*, 111–26. Minneapolis: Fortress, 2003.

———. *God in Creation: An Ecological Doctrine of Creation*. Translated by Margaret Kohl. London: SCM, 1985.

———. *God in Creation: A New Theology of Creation and the Spirit of God*. Translated by Margaret Kohl. Minneapolis: Fortress, 1993.

———. "God's Kenosis in the Creation and Consummation of the World." In *The Work of Love: Creation as Kenosis*, edited by John Polkinghorne, 137–51. Grand Rapids: Eerdmans, 2001.

———. *History and the Triune God: Contributions to Trinitarian Theology*. Translated by John Bowden. London: SCM, 1991.

———. *Hope and Planning*. Translated by Margaret Clarkson. London: SCM, 1971.

———. *How I Have Changed: Reflections of Thirty Years of Theology*. Translated by John Bowden. London: SCM, 1997.

———. *Jesus Christ for Today's World*. Translated by Margaret Kohl. Minneapolis: Fortress, 1994.

———. "Justice for Victims and Perpetrators." *Reformed World* 44.1 (March 1994). Online: http://warc.ch/pc/rw941/01.html

———. "A Lived Theology." In *Shaping a Theological Mind: Theological Context and Methodology*, edited by Darren C. Marks, 87–95. Hants, UK: Ashgate, 2002.

———. *Man: Christian Anthropology in the Conflicts of the Present*. Translated by John Sturdy. Philadelphia: Fortress, 1974.

———. *On Human Dignity: Political Theology and Ethics*. Translated by M. Douglas Meeks. Philadelphia: Fortress, 1984.

———. "An Open Letter to José Míguez Bonino: On Latin American Liberation Theology." *Christianity and Crisis* (1976) 57–63.

———. *The Passion for Life*. Translated by M. Douglas Meeks. Philadelphia: Fortress, 1978.

———. "A Pentecostal Theology of Life." *Journal of Pentecostal Theology* 9 (October 1996) 3–15.

———. *The Power of the Powerless*. Translated by Margaret Kohl. San Francisco: Harper & Row, 1983.

———. "Progress and Abyss: Remembrances of the Future in the Modern World." *In The Future of Hope: Christian Tradition amid Modernity and Postmodernity*, edited by Miroslav Volf and William Katerberg, 3–26. Grand Rapids: Eerdmans, 2004.

————. "The Reconciling Power of the Trinity in the Life of the Church and the World." In *Triune God: Love, Justice, Peace*, edited by K. M. Tharakan, 32–50. Mavelikkara, India: Youth Movement of Indian Orthodox Church, 1989.

————. "Reflections on Chaos and God's Interaction with the World from a Trinitarian Perspective." In *Chaos and Complexity: Scientific Perspectives on Divine Action*, edited by Robert J. Russell et al., 205–10. Vatican City State: Vatican Observatory Publications, 1995.

————. *Religion, Revolution, and the Future*. Translated by M. Douglas Meeks. New York: Scribner's Sons, 1969.

————. *Science and Wisdom*. Translated by Margaret Kohl. Minneapolis: Fortress, 2003.

————. *The Source of Life: The Holy Spirit and the Theology of Life*. London: SCM, 1997.

————. "The Spirit Gives Life: Spirituality and Vitality." In *All Together in One Place: Theological Papers from the Brighton Conference on World Evangelization*, edited by Harold Hunter and Peter D. Hocken, 22–37. Sheffield, UK: Sheffield Academic, 1993.

————. *The Spirit of Life: A Universal Affirmation*. Translated by Margaret Kohl. London: SCM, 1992.

————. *Sun of Righteousness, Arise! God's Future for Humanity and the Earth*. Translated by Margaret Kohl. Minneapolis: Augsburg Fortress, 2010.

————. "Theological Basis of Human Rights and the Liberation of Man." *Reformed World* 31 (1971) 348–57.

————. *Theologie der Hoffnung. Untersuchungen zur Begründung und zu den Konsequenzen einer christlichen Eschatologie*. Munich: Kaiser, 1966.

————. *Theology of Hope: On the Ground and the Implications of a Christian Eschatology*. Translated by James W. Leitch. New York: Harper & Row, 1967.

————. *Theology Today: Two Contributions towards Making Theology Present*. Translated by John Bowden. London: SCM, 1988.

————. *The Trinity and the Kingdom of God: The Doctrine of God*. Translated by Margaret Kohl. London: SCM, 1981.

————. *The Way of Jesus Christ: Christology in Messianic Dimensions*. Translated by Margaret Kohl. London: SCM, 1990.

————. *The Way of Jesus Christ*. Translated by Margaret Kohl. Minneapolis: Fortress, 1993.

————. "The World in God or God in the World?: Response to Richard Bauckham." In *God Will be All in All: The Eschatology of Jürgen Moltmann*, edited by Richard Bauckham, 35–42. Edinburgh: T. & T. Clark, Edinburgh, 1999.

————. "Wrestling with God: A Personal Meditation." *The Christian Century* 114 (August 13, 1997) 726.

Moltmann, Jürgen, and Ellizabeth Moltmann-Wendel. *Humanity in God*. New York: Pilgrim, 1983.

Moltmann, Jürgen, and J. Weissbach. *Two Studies in the Theology of Bonhoeffer*. New York: Scribner, 1967.

Moltmann, Jürgen, and Karl-Josef Küschel, eds. *Pentecostal Movements as an Ecumenical Challenge*. London: SCM, 1996.

Moltmann, Jürgen, Nicholas Wolterstorff, and Ellen Charry. *A Passion for God's Reign: Theology, Christian Learning, and the Christian Self*. Edited by Miroslav Volf. Grand Rapids: Eerdmans, 1998.

Müller-Fahrenholz, Geiko. *The Kingdom and the Power: The Theology of Jürgen Moltmann.* Minneapolis: Fortress, 2001.

Muller, Richard A. *Post-Reformation Reformed Dogmatics: The Rise and Development of Reformed Orthodoxy, ca. 1520 to ca. 1725,* 4 vols. Grand Rapids: Baker Academic, 2003.

Neal, Ryan A. *Theology as Hope: On the Ground and Implications of Jürgen Moltmann's Doctrine of Hope.* Princeton Theological Monograph Series 99. Eugene, OR: Pickwick, 2008.

Nolland, John. *Luke 9:21–18:34.* Word Biblical Commentary 35b. Dallas: Word, 1993.

O'Brien, Peter T. *Commentary on Philippians.* New International Greek Testament Commentary. Grand Rapids: Eerdmans, 1991.

O'Donovan, Oliver. *The Desire of the Nations Rediscovering the Roots of Political Theology.* Cambridge: Cambridge University Press, 1999.

Otto, Randall. "Moltmann and the Anti-Monotheism Movement." *International Journal of Systematic Theology* 3.3 (2001) 293–308.

Parker, Paul. "God and the Moral Life: Beliefs about God in Selected Moral Arguments of Bernard Häring and Jürgen Moltmann." PhD diss., The Southern Baptist Theological Seminary, 1986.

Peterson, Erik. "Der Monotheismus als politisches Problem." In *Theologische Traktate,* edited by Erik Peterson, 45–147. Munich: Kösel, 1951.

Pinnock, Clark H. *Flame of Love: A Theology of the Holy Spirit.* Downers Grove, IL: InterVarsity, 1996.

———. *Most Moved Mover: A Theology of God's Openness.* Carlisle: Paternoster Press, 2001.

———. et al., *The Openness of God: A Biblical Challenge to the Traditional Understanding of God.* Downers Grove: InterVarsity, 1994.

Prooijen, Ton van. *Limping But Blessed: Jürgen Moltmann's Search for a Liberating Anthropology.* Amsterdam: Rodopi, 2004.

Rahner, Karl. *The Trinity.* Translated by Joseph Donceel. New York: Crossroad, 1997.

Rasmusson, Arne. *The Church as Polis: From Political Theology to Theological Politics as Exemplified by Jürgen Moltmann and Stanley Hauerwas.* Notre Dame, IN: University of Notre Dame Press, 1995.

Rossi-Keen, Daniel E. "Jürgen Moltmann's Doctrine of God: The Trinity beyond Metaphysics." *Studies in Religion/Sciences Religieuses* 37 (September 2008) 447–63.

Ross, G. MacDonald. *Leibniz.* Oxford: Oxford University Press, 1984.

Sachs, J. R. "Apocatastasis in Patristic Theology." *Theological Studies* 54 (1993) 617–40.

Scholem, Gershom. *Major Trends in Jewish Mysticism.* New York: Schocken, 1954.

Scholder, Klaus. *The Churches and the Third Reich,* Vol. 1. London: SCM, 1987.

Sedgwick, Peter. *Anglican Theology.* Edited by David F. Ford. Oxford: Blackwell, 2006.

Sepúlveda, Juan. "The Perspective of Chilean Pentecostalism: Review of Jürgen Moltmann's, *The Spirit of Life: A Universal Affirmation." Journal of Pentecostal Theology* 4 (1994) 47–49.

Shepherd, William H. *The Narrative Function of the Holy Spirit as a Character in Luke-Acts.* SBLDS 147. Atlanta: Scholars, 1994.

Snyder, H. A. *EarthCurrents: The Struggle for the World's Soul.* Nashville: Abingdon, 1995.

Sobrino, Jon. *Christology at the Crossroads: A Latin American Approach.* Translated by J. Drury. Maryknoll, NY: Orbis, 1978.

———. *Jesus the Liberator: A Historical-Theological View.* Translated by P. Burns and F. McDonagh. Maryknoll, NY: Orbis, 1993.

Stassen, Glen H. *Just Peacemaking: The New Paradigm for Ethics of Peace and War.* 3rd ed. Cleveland: Pilgrim, 2008.

———. *Just Peacemaking: Transforming Initiatives for Justice and Peace.* Louisville: Westminster/John Knox, 1992.

Stibbe, Mark W. G. "A British Appraisal: Review of Jürgen Moltmann's, *The Spirit of Life: A Universal Affirmation.*" *Journal of Pentecostal Theology* 4 (1994) 11.

Sykes, Stepen W. *Power and Christian Theology.* London: Continuum, 2006.

Tacey, David. *ReEnchantment: The New Australian Spirituality.* Sydney: HarperCollins, 2000.

Thiemann, Ronald. *Revelation and Theology: The Gospel as Narrated Promise.* Notre Dame, IN: Notre Dame University Press, 1985.

Thiselton, Anthony C. *Interpreting God and the Postmodern Self.* Edinburgh: T. & T. Clark, 1995.

Torrance, Alan J. "*Creatio ex Nihilo* and the Spatio-Temporal Dimensions, with Special Reference to Jürgen Moltmann and D. C. Williams." In *The Doctrine of Creation: Essays in Dogmatics, History and Philosophy,* edited by Colin E. Gunton, 83–103. Edinburgh: T. & T. Clark, 1997.

Torrance, James B. *Worship, Community, and the Triune God of Grace.* Carlisle, UK: Paternoster, 1996.

Torrance, Thomas F. *Divine and Contingent Order.* Oxford: Oxford University Press, 1981.

Travis, Stephen. *Christian Hope and the Future of Man.* Leicester, UK: InterVarsity, 1980.

Vanhoozer, Kevin J. *The Drama of Doctrine: A Canonical Linguistic Approach to Christian Theology.* Louisville, KY: Westminster John Knox, 2005.

Volf, Miroslav. "A Queen and a Beggar: Challenges and Prospects of Theology." In *The Future of Theology: Essays in Honor of Jürgen Moltmann,* edited by Miroslav Volf, Carmen Krieg, and Thomas Kucharz, ix–xviii. Grand Rapids: Eerdmans, 1996.

Walsh, Brian J. "Theology of Hope and the Doctrine of Creation: An Appraisal of Jürgen Moltmann." *Evangelical Quarterly* 59 (1987) 53–76.

Webster, John. "God's Perfect Life." In *God's Life in Trinity,* edited by Miroslav Volf and Michael Welker, 143–52. Minneapolis: Fortress, 2006.

Weil, Simone. *Waiting on God.* London: Collins, 1963.

Williamson, Edwin. *Borges: A Life.* New York: Viking, 2004.

Willis, W. Wade. *Theism, Atheism and the Doctrine of the Trinity.* Atlanta: Scholars, 1987.

Wolff, Hans Walter. *Anthropology of the Old Testament.* Translated by Margaret Kohl. London: SCM, 1974.

Wolterstorff, Nicholas. "Is There Justice in the Trinity?" In *God's Life in Trinity,* edited by Miroslav Volf and Michael Welker, 177–88. Minneapolis: Fortress, 2006.

Wright, N. T. *Jesus and the Victory of God.* Christian Origins and the Question of God, vol. 2. London: SPCK, 1996.

———. *The Resurrection of the Son of God.* London: SPCK, 2003.

Zizioulas, John D. *Being as Communion.* New York: St. Vladimir's Seminary Press, 1985.

Subject Index